THE
ENGLISH TEACHER'S
ACTIVITIES HANDBOOK

An Ideabook for Middle & Secondary Schools

SECOND EDITION

with text and illustrations by

FLOYD L. BERGMAN

ALLYN AND BACON, INC.
Boston   London   Sydney   Toronto

To my wife,
Virginia,
and all other contributors
&
To the memory of my mother,
Anna Josephine

Library of Congress Cataloging in Publication Data

Bergman, Floyd L., 1927—
　　The English teacher's activities handbook.

　　Bibliography: p. 311
　　Includes indexes.
　　1. English language—Study and teaching (Secondary)—
Handbooks, manuals, etc.　I. Title.
LB1631.B39　　　　428'.007'12　　　81-7884
ISBN 0-205-07383-2　　　　　　AACR2

Managing Editor: Robert Roen

Printed in the United States of America.

10　9　8　7　6　5　4　3　　　　91　90　89　88

Contents

Foreword

A sign in a Montreal bus advertises "Canada's like this: 'Our unity is our diversity.'" And that's true of English, too.

For "What's English?" keeps coming up, year after year, when teachers stop teaching it and start talking about it—at conferences, in planning meetings, in teacher training sessions. We seem to agree about general goals although not about how to state them nor evaluate them. We are always looking for methods that work. That's what this book is about.

Admittedly a cafeteria offering, Bergman's collection reminds experienced teachers of methods that may work again and gives beginners enough ammunition for the first two years, at least.

It's a troublesome book, in a way, because it puts to rest the complaint, "I can't think of anything to do to awaken interest." And it's dangerous, too, because administrators or parents may see it and wonder why more of these ideas aren't being tried in their school.

But it's meant to be a help, a resource to keep handy, a refresher, a prod to the imagination of the English teachers. As long as that "faculty" is at work, learning's more likely.

In the end, this book is for students—to help make English lively, profound, useful, and fanciful; never dull, repetitious, or senseless.

I hope, for the student's sake, this book helps us all.

William E. Hoth
Professor of Education
Wayne State University

Preface

Graduate and undergraduate teacher education students as well as classroom teachers, through the years, have shared with me hundreds of practices for teaching English. In college classes we often duplicated and distributed the ideas. These booklets became one of our most popular innovations, sought after even by others. Class members frequently suggested an expanded book of ideas which more teachers could share. This book is the result: the best of the class collections, some of my own favorites, and those gleaned from visiting classes in action.

These ideas are not offered as unique curriculum changes but simply as succinctly phrased, proven classroom practices for the new or experienced English teacher.

Some readers might prefer more complete descriptions than this book offers: materials to use, steps to take, results of past trials, lists of resources, and the like. Such articles are found in abundance elsewhere, many listed in the comprehensive bibliography.

This book is designed to save preparation time and to encourage planned creativity. The approach here reflects several fairly safe assumptions about teachers. They do not always need detailed descriptions of techniques; they can readily expand an abbreviated idea; and they prefer to innovate rather than copy.

As acknowledged above, many "coauthors" contributed to this collection—actually more than 300. I would have liked to show my appreciation by listing their names. Over the years, however, some names and ideas have become separated, and there have been many duplications. Then too, although originality was always encouraged, some suggestions probably have been passed along from various sources. Thus, all ideas, liberally edited, are published in this volume as "author unknown." Individuals whose suggestions appear here, I'm sure, will overlook the credits and understand that their contributions to the profession are appreciated.

How to Use This Book

Those who support an English curriculum guided by cognitive—even affective—objectives will find the content and classification system of this book helpful. Those who cannot accept English structured along the performance objective route need not be turned away by the rather elaborate labeling. The ideas will still be useful and not difficult to find.

In whatever camp you find yourself, taking the time to read this short introduction will help you get the most from this book.

All formal teaching and learning require some structure. That basic framework must be both simple and commonsensical, relying on the natural abilities of students. First, some information or concept is introduced. Then students begin to mesh new and earlier learnings, deliberating about the new until new ideas are fitted into familiar frameworks of past experience.

To prove this is not false comfort, the students need an evaluation, even if it is completed privately. The new-found information must then be applied in some lifelike, if not actual, situation. Otherwise, the previous three steps may be wasted effort.

These steps have grown into the four-phase process which is this book's organization. And it is process rather than content which the Ideabook attempts to emphasize—process because students need to practice different methods for handling any new situations which might come along.

If we can use our best content to form long-range, useful operations that can apply to any content, education will have succeeded in one of its basic purposes, perhaps the main one.

THE FIVE PARTS AND SUBDIVISIONS

To help locate ideas quickly, the Ideabook has been divided into the typical English areas: Composition, Grammar/Language, Literature, and Reading. These, with an added section called Room Management, form the five parts.

As a further aid for locating ideas, suggestions in each main section have also been grouped according to four generally accepted steps in the teaching-learning sequence: Introduction, Deliberation, Evaluation, and Application. They are explained briefly below as well as in the Glossary, page 304, and in the Appendix.

Key to Steps in Teaching-Learning Sequence

Introduction—learner receives new information from various sources

Deliberation—learner derives meaning from information and fits it into familiar frameworks

Evaluation—learner or teacher discovers if the first steps have been achieved

Application—learner puts new knowledge to use, ideally outside the classroom or if relearning must take place

These groupings also contain typical subject matter subdivisions. For example, Composition ideas are designated by Argumentation, Description, Exposition, Narration, and several other related descriptors, all arranged alphabetically for easy locating. These classifications are designed to serve the various purposes explained in the following pages.

THE IDEAS

All ideas are numbered sequentially from 1 to 1,001. Each number is followed by a code letter enabling the user to quickly locate the activity's scope. The letter "C" indicates an idea for the entire class, "G" for groups, and "I" for independent study and tutoring. All ideas coded "T" are specific helps for the teacher.

> COMPOSITION
>
> Introduction
>
> Narration
>
> 25-C (Read/Book) "Ncmbei in tha ot."
> many in Ite xmll nnemt y guoit in
> An I wheii hall tny moving fomi.
> IIt wh oll f yoii Ih III mev tI(velni
> Oun thing.

Besides being located under headings for content, subdivisions, and steps in the teaching-learning sequence, each idea is further identified by an entry word in the parentheses preceding the idea. There are twenty such words representing specific processes in the teaching-learning sequence—five for each step. (See the Appendix.)

Each process word also shares parentheses with a second word which identifies the "vehicle" used to aid learning—tools such as books, bulletin boards, filmstrips, games, pictures, skits, and television. For instance, *Observe* (a process under Introduction) may be teamed with a number of different vehicles: (Observe/Filmstrips), (Observe/Movies), (Observe/Plays), (Observe/Television). The processes and vehicles can be used not only to locate ideas but also to form key words when writing objectives. (See the Appendix.)

The following suggest ways to locate ideas dealing with composition in the Ideabook.

Locating General Ideas in a Content Area

Besides thumbing through the book until something appropriate comes along, a reader may want general ideas for evaluating compositions. In Part 1, the Composition section, various ideas can be found under Evaluation and then under the five processes: Compare, Extrapolate, Identify, Judge, and Restructure.

Locating Specific Processes in a Content Area

A teacher may be interested in only one approach to evaluating compositions—through comparison. The best way to locate suitable ideas is to check under Compare in the Index and then refer only to the Composition entries.

Locating Specific Processes in One Aspect of the Content Area

A teacher working in a composition unit may want to locate ways to evaluate narration by judging. Specific ideas can be found by turning to the content area Composition (Part 1), then to Evaluation; next to Narration; and finally to Judge (the specific process).

THE RATIONALE

This book has been designed to provide two types of resources: a handy reference for locating classroom activities when variety is needed and a guide for framing cognitive objectives and affective goals. All practices in the book are gathered under four basic teaching-learning steps—Introduction, Deliberation, Evaluation, and Application—and their twenty process entry words adapted from two reliable curriculum sources.

Introduction is actually the "Knowledge (1.00)" and "Comprehension (2.00)" components of Bloom's taxonomy,[1] or what Parker and Rubin[2] call "Memory and Information Input" or Step One of their suggested teaching-learning sequence.

1. Copyright © 1956 by the David McKay Company. From B.S. Bloom, *Taxonomy of Educational Objectives, Handbook I: Cognitive Domain* (New York: David McKay Company). Used with permission.
2. J. Cecil Parker and Louis J. Rubin, *Process as Content: Curriculum Design and the Application of Knowledge* (Chicago: Rand McNally & Co., 1966), pp. 55–56.

Deliberation grows out of Bloom's categories of "Analysis (4.00)" and Parker and Rubin's "Deriving Meaning." The term *Evaluation* is listed in the Bloom taxonomy as "Evaluation (6.00)." Freely interpreted, this is the same step Parker and Rubin call "Attaching Significance," in which "testing for usability" figures prominently.

Finally, the term *Application* combines Bloom's classes of "Application (3.00)" and "Synthesis (5.00)." Parker and Rubin call this step "Action."

Perhaps the easiest way to show how the Ideabook has incorporated both the Bloom taxonomy of cognitive objectives and the Parker and Rubin Teaching-Learning Sequence is to lay out the three plans side by side and let the reader find the similarities. Since Parker and Rubin based much of their material on the Bloom taxonomy, the similarities among all three are striking. Refer to the chart on page xiii entitled Key Classifications of Cognitive Processes Compared.

Of course, liberties have been taken to establish the classifications in the Ideabook, but the original contention that there is a sequence in the teaching-learning process has been retained. The I-D-E-A organization, therefore, is more than an attempt to contrive an appropriate acronym for the Ideabook.

The notion of a teaching-learning sequence extends much further back in history than Bloom and Parker and Rubin. In the early nineteenth century, Johann F. Herbart established five inductive principles of teaching and learning: preparation, presentation, association, generalization, and application. His work and many writings earned him the title of "father of teaching training." With a resemblance to Herbart's classic approach, the case for I-D-E-A is strengthened.

The next major contribution in sequencing curriculum and instruction came from Tyler, writing in the mid-1900s. He proposed four fundamental questions for developing any curriculum and plan of instruction:

1. What educational purposes should the school seek to attain?
2. What educational experiences can be provided that are likely to attain these purposes?
3. How can these educational experiences be effectively organized?
4. How can we determine whether these purposes are being attained?[3]

Tyler's emphasis on objectives, experiences, organization of experiences, and evaluation are seen as part of Taba's seven steps of curriculum development:

Step 1: Diagnosis of needs
Step 2: Formulation of objectives
Step 3: Selection of content
Step 4: Organization of content
Step 5: Selection of learning experiences
Step 6: Organization of learning experiences
Step 7: Determination of what to evaluate and of the ways and means of doing it[4]

3. Ralph W. Tyler, *Basic Principles of Curriculum and Instruction* (Chicago: The University of Chicago Press, 1950, 1957), pp. 1–2.
4. Parker and Rubin, *Ibid.,* p. 17, citing Hilda Taba, *Curriculum Development: Theory and Practice* (New York: Harcourt Brace and World, 1962), pp. 347–378.

Tyler also influenced Bloom and associates who, in turn, influenced Parker and Rubin, and so on.

Risking some degree of presumptuousness, then, I suggest that the teaching-learning sequence—Introduction, Deliberation, Evaluation, and Application—was duly influenced by the combined contributions of Herbart, Tyler, Bloom and colleagues, as well as Taba, and Parker and Rubin. In these days of accountability, performance objectives, and competency-based education, one couldn't ask for better models even without direct references to Bruner and Piaget. Both, however, are cited frequently by the authors mentioned.

Key Classifications of Cognitive Processes Compared

Bloom* (summarizea and reordered)	Parker and Rubin Model I†	Ideabook Teaching-Learning Steps & Processes
1.00 Knowledge Recall Understand Identify	I. Memory and Information Input Formulating questions Reading expository material Observing a phenomenon Collecting evidence	1. Introduction Discover Listen Observe Read
2.00 Comprehension Translation Interpretation Extrapolation	Listening to a presentation Discovering principles	Research
4.00 Analysis (of elements) (of relationships) (of organization)	II. Deriving Meaning Analyzing the material Experimenting with the material Reorganizing the material Consolidating the material Integrating the material	2. Deliberation Analyze Consolidate Experiment Interpret Organize
6.00 Evaluation Judgment Comparison	III. Attaching Significance Inferring generalization Reconstructing the general structure Relating the material to other situations Testing for usability	3. Evaluation Compare Extrapolate Identify Judge Restructure
5.00 Synthesis Communication Construction Organization Discovery Solution	IV. Action Using the material to solve a problem Using the material to create a problem Using the material to clarify a problem	4. Application Construct Perform Solve Speak Write
3.00 Application		

* B. S. Bloom, *Taxonomy of Educational Objectives, Handbook I: Cognitive Domain* (New York: David McKay Company).

† J. Cecil Parker and Louis J. Rubin, *Process as Content: Curriculum Design and the Application of Knowledge* (Chicago: Rand McNally and Co., 1966), pp. 55, 56.

The I-D-E-A format is only a portion of the needed planning for teaching, and a small portion at that. It deals with one activity at one stage of development as it might be introduced, deliberated, evaluated, or applied to extra-class environments. Before the Introduction phase even begins, the teacher must diagnose needs, set goals, formulate objectives upon these goals, and select and organize content and experiences (including tools) to help achieve the goals and objectives. At this point I-D-E-A enters the picture.

The Teaching-Learning Sequence

Although an English teacher does not need explanations of the five content divisions—Composition, Grammar/Language, Literature, Reading, and Room Management—the I-D-E-A sequence and related processes warrant more definition than has been given to this point. The following explanations are also summarized in the Appendix.

Introduction, as is evident in the term, becomes the first step in the teaching-learning sequence, when students are exposed to information for improving skills and building concepts. This is the information-intake step during which new generalizations are built upon past learning and knowledge, and it is usually the first portion of a lesson covering new material. The ideas included under Introduction suggest ways to begin teaching a concept, lesson, or unit.

Under this step are five main Introduction processes: *Discover*—asking questions and using other inquiry methods; *Listen, Observe*—reviewing something such as films or slides; and *Read*—translating both literal and nonliteral information (the latter including metaphor, symbolism, irony, and exaggeration). *Research,* the fifth method, generally takes place out of class in libraries or among authorities, and it relies on its companion processes, particularly *Read.*

Admittedly, selecting only five processes (and always the same number) for each of the four phases in the teaching-learning sequence is an arbitrary decision, reducing the number of processes to be kept in mind. Thus, to the Introduction phase processes described here could be added many other ways to receive the information needed for making generalizations and increasing knowledge. The Appendix lists some of the possibilities.

The purpose of an Introduction step is to give the learner some information and background to add to what is already known, in an effort to build generalizations about the new material. Once this is accomplished, the generalizations and associated information must be manipulated to make them more understandable and, therefore, more retainable. This becomes the function of the second step.

Deliberation suggests meditating, reflecting, considering, pondering, and reasoning. The Deliberation phase ideas collected here attempt to place recently acquired information into familiar frameworks of experience. Here the student engages in a number of different processes of which five are most frequently used.

One process in the Deliberation phase is for the student to *analyze* information—recognizing unstated assumptions and distinguishing facts from hypotheses, seeing how elements are related, and studying their structure and peculiarities. Sometimes students must *consolidate* information, selecting specific and useful new information and relating it to other previously accumulated but similar knowledge.

To understand new ideas, students must often practice using skills and concepts. They often *experiment* through in-class activities and practice exercises. Occasionally they need to *interpret* the information, for example, to grasp the complete thought of a literary work to determine purpose, theme, or moral. Finally, in the Deliberation phase, the learners may have to *organize* incoming information, because classifying and ordering can make information easier to recall for later use and for conveying to others.

The third level of the teaching-learning sequence is called **Evaluation.** Here the learner performs one or more oral, written, or mental "tests" to determine if the information being learned is significant or even useful. Here also is a chance to discover if one's knowledge of the new material is sufficient. It also gives the teacher a chance to measure teaching effectiveness.

One way to evaluate is to *compare* or seek similarities and differences among situations, ideas, and products usually based on observable external qualities. True knowledge of material is measured by the ability to *extrapolate* beyond the given situation and data. By this process, the learner determines implications and consequences of a work and predicts what might occur when similar conditions are present in another context. Such reasoning is assisted by relating to past similar experiences.

Typical among evaluation approaches is the need to *identify* or differentiate among various ideas and structures and to select meanings and definitions that belong to particular sources. The two remaining processes in the Evaluation phase are the abilities to *judge* and to *restructure*. In the former, the learner tests an idea or product for usability, accuracy, logic, or other internal traits. Restructure is sifting data and arranging what is appropriate to fit a function similar to but not exactly like the original instances.

Little new information remains with a learner unless it can be applied somehow to ongoing daily life. The **Application** phase, probably the most important but least understood and used, includes processes that permit knowledge and information to be implemented or applied in different settings and contexts, preferably in ways that reflect or even utilize true-to-life situations.

One way to apply learning is to *construct* something such as a model, a structure, a work of art, or a product that does not fit into any of the following Application processes. Frequently a learner uses learnings to *perform:* acting in plays or working at tasks requiring specially acquired skills. Another way to apply learning is through the need to *solve* anything from life's daily problems to completing a puzzle. Finally, a learner may put learnings into play by choosing to *write* or *speak*.

These constitute the four steps in the teaching-learning sequence along with their associated processes, twenty in number for convenience. Once again, even though more processes could have been added, those selected seem to represent the needs in the typical school. An expanded list of process words can be found in the Appendix.

In conclusion, if at least three principles of I-D-E-A are followed in each day's lessons, no pupils should be bored, at least from lack of variety. Each step in the sequence requires a switch in procedures. This book's purpose is to enhance "switching."

The Ideabook, the Methods Class, and Student Teaching

Although it is written particularly for in-service teachers, this book also has potential value in English methods classes and student teaching.

Any idea, wherever it appears in the I-D-E-A sequence, can be hypothetically traced forward or back. An idea listed in the Evaluation phase, for instance, can be described three more times: as it might have begun in the Introduction phase, as students might work with it in the Deliberation phase, and then as it might be handled in Application. One idea should suggest three others at different stages with different approaches but with the same content.

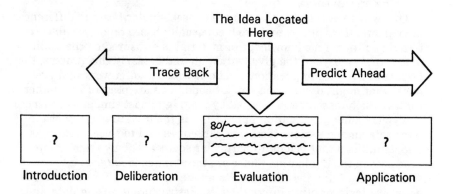

Depending on its complexity, a single tip can also be expanded from one day to several days or even several weeks. Here, then, is a resource for treating unit and daily lesson plans, developing micro- and macro-teaching demonstrations, stating objectives and competencies, developing learning modules, and pursuing many other related projects.

Even further, some ideas in this collection can be discussed orally or in writing to see how they might be improved, or, on the positive side, to determine why they are good techniques.

In the following examples, one basic idea has been described in all four phases by expanding upon an idea that could have been listed in the Evaluation phase of the Grammar/Language section.

GRAMMAR / LANGUAGE

Vocabulary   *Introduction*

00–C   *(Discover/Read) "Word Watchers"*

Encourage the students to build a source of useful words by having them keep pocket-sized spiral notebooks in which to place new vocabulary encountered in various reading experiences. Collect the notebooks periodically to build a relevant supply for class use. Dividing a notebook into sections will add more interest. These are suggested: Words from Novels, Words from Classes (textbooks), Words from the Media, Words from Being a Good Listener.

* * * *

GRAMMAR / LANGUAGE

Vocabulary *Deliberation*

00–I   *(Consolidate/Lists) "Words with Personality"*

Using the new vocabulary words, students write brief definitions for the words. To help place the new word into a familiar area, a word describing human characteristics can be paired with fictional or actual personalities:

garrulous: the nurse in *Romeo and Juliet*
philanthropist: Andrew Carnegie

By associating new vocabulary with personalities and familiar landmarks or events, students will reinforce the retention of word definitions.

* * * *

GRAMMAR / LANGUAGE

Vocabulary *Evaluation*

00–I   *(Identify/Tests) "Why Not?"*

To test students' comprehension of newly introduced vocabulary, prepare a special true-false test. Give correct definitions for some words, for others give incorrect definitions. If the given meaning is wrong, students must also supply the correct definition. For an extra point, they could also supply a word which fits an incorrect definition.

* * * *

GRAMMAR / LANGUAGE

Vocabulary *Application*

00–C,I   *(Construct/Bulletin Boards) "Who Said That?"*

After they have learned a particular set of new vocabulary words, students can locate pictures, articles, and other instances from outside sources (magazines, newspapers, literature, speeches) where they have seen the same words. Place a large "graffiti board" in the room so students can share words, contexts, and sources. If they will recognize how frequently these words are used in everyday living, students will begin to use this new vocabulary in their own speaking and writing.

THE REST IS UP TO YOU

If you have had time to read this introduction, you are now better informed on the rationale for this Ideabook and on ways to use it. If you are interested in studying English methodology in teacher preparation, you have found suggestions for expanding one idea to cover the four phases of the teaching-learning sequence. If you want to see how classroom activities can become models for practice in writing cognitive objectives, you are invited to turn to the Appendix. There you will also discover how to help an affective goal.

Since this is not a methods book, the explanations are brief, perhaps even superficial. Readers who want more depth must locate additional readings (see Resource Bibliography).

Those who did not read the Introduction will, through trial and error, learn how to find specific classroom activities in the Ideabook. But they will certainly not understand its full potential. Lack of understanding, however, may not be a complete obstruction to either the introduction-skippers or yourself. The more you use this book and work it into your own teaching preferences—interweaving these ideas with your own—the more useful the book will become. You may even want to build a file of new ideas you encounter. A suggested format such as found in the Ideabook is in the Appendix.

The Ideabook cannot be a panacea. It is simply a handy supply of proven classroom activities adaptable to the unique teaching style of an individual teacher for a specific group of students. Since no two classes are exactly the same, what works for one class may not work for another. Similarly, an idea that works for one teacher may not work for another—even with the same students. The ideas in this book worked for those who suggested them. The best way to use this handbook, therefore, is to let it jog the imagination when you believe or when your students indicate that a "shift of gears" is needed.

Part One

COMPOSITION

1 Introduction

ARGUMENTATION

1-C *(Discover/Discussions) "Writing Relevantly"*

Most problems in teaching written composition would be solved if *all* topics were interesting to *all* students. Argumentative compositions come closest to the life style of youth as well as adults. Our very existence depends on good debate as it occurs in a democracy. Composition topics that pair current world issues with the class material heighten interest in and awareness of history-in-the-making and in ways to communicate the knowledge. Introduce ways to write on polarized topics such as: "Why everyone should support (issue or idea) instead of (opposing issue or idea)."

2-C *(Observe/Magazines) "Unhidden Persuaders"*

Part of a unit on argumentation should be devoted to the art of persuasion. Clipping, collecting under types, and studying model ads from magazines can be helpful. Add a little more fun by deleting from the ads references to the products' names and their manufacturers. Let the class guess the product as well as analyze to what basic human need the advertiser is appealing.

3-C *(Observe/Periodicals) "News No-Nos"*

In a unit on argumentation, have individuals bring in newspaper and magazine clippings (ads and articles) with models of fallacies underlined. Place the items attractively on a bulletin board carrying an interesting title such as "Writing Fallaciously" or "Fuzzy Thinking." Suggest the errors and prejudices that often cause reasoning to go faulty, such as being: (1) too humane, (2) overly selfish or egocentric, (3) strongly influenced by word and symbol, (4) swayed by formal thought (philosophy, religion, politics), (5) impressed by change for sake of change, and (6) attracted to the status quo.

DESCRIPTION

4–C   *(Research/Field Trips) "Something to Behold"*

Writing creatively requires time to put all the senses to work as ideas are being formed. Students need to practice this "lost art." Expose the class to serious contemplation by suggestions such as: (1) Sit in a park or anywhere slightly apart from the hustle and bustle. Listen for and identify all the sounds you hear. List them so as not to forget them. (2) Search for something unusual in nature such as a four-leaf clover or a branch covered with lichens. (3) Curl up in a comfortable chair to listen with closed eyes to a symphonic movement, e.g., the fourth movement ("storm movement") of Beethoven's *Sixth* ("Pastoral") *Symphony.* Then think deeply of what you have just experienced and consider how to describe the sensations. Such activities often become unique experiences to those who have never been very perceptive. Through close observation, students learn to recognize the experiences needed for quality creative writing.

5–C   *(Research/Field Trips) "Triptoe through the Tulips"*

Obtain permission to take the class on a short excursion around the school neighborhood. Remind students to keep all senses open. Upon returning, have them jot down observations in readiness to practice organizing thoughts about an individual met along the route, a situation encountered, or simply an aesthetic description of a scene. Perhaps for the first time they will really observe the mailman's actions or the condition of the empty shopping center lot after a busy evening.

DRAMA

6–C   *(Read/Plays) "Daily Forum Mirror"*

To help students appreciate the difficulty and artistry involved in good writing, select a scene such as Caesar's assassination or a scene from any Elizabethan drama that has been rewritten in the style of modern journalism or in another expository form. Analyzing the original version and the rewrite will readily show the differences between the literary styles.

EXPOSITION

7–C   *(Discover/Critiques) "Eye for Art"*

Let students discover how a powerful writing style can influence people to accept or reject a finished product. Reviews of popular books, concerts, and films furnish examples of exposition designed to change minds. Studying the techniques of the critic helps to develop a sharper prose style as well as an analytical mind. Most important, the examples are readily available and students don't mind looking for them.

8–I   *(Discover/Questions) "Shares that Gather Interest"*

Everyone wants to be recognized for some skill or knowledge. Capitalize on this psychological phenomenon when helping students choose expository topics. Ask such questions as, "What do you know that you could share with others?" "What do you really care about?" Few will say "nothing" and mean it.

9–I   *(Listen/Sentences) "Least for the Most"*

Explain the functions of short, choppy, sometimes incomplete sentences where extreme succinctness is required. Discuss how this style may be acceptable for telegrams and classified advertisements but not for most compositions. Prepare a set of terse telegram messages for the class to rephrase into acceptable complete sentences.

10–C   *(Observe/Paragraphs) "Strip Tease"*

With a paragraph board, demonstrate the principles of writing expository paragraphs. Write each sentence of the paragraph on a long strip of poster board or paper. Using a bulletin board, place the cards in the wrong order, then ask the class to tell why they are wrong. The paragraph can be corrected by changing the card positions, removing cards, or by adding new cards. For example, to teach emphasis, the main point of the paragraph could first be buried in the middle of the paragraph and then be moved to the beginning or end. Sentences can also be printed on strips of clear plastic for the overhead projector.

11–C   *(Observe/Pictures) "Introduction to Introspection"*

Part of being able to write a good composition is to have something to say about the immediate environment. This comes through careful observation and not superficial glances. Demonstrate by showing (or projecting) a picture for a minute or less. The students write one descriptive paragraph to include everything they remember about the picture. At first the picture can be rich with possibilities to make the task easier, but after giving the students several tries, narrow the choice to very simple objects such as a paper clip or a light bulb.

12-I   *(Research/Authorities) "Research Travel-Log"*

Build a unit around the theme "Travel." Each student chooses a place he or she would like to visit. The student must research it thoroughly to present an authoritative written paper. Related work can include such activities as business letters requesting information from the source, thank-you notes, conversations with people who have been there, or posters from travel agencies. The kinds of writing appropriate to this assignment are varied and reflect just about any writing situation one can encounter. This activity also introduces the student to the needs for and methods of research.

13-I   *(Research/Authorities) "Super Snooper"*

Understanding the community and its workings is important, especially at the upper levels of high school. Incorporate English composition with problems of the city. Build on student outside interests. For one assignment, the class might spend a month gathering information on some aspect of city organization and then write papers on their findings. Students could speak with persons who work in the departments they are studying. They might also make comparisons by gathering additional information from other communities.

14-G   *(Research/Books) "Telling It Like It Was"*

In a unit such as "Our American Founders," students form small groups to read numerous biographies and autobiographies. For class presentations, each group shares its research through any approach (individual or group)—a skit, audiovisual presentation, panel discussion, and the like. Prizes might be awarded for the best presentation.

15-I   *(Research/Circulars) "Firm Footnoting"*

When students are asked to document an opinion paper or research, have them go further than just providing footnotes. Have them also make a collection of other pertinent sources of information. For example, if a student is asked to present and substantiate his political viewpoint, he could collect flyers, advertising brochures, or booklets from organizations that support his position, or clip newspaper headlines and magazine illustrations that reflect a political viewpoint he could support or reject. Display items can then be put into a notebook along with the composition. More creative students might prepare collages (montages) on large sheets of tagboard to be displayed in the room.

16-I   *(Research/Letters) "Mail Order Topics"*

Most students are eventually asked to write a term paper about a foreign country, and there are always those who don't know where or how to begin. In a joint effort with the social studies department, the English class can help. Encourage the students to write letters to the United Nations Office of Public Information, New York City, to obtain a free list of information, services, and foreign embassies in the United States. Students then write letters requesting free maps, pictures, flags, booklets, and printed material for projects.

17-T   *(Research/Libraries) "Communicate to Teach"*

Research techniques can be more practical than they usually are. The teacher might open class discussion by posing a question about which he or she needs more information. For example, the problem might be deciding on the best car to buy. The teacher must know in advance the kinds of things one needs to know about a car before buying and can then guide the students in finding and citing sources of information to get the answers. By finding and documenting information usually found in the library, the students compile their reports, hoping the teacher decides on their favorite car. Not until the end of the project is it mentioned that they have been introduced to the "research paper."

FILM MAKING

18-C   *(Discover/Books) "Film-m-m-making"*

If your school has or has access to a motion picture camera, some English classes might produce a short film. Students should first learn about the strengths and limitations of film as a communication medium. They should also learn some of the techniques: sequencing, cutaway, fade, and so on. After a theme has been proposed for a film, a lesson on script writing is due. Scripts can be very simple or complex depending on available equipment. For example, the silent movie or mime script with tape-recorded narration, music, and sound effects can be very effective when sound-film synchronization is not possible. Either way everyone has a job to do: write script, develop sound effects, choose background music, create costumes and scenery, do makeup, operate camera, and act. If some students still do not have jobs, become more technical and involved. Select a producer and director. Set up an advertising and publicity committee. At this point, funding might be a problem. So, early in the planning, let the producer head up a finance committee to sponsor events to raise money for the extravaganza.

19–C   *(Observe/Projectors) "Calling the Shots"*

Typical projection equipment available to almost any classroom can be used to explain the various movie camera shots. On one side of the front wall (or screen) an overhead projector displays a list of camera shots with brief explanations. Nearby, an opaque (or slide) projector shows appropriate pictures demonstrating each shot. For example, an airplane view of New York City depicts a long shot (a pan shot by moving a rectangular light mask across the picture). A shot of a tenement house reflects another camera angle. A close-up shot might be a child sitting on a stairway and eating an apple. Fade-ins and fade-outs, though tricky, can be shown by manipulating two L-shaped pieces of cardboard to mask the light gradually. All these techniques can be used to illustrate student movie scripts or scenarios.

JOURNALISM

20–C   *(Discover/Magazines) "Variety Variation"*

Arrange for copies of a popular variety magazine to be sent or brought to class once or twice a month. Point out concerns such as format, regular features, themes, slant, and advertising. Also encourage students to read some of the new books the magazines review. This will provide variety to the "required reading list." By reading book reviews and then the book themselves, advanced classes should be able to write book reports that resemble magazine book reviews rather than the traditional title-author-plot variety.

21–C   *(Listen/Radio, Television) "People Baiter"*

In a journalism or composition unit, include the skills of obtaining and writing interviews. Prepare students by discussing the different interview approaches and special preparations for conducting and writing them. Use carefully selected radio or television interviewers as study models. Later, as a culminating task, find someone to interview. The guest need not be famous. All people can be interesting if the interviewer is creative and skillful. A student, the principal, custodian, city librarian, museum curator, or a parent can make good subjects. The finished products can be discussed and the best ones written up for the school paper. Different interview techniques uncovered (glibness, frothiness, aggressiveness among others) can be discussed.

22–C *(Read/Newspapers) "Newsworthy Idea"*

Newspapers are cheap, readily available, and offer a variety of subjects interesting to everyone. Students can also mark and cut newspapers. Besides reading and studying news articles, editorials, and features (the usual procedure), students can use them in other ways: reorganize or rewrite paragraphs of sections of articles if not the entire one, restructure sentences and strip them of excess verbiage, or write imaginative stories based on news items, even putting themselves in the story. Other activities include looking for slanted news articles and locating fallacies.

23–C *(Research/Mixed Media) "Potpourri"*

Students clip articles, pictures, cartoons, advertisements, or interesting famous quotes from newspapers or magazines. These are pasted in a loose-leaf notebook or spiral journal. By answering the question "Why did you choose this item?" students will automatically emerge with many ideas which they can later use for various composition assignments.

NARRATION

24–C *(Listen/Anecdotes) "Anecdote-tell"*

Telling short, true, or fictitious stories aloud is good practice as well as fun. It prepares students for the more interesting job of writing a longer story and helps them organize thoughts. The teacher can create initial interest by telling two or three humorous anecdotes, then asking students to think about what makes each story funny, where the most humorous part occurs, and what makes a good anecdote. Finally, set up some guidelines for choosing an incident, making it interesting, using conversation for reality, building suspense, and ending quickly with a strong line.

25–C *(Read/Books) "Anapest No Bug"*

Next to nursery rhymes, perhaps the children's books by Dr. Seuss are the best known to today's youth. Even adults enjoy reading the mainly anapestic feet gamboling through his delightfully different stories. Take advantage of this natural interest and bring in some Dr. Seuss books to be read for the purposes of studying meter and their appealing qualities.

26–C   *(Read/Chalkboards) "A Bird in Hand"*

Proverbs are useful for teaching literal and figurative meaning. A new proverb can be written on the chalkboard daily and then be discussed at the start of each class. This activity promotes oral discussion and suggests topics for impromptu and short compositions.

OVERVIEW

27–C   *(Discover/Discussions) "What's Your Bag?"*

The class can brainstorm during one full class period—more if effective—to come up with topics that interest them. During some of the tangent discussion that is bound to occur, list the best ideas as a source of composition topics which will meet most interest levels.

28–I   *(Discover/Handouts) "Favor or Disfavor"*

At an early-in-the-year class session, ask each student to complete sentences such as these: The thing I fear (or dislike) most is…. A thing that bothers me most about people (life) is…. I think least about…. The contributors should remain anonymous. The various replies may be duplicated for the class and become sources for future composition assignments.

29–I   *(Discover/Notes) "Recall Experiences"*

When starting a composition unit, obtain a card file to use as a Topic Box. A student fills out 3×5 cards outlining three ideas on which he or she would like to write. New ideas can be added any time from discussions or reading. The teacher uses the cards to help individualize future assignments. All members use the box when they need theme topics.

30–C   *(Listen/Music) "Music to Write By"*

Music that evokes a strong emotional response can enhance instruction or stimulate imagination. Find a disc or tape recording of some unfamiliar music, such as "Fetes" by Debussy or a portion of any symphony. Play the music through at least three times while students jot down their thoughts as they feel the music. Suggestion questions: Does the music make you feel happy, sad, excited, or what? If this were background music for a motion picture, what would you expect to see on the screen? Then help them choose an appropriate vehicle that will convey their feelings: a personal anecdote, an essay, a poem, a descriptive scene captured in a few words, or any idea that could later be developed into a longer composition. This exercise introduces to students the variety of ways they have to express the many, many emotions that affect them each day.

31-C *(Listen/Music) "New Days a 'Dawnin'"*

To introduce new ideas for compositions, have a "Someplace Day" several times a month. For example, several students might plan a "Hawaiian Day" when they play Hawaiian music (recorded or live), demonstrate native dances, show pictures or slides, and possibly even end up with a luau produced in cooperation with the home economics department. Following each "Day," students move into the writing practice phase by either doing narratives, descriptions, or expositions on whatever aspect interested and inspired them most.

32-C *(Listen/Radio, Television) "On the Air"*

Students listen to the radio a lot. Various opinions have been offered as to how well they really listen. To emphasize the need to be more consciously observant, assign a short paper (or discussion) on the past week's radio menu. Typical questions may be: (1) What kinds of programs characterize most of your listening? (2) Why did you make the selections you did? (3) Were the programs mainly local or network? (4) What were the call letters of the station you listened to most? Then have them zero in on one favorite program: (1) Was it sponsored or not? By whom? (2) What were the products advertised? (3) What was one "near-quote" you can remember? (4) Who was on the program (name singers, actors, announcers)? Many other questions can be asked and could be applied to television as well as radio. If students do poorly on this assignment, it becomes a case in point that people do listen—even view—unconsciously. Or they may listen or view selectively. Discuss whether unconscious and selective viewings are good or bad.

33-I,C *(Observe/Bulletin Boards) "Words of Wisdom"*

Let your students install a collective bulletin board. They can bring in sayings and quotations (with pictures if possible) by famous people who have influenced lives with what they have written or spoken: Benjamin Franklin, Confucius, Jesus Christ, Kahlil Gibran, Solomon (Proverbs in the Bible), William Shakespeare, Winston Churchill, some of our presidents, and others. This words-of-wisdom corner serves to introduce discussion and eventually composition topics.

34-I   *(Observe/Pictures) "Kids on Display"*

On a file folder panel each student pastes a display of magazine and catalogue pictures reflecting his or her own personality and interests. On another face of the folder, the student may attach a brief writing sample which explains his or her creation. When all have completed their "personality" folders, display them (names hidden) on the bulletin board under the banner *Guess Who*. When the identification game is over, folders are filed for conferences, assignment storage, and for reading and writing suggestions.

35-C   *(Read/Handouts) "What's Due?"*

Provide the class with a list of composition topics for the entire semester. As each of the compositions is completed and corrected, check it off. The master list then becomes a progress chart.

36-G   *(Research/Authorities) "Stations, Everyone"*

Reflect on a topic such as "life and death" or "war and peace." Set up several stations around the room (they may be numbered). Split the class into small groups with each starting at a different station and proceeding until all have been covered. Possible stations are: (1) chalkboard with short quotations (students add their own); (2) folder with short newspaper article(s); (3) a picture bulletin board to which students may add; (4) a participatory graffiti wall (wide wrapping paper); (5) a slide-tape show; (6) a tape-recorded radio newscast; (7) a film or field trip (if topic is war and peace) to the museum to see war relics then to the art gallery to see art depicting peace and war; (8) a wrap-up station where students can hear past comments on projects and record new comments. After they have visited all stations, have students write about their feelings, thoughts, and emotions that were evoked by materials at the stations. They can use whatever style they wish: essay, poetry, stream-of-consciousness, or other.

37-G   *(Research/Games) "Sh-h-h!"*

After studying library procedures from a book, students need to experience what was introduced by going to the library. Divide the class into teams. Give each team a list of books by author, title, subject, or call number. The students must determine which books are in the card catalogue and then find them on the shelves. Articles from periodicals could also be included in the list. The team that locates all of the references first wins the competition. A natural follow-up, of course, is to research a topic for a report.

38-G   *(Research/Libraries) "Class Cutter"*

Besides the regular class work, individuals work on outside projects or term papers. To research the work, small groups can go to the library each day on a rotating basis. Besides decreasing daily class size by four or five students, the approach teaches students how to work without supervision. It also presents the chance to concentrate on something really interesting. This is a good opportunity to involve student teachers, teacher aides, or even student cadets.

POETRY

39-C   *(Listen/Music) "Un-Musical Sounds"*

To help students get more use out of descriptive words, introduce onomatopoeia by using a record featuring musical instruments that imitate nonmusical sounds (e.g., Prokofiev's *Peter and the Wolf*). Students can write what they hear. Later they can build their own lists of words that have built-in sounds, such as grumble, clink, lumber, plop, and splash.

40-C   *(Observe/Artwork) "Poetic Bars"*

In teaching poetry as an art form, explain that the first poetry was always sung. Other relationships between poetry, music, and art can be demonstrated by presenting recordings and paintings that express the same mood as a particular poem.

Call attention to certain aspects of the painting that are also conveyed by the selected music and by an appropriate quotation from poetry. A good example might be a poem by Frost such as "Stopping by Woods on a Snowy Evening" or "The Runaway" juxtaposed with a winter scene by Grandma Moses, Norman Rockwell, or less contemporary painters.

As for music, select any symphonic movement that conveys the New England countryside in a muffled snowfall. Mozart and Beethoven are always reliable sources as well as Ralph Vaughn Williams or Ravel. Stress similarities in design (repeated motifs) and deliberate breaks in the design for variety. Then explore the dominant impressions created by space, form, words, or sounds. It is this dominance that creates the most distinguishable parallels. (Also see idea 531.)

41-I   *(Observe/Chalkboards) "Green Poets"*

To introduce the value of word associations in poetry, give the word *green*. Class members call out the words or images they associate with the color. Then the class reciprocates by giving an evocative word to the teacher who lists on the board the associations, some of which are later formed into a simple word poem.

This List	*And This*	*Become*
green	cattle	*Grass*
grass	hay	*lush-green,*
carpet	food	*carpet,*
cucumber	mow	*cool—*
cool	peas	*spring.*
aroma	lush	*Fresh-mown*
beans	spring	*hay.*
		Aroma.
		Cattle-food.

The "poem" in the right column is largely formed by listing all the related words from the first two columns. Next, the class is given a word, and the members list on paper all words and phrases that seem to relate. Then each student creates his or her own poem.

42-C   *(Observe/Models) "Haiku! Bless You"*

A short poetic form developed in Japan centuries ago, haiku has become the achievable goal for many budding young poets. Its three unrhymed lines (with 5, 7, and 5 syllables respectively) usually reflect a season, catch a mood or an emotion, and unite for a brief moment poet and reader in a common life experience.

Autumn came crisply
Showing its reds and yellows
In each dancing leaf.

Resembling haiku, tanka—another Japanese poetic device—uses five unrhymed lines of 5, 7, 5, 7, and 7 syllables. Before letting the class write their own, show and read some samples.

WORDS

43-C   *(Listen/Lists) "Going Jotting"*

Bring in a list of words (preferably adjectives). The class jots down each word as it is read. They also include the first word(s) called to mind as they hear the trigger-word. Try to make the original word list as interesting and provocative as possible. The words can be reorganized into a poem, essay, or a narration. A simple word like *blue* may evoke anything from the flashing blue light of the county sheriff's car to the sparkling water of a mountain stream.

2 Deliberation

ARGUMENTATION

44–C *(Analyze/Models) "Fallaciously Speaking"*

Students are interested in analyzing sentences for fallacies in reasoning such as these models: (1) Appeal to force: "Your grandchildren will live under communism" (Khrushchev); (2) Appeal to mass emotion by using almost any political speech; and (3) Non sequitur: "Smith is a good lawyer, and he attends church." Many more models appear in any logic book. Commercial advertising fits nicely in this study, as well as comments in the Letters to the Editor newspaper columns.

45–I,G *(Experiment/Discussions) "Better Half"*

To give practice in understanding principles of persuasion, assign a composition on any controversial topic. After each pupil has completed a brief paper taking one side of the argument (for example, a supportive stand on the military draft), assign another paper in which the student must take the opposite view. When the students see that there are two sides to most issues, they can be introduced to a practice used by debate teams. Divide the class into two groups: X and Y. Present a highly debatable topic (thesis), assigning the affirmative position to one group and the negative to the other. Allow both groups a few minutes to discuss arguments for their side. The first person in group X makes a statement to be refuted by the first in line from Group Y who then follows by giving a statement his or her side supports. The second X team member responds with a refutation and offers another statement from his or her side. The response pattern is X_1, Y_1, X_2, Y_2, X_3, and so on. If the class happens to agree on a particular issue, the teacher takes the opposing side and lets the students challenge one at a time. Finish the exercise by pointing out examples of good and bad arguments that were made.

46–I *(Experiment/Role Playing) "Pro in Conning"*

After selecting a controversial topic that lends itself to argumentation, the student decides to be either pro or con. In a written exercise she argues her point as if she were, for example, a journalist, politician, or a philosopher, writing in the style of each. This exercise gives the student a chance to experiment with various argumentative approaches.

47-I   *(Organize/Papers) "About Face"*

To give practice in understanding principles of persuasion, assign a composition on any controversial topic. When each pupil has completed a paper taking, say, a supportive stand, assign another in which he or she must take the opposite view. Debate teams sometimes use this practice, but any English classroom could also use it because it forces students to see that there are two sides to most issues, each side making sense to the proponent.

DESCRIPTION

48-C   *(Analyze/Papers) "Details, Details!"*

Students can analyze the importance of detail and exactness in writing by briefly describing what they observed in the classroom during the previous five minutes. When the papers are read, the differences in the way each student perceives the same situation will be enlightening.

49-G   *(Analyze/Games) "Com-pairing"*

Students can be helped to write imaginative descriptions if they learn to observe familiar objects in new ways. To obtain some models as inspiration, play the comparison game. Select two familiar yet dissimilar objects. Competing groups try to list in a given time (five or ten minutes) as many ways as possible in which the two objects are alike. For example, a *chalkboard* is like a *window:* both are rectangles, both "shed light" on a subject, they are vertical, hard to the touch, and for both, sand is used in the manufacturing process. Have some of the comparisons read orally. Each participant is awarded two points for each comparison which he or she alone suggested, one point for a comparison which two or three have contributed.

50-I,G   *(Consolidate/Papers) "About a Minute or Two"*

For about a minute or two, students watch the actions of a person on the street, on a subway train or bus, in a store, or at home. Then each prepares short descriptions of the incident as though he or she was a detective or spy. Later the papers can be read in class. Students attempt to guess where the person was and what the person was doing—an easy job if the description is good.

51–G *(Consolidate/Papers) "Character-eyes"*

To develop a model for the processes of characterization, each class member picks a personal acquaintance to describe as it might be done in a short story or novel. Characterizations must include physical qualities, mannerisms, attitudes, actions, and speech habits. The presentation should show how others view and interact with the character and how the character views himself or herself.

52–C *(Experiment/Chalkboards) "Four Across"*

Using the same four-column format, place these sound words on the chalkboard:

baying	sputter	patter	cackled
shrieked	ticked	hum	thumped
crash	swished	crunch	whined
tapped	crackle	roar	hissed
sputtered	moaned	bleated	screeched

Tell the class to note that there are four columns. They are to take one word from each column and then use those four words as key ideas in a short descriptive piece of practice writing that really has a "sound" to it. We want to *hear* as well as see.

53–I *(Experiment/Displays) "Brilliant Idea"*

Children need every opportunity to use their imaginations and their senses. A surprising number, however, have not even engaged in the joyful pleasures of conjuring images from cloud formations. Similar in-class displays can evoke similar responses through use of the overhead projector, if going outside is not feasible. Place various opaque objects or cutout shapes on the projector table. Encourage imaginations to wander.

In another approach, obtain two pieces of clear white acetate (plastic sheets). Place several separated drops of colored liquids—as from food dyes or water colors—on one sheet. Then place the second sheet on top. Seal the edges with tape and project on an overhead. The heat will cause the colors to rearrange themselves in different patterns. Pressing the sheets changes the pattern. Also apply multicolors to clear 16 mm film. Show through a projector for startling effects. Even ink blots, as in the Rorschach test, will provide additional stimulation for descriptive paragraphs or essays.

54–C *(Experiment/Games) "What Am I?"*

Paste some magazine illustrations of common objects on file cards, putting the name of the object below. Or make up cards with only the name on them. Students draw cards at random and write a description of the object pictured or labeled. Each student has a different object to describe without naming it. Descriptions must include ten qualities based on sight, touch, taste, smell, and sound. Then the descriptions are read aloud while the other students (or teams) try to guess what is being described. The faster the object is guessed, the more credit students would get for their work because they have learned to use description so well.

55–C   *(Experiment/Lists) "No Peeking"*

To become aware of style in good writing, students need practice in visualizing concrete images from words—building visual images by expanding on details. Reading carefully selected sentences, ask the class to close their eyes and imagine a scene complete with sounds. Then they list all the details. They can later expand these lists into descriptive compositions. Two good stimulus sentences to read are: (1) A great, dead, sun-bleached city lay waffle-like on white-hot sand. (2) There is nothing quieter than the blackened skeleton of somebody's house the morning after a fire.

56–C   *(Experiment/Pictures) "Going on Record"*

The tape recorder can be used to help students realize composition is oral communication symbolized. After presenting a brief introductory lecture, such as "Words—Vehicles for Feeling," show pictures (using slides, opaque, or bulletin board) to arouse emotions. Then allow time for students to record their emotions on tape. Point out that each has produced a mini-composition. Just as they have spoken to let others know how they feel, at times they must also write. To follow through, the teacher might have some taped descriptions transcribed and duplicated for the class to study and discuss.

57–I   *(Interpret/Biographies) "Guess Who"*

To illustrate the importance of describing personalities when writing about people, have each student write a brief personality sketch of anyone. Later the teacher reads the sketches, not revealing the writer or subject. The class tries to guess the subject in each case. This procedure shows that personalities are important and quite different—as different as each person writes. To illustrate the importance of details when writing about people, have each student write a brief personality sketch of the same character just studied in a novel. These are discussed for the differing interpretations and possibly why some are better than others. Then, as a follow-up practice, students write about anyone they all should know, choosing different subjects well-known in the community or the nation.

Later these sketches are read without revealing the subject. The class tries to guess the subject in each case, depending on rich descriptive details.

58–I   *(Interpret/Demonstrations) "Nose for Writing"*

Bring some object to class that has a pervasive but recognizable odor. Assign a short paper on what the odor reminds them of and why, e.g., a particular place, a season of the year, and the like. Kitchen spices and liquid flavorings are good to use because they can evoke memories of a variety of situations and settings. Read some of the results.

59–I,C   *(Interpret/Games) "Where Am I?"*

Each class member writes with clear, precise imagery a scene that would be familiar to all students in the class. They relate what they see, hear, smell, and touch when they are there, but cannot refer to the place by name. When the pieces are read aloud, the rest of the class tries to guess the location.

60–I,G   *(Interpret/Pictures) "No Foldouts"*

Students select a picture from a magazine, a calendar, or a collection of famous prints. They can find their own or use one from the teacher's collection. The object is to express in writing the emotions that the illustration has created. Then they must include why they think the picture made such an impression. The reasons usually run the gamut from childhood memories to recollections of a particularly impressive movie or television program. These are shared in groups to save time. Perhaps each group chooses the best; these are offered to the class.

61–C   *(Interpret/Skits) "Caught in the Act"*

To provide students with a single event about which all could write descriptions, arrange to have some students (three is a good number) come into the class and perform several pre-arranged activities—one student could write a word on the board and then erase it, another could say something and move in an interesting way. They would remain in the room about a minute, then leave. (The actors could be from another teacher's class.) The class that observed the unexpected event would then write a brief description of what transpired, including what each actor wore. Besides being interesting, this activity also points out the need for careful attention to details. Papers will reflect a great variety in quality and accuracy.

62-I *(Organize/Pictures) "Cutting the Family Tree"*

Provide magazines so the class can cut out faces of men, women, and children, all of varying ages, to create a hypothetical family. They paste faces on a simple family tree drawn on construction paper, give names to all members of the family, and then write about each person (age, hobbies, personality, and so on) until they have created as complete a family background as they can. A follow-up would be to locate a picture of the type of house the main family would have, describe it on paper, and draw simple floor plans. Display some projects on the bulletin board.

DRAMA

63-I *(Interpret/Letters) "Man Called Wil"*

After reading a Shakespearean play such as *Hamlet*, students pretend they live in England at the time the play was written. They have just seen a play written by the relatively unknown playwright William Shakespeare. They then write a letter to a friend who has not seen this play. The result is a play review. The unified studies program would find this an excellent way to enliven history through immersion in both time and language. Producing an authentic letter requires some research and an ability to draw inferences.

EXPOSITION

64-C *(Analyze/Books) "Topical Topics"*

After the class has considered what a topic sentence is, have students look for the topic sentences or developing ideas in their various textbooks as well as in periodicals. Seeing that professional writers need and use topic sentences encourages students to try for better-structured paragraphs in their own writing.

65-I *(Consolidate/Displays) "Grab This"*

As practice in writing descriptive exposition, each student prepares a grab bag including a dozen or so items such as bits of uniquely shaped macaroni, some rubber bands, a few tiny toys, two or three empty spools, and some small objects from Dad's workbench or the kitchen junk drawer. Mix up the brown paper bags so that each student gets someone else's. Then each constructs something from the collection in his or her bag. The next activity is to come to class prepared to describe step by step (oral or written) how the creations were built. Vote on the best descriptions to be used as models for class study.

66-I   *(Consolidate/Displays) "The Plane Facts"*

To practice expository writing, one student—an expert at folding—folds a paper into a sleek airplane that flies. Students then fold their own, following the modeling repeated by the demonstrator. Then comes the test. Students write the instructions so that a stranger could make the same plane. Other objects besides a plane may be folded, of course, or cut or even glued.

67-I   *(Consolidate/Essays) "Squeezey Writing"*

Let class practice condensing a three- or four-page printed essay into 250 words, preserving meaning and as much of the style as possible. This paraphrasing assignment illustrates that omitting details from a well-written essay destroys its style and often its meaning.

68-C   *(Experiment/Discussions) "Emote-shuns"*

This approach helps reaffirm methods of definition and stimulates vital discussion. The teacher begins class by asking students for a paragraph defining "son" or "daughter," depending on which they are. The results are collected or read aloud by volunteers. The ideas contained in these definitions are sources of discussion on how these common words have a wide variety of meanings to different people and how words can trigger a range of emotions.

69-C   *(Experiment/Journals) "Random Thoughts"*

For an alternate approach to the usual journal assignment, give the class a topic of current interest and ask them to list in their journals random thoughts on the topic. They need not consider mechanics or grammar. The purpose is to practice the art of thinking on paper.

70-I   *(Interpret/Periodicals) "Clipped Topic"*

Newspapers and magazines can be used to practice creative writing. The teacher clips from a newspaper or magazine an article that involves many people, e.g., 900 people on strike at X Factory, 100 families homeless following a tornado, and so on. After reading the article to the class, the teacher directs each student to do the following: Imagine what might happen to a person involved in the incident, jot down the important ideas as they occur to you, rearrange them in a sequence by preparing a simple outline, then write a paper on this broad news event, narrowing it to its effect on a single individual.

71-C   *(Organize/Papers) "Forward in Reverse"*

Often students are asked to complete a story that has an unfinished ending. Reverse this idea, in a sense. For one attempt, show an object such as a model ship or a decorative table ornament. Have the students think about how the item must have been constructed from planning stage to completion. Students practice writing an exposition that explains the steps that must have been followed to complete ccnstruction. This idea can also be used for narrative writing by giving the ending and having students write what came before.

72-T   *(Organize/Papers) "Your Order, Please"*

To demonstrate transitional signals and logical progression, make an easy-to-read-from-a-distance chart that lists by numbered sequence the various transitional devices (words, phrases, sentences, and paragraphs) that keep compositions moving. Then students may be referred to these devices as needed by calling attention to a "T-number." The same chart may be duplicated on a sheet of paper to be placed in student notebooks.

73-I   *(Organize/Papers) "First Priority"*

In learning how to write well, students must first become fluent in their own use of language to express ideas. Before attempting to improve syntax and grammar, students should have something to say. The first concern, then, is a message. Encourage students to write first drafts as if explaining something aloud to a friend. A tape recorder would help. In this manner, content is emphasized and all mechanical concerns that impede the flow of thought are pushed into the background until later. If students are allowed to feel they have an interesting message worth sharing, they will feel more justified going through the arduous task of rewriting and polishing.

74-C   *(Organize/Sentences) "Mini-Mini Comps"*

Many students entering college or the business world discover they can't communicate their ideas to others. To help eliminate this problem, require students to write and hand in *one* sentence each day on any topic chosen by the student. The assignment, which can later be structured to give practice in using learned grammar rules, reduces the fear of writing and increases the natural flow of written speech. Gradually most students will feel the need to write an entire paragraph to express ideas once they see that it is nothing more than a collection of related sentences. The last step would be sentence combining. Give students suggestions for connecting thoughts through simple coordination in compound sentences or through subordination using phrases and clauses.

HUMANITIES

75-T *(Experiment/Journals) "Jogging Journals"*

Too often teachers let students generate their own motivation to write in a journal. Some students *do* find it difficult to write anything without a little push—even a good writer, from time to time. Give "journal joggers," such as showing some interesting slides or a film and having students write some reactions without fear of grade. Someone could give a talk—even a book report—to stimulate journal reactions. For other ideas, have students fasten an envelope inside the back cover of the journal in which they can store a few newspaper or magazine articles or comments written on scraps when time was a problem. Even a single word written down could set off pages of journal entry when time is available and when the blank page meets a blank mind.

76-I *(Interpret/Artwork) "Find Arts"*

To teach creative writing and art appreciation at the same time, bring to class prints of contemporary paintings by famous artists. After several days in art appreciation discussion, each student selects one print to use for a practice project. First, the student writes a description of the painting and its apparent theme. Then he or she develops the scene and theme into a creative story or poem.

JOURNALISM

77-C *(Analyze/Newspapers) "Press of English"*

Slower students often find nothing in the English class that interests them. Bring in something that will capitalize on their natural concern for world conditions—the daily newspaper. After a time of discussing interesting articles, branch out to other aspects: analyzing news coverage and writing styles, recognizing article types, or locating examples of doublespeak. (See idea 79.) As interest grows, arrange to tour a newspaper plant. This could be followed by publishing a class newspaper using ideas learned in class and on the field trip.

78-C *(Analyze/Newspapers) "Publisher Psychout"*

Purchase or borrow some of the nation's leading newspapers. Read different accounts of one event in the various papers. Note the differences in word choice, pictures, placement, and the like. Collect some of these articles in scrapbooks or on the bulletin board. For a related activity over a period of time, trace one story in a single newspaper. Notice how the placement changes, how it is sometimes featured and then played down, depending on latest developments.

79–C *(Analyze/Newspapers) "Word Pollution"*

After an introduction to doublespeak (ambiguous, sometimes deceptive language, frequently using euphemisms, vague terms, and abstract ideas that often confuse the public), have the class locate samples of advertisements as well as news items about education, politics, and the military. All are usually good sources for doublespeak terms. Sentences like this abound: "If prompt actions are implemented within the disinvestment parameters, the core area's meaningful objectives may be maximized." (Also see ideas 77 and 287).

80–C *(Experiment/Bulletin Boards) "Gigantic Antic"*

Make a bulletin board display of a giant newspaper layout. Draw in the columns and provide space for news items, editorials, features, and sports, but leave columns empty. The class provides accounts of school, community, and national events by writing articles for the proper columns. Adding machine tape can be used as paper for the typed or hand-lettered copy. These contributions serve as models for further study.

81–I *(Experiment/Cartoons) "Captured Captions"*

After an introduction to caption writing—really a lesson about inferential thought—supply a quantity of editorial or situation cartoons with captions removed. Each student randomly selects five and writes his or her own captions. Different ways to share these among class members can be devised, but the opaque projector is the simplest method. Perhaps a chance to compare student captions with the originals should be provided.

82–G *(Experiment/Interviews) "Journal-ease"*

After presenting information on the interview technique, don't do the usual practice of pairing up and interviewing each other or interviewing parents or the teacher. Instead, bring a relatively unknown person to your class after giving some significant facts. Have the class conduct its own interview in press conference format. Have each student write up the interview as a culminating activity. Some of the best papers should be shared, with the very best sent to the school newspaper if the interview subject would interest the student body.

83–C   *(Interpret/Newspapers) "Matchmakers"*

Select short, interesting news items with well-worded headlines. Number the headings and corresponding articles so they can be matched later. Remove the headlines and keep them at the teacher's desk. Each student reads an article and writes an original headline for it. As the teacher calls article numbers, each student reads the article and new headline. Then the teacher reads the original headline. The exercise provides good practice in getting the key idea from a piece of writing.

NARRATION

84–C   *(Analyze/Models) "And Lo, There Was a Time"*

As an exercise analyzing narrative style, rewrite a familiar children's story ("Goldilocks," "Little Red Riding Hood," or "The Three Little Pigs," for instance) as Chaucer might have written them or as a popular news magazine or even the Bible might have presented the story. Papers are read to the class or displayed on the bulletin board.

85–I   *(Consolidate/Models) "Grand Finale"*

Combine knowledge of fiction and composition. Individuals write their own endings for a novel or short story they have recently studied, changing it in any way they wish. This activity provides opportunities to combine theme, tone, characterization, structure, and dialogue into a single project. An advanced class can try writing in a certain author's style.

86–G   *(Consolidate/Pictures) "Captured Moments"*

Prepare a bulletin board using thought-provoking magazine pictures without captions. Divide the class into small groups. Each group chooses a picture to discuss for ten to fifteen minutes for the purpose of building a story around it—a group-written story. Split the workload so certain individuals specialize in perfecting certain aspects of the story. For example, various members would be responsible for embellishing each of these based on an agreed-upon outline: time and place (the setting); the sounds, colors, shapes; the mood; and the dialogue for the characters. Major items of plot, characterization, and theme would be handled by the group as a whole.

87-G *(Experiment/Audiotapes) "Off the Record"*

Divide the class into groups of five or six. Each group is given a tape recorder and an opening sentence for a narrative (all groups can work with the same sentence or each may have a different one). One student in each group begins a story using this sentence. Each student in the group adds a sentence. The aim, of course, is to develop a story with plot, climax, and conclusion. When completed, the story is played back and perhaps edited to satisfaction. Although some stories are shared orally, others may be duplicated for more careful attention to organization, grammar, format, originality, and such specific narrative devices as subplots and foreshadowing.

88-I *(Experiment/Cartoons) "Balloon Talk"*

After a study of comics and how they are simple narratives, cut out entire sets of comic strips from Sunday papers. Remove the dialogues from the balloons. Each student receives a strip and supplies dialogue appropriate to the characters and to the situations so that the story can be told succinctly. Print dialogue directly on the strip or on separate paper containing numbers corresponding to numbered balloons. As a continuation of this idea, students could devise their own cartoon characters for a strip, drawing one frame each day. Each new frame is related to the previous day's frame. The final frame at the end of the week concludes the short narrative. Even if drawings are just stick figures, students will receive practice developing simple plots through dialogue, action, and setting, along with good punctuation practice.

89-I *(Experiment/Magazines, Newspapers) "Cut It Out!"*

Students can obtain good practice writing dialogue by cutting out magazine or newspaper pictures of two individuals (some famous). Paste the pictures (pairs of individuals) on construction paper backing. Then students write what these people would say to each other. These dialogues are either typed or printed on strips of paper (or written as comic strip balloons) which are then pasted next to each speaker. Results can be very humorous.

90-C,G *(Experiment/Models) "Telling It Like It Is"*

Place a chair or table (or any common object) in front of the class. Tell the students this is a very special object. Tell them to write down answers to these questions, being as creative as possible: Where is it? What is special about it? Who is using it? What happened to it? When did it happen? Students then get into small groups and tell their stories to each other. When the groups decide the best plot, all students in that group contribute to make up one excellent story. Then one good reader in each group shares the narrative with the class.

91-G   *(Experiment/Mysteries) "Who, What, When, Where, Why— and How!"*

A study of mysteries can readily include the four types of discourse: (1) narration—giving basic plot; (2) description—setting the scene of the crime; (3) exposition—presenting the evidence; and (4) argumentation—hearing defense and prosecution. For practice, have students form groups to write a class mystery. The groups vote on basic plot as a start (something stolen, someone murdered, somebody blackmailed, for example). Each group then writes part of the story—characters and setting, the crime being committed, the investigation, and the solution. Group chairpersons and the teacher are responsible for continuity. The story can be read aloud with assigned speaking parts. Discuss strengths and weaknesses of each group's contribution.

92-I   *(Experiment/Skits) "Sets of Vignettes"*

Point out vignettes such as those throughout Hemingway's *The Sun Also Rises* or in a more contemporary novel. With these examples students can practice writing some of their own, representing humorous or dramatic scenes from their own experiences. Some papers should be read to the class or posted on a bulletin board.

93-I   *(Interpret/Movies) "Selected Short Subjects"*

To expand a study of narration, show a short narrative film in its entirety without turning on sound. Students write a short story giving it a title, character names, setting, dialogue, and plot based on what they think is happening. Show the film again, in short segments if needed. When the projects are in and some have been shared in class, show the film once more, this time with sound.

94-C,I   *(Interpret/Records) "Sound Off"*

Use sound effects records to create a background of sequential sounds which could evoke a story, e.g., car motor, motor stops, car doors slam, footsteps, and so on. Students then build a short narrative on what they have heard. Most suppliers of recordings for schools have such records. If you can't locate some, ask the drama coach, local radio station, or community library.

95-I *(Organize/Pictures) "Get the Picture"*

Bring in numerous copies of popular pictorial magazines. Students select and clip about twenty pictures on a single theme or idea. Do not break the news until they are finished collecting pictures that they must create a picture story complete with captions. This assignment is handled very simply— almost in storybook fashion. It offers practice in organizing thoughts, stimulates creativity, and is suitable for both younger and older children.

96-I *(Organize/Short Stories) "Starting at the Start"*

To practice narrative organization, students complete a short story beginning with a line like this: Mr. Smith opened the door and peeked out.

97-I *(Organize/Talks) "Follow the Leader"*

A student starts an original narrative. After a sentence or two, the student chooses a second person (or volunteer) to continue the same story. The second moves the story line along and then designates a third. Students continue until a completion point is reached. To promote originality along with unity and coherence, do not allow anyone to repeat or contradict what has been said. Anyone doing so must take notes, writing down the story for later discussion. The entire approach—even the punitive measure—is excellent practice for organizing thoughts, a skill that will carry over to longer papers.

OVERVIEW

98-I *(Analyze/Models) "Copy Break"*

After a composition assignment is turned in by the students, do more than simply evaluate. To get more mileage from the compositions, take at least one full class period integrating the assignment with grammar study. This provides variety and makes grammar more relevant. Students also benefit from analyzing their own writing models rather than using some- one else's.

99-C *(Analyze/Models) "Item-eyes"*

Here is an opportunity to experiment with all three composi- tion forms: description, exposition, and narration. Tell stu- dents to write a description of any common object without naming it, so that the reader knows what it is. Then using some of the same wording, students imagine a story involving the object (an ink pen, lunch box, purse, wallet, knife, doll, toy, cup, etc.). Finally, they make an exposition on the same item, such as its uses, how it is made, or what its benefits and disadvantages might be.

100–T *(Analyze/Models) "Join 'Em"*

To be able to teach writing well, an English teacher must participate in some class assignments. At times prepare a written paper before assigning it to the class. Not only will it provide a model for class analysis, but it will also alert you to problems the students may have. Occasionally insert errors to provoke discussion. Some assignments can be completed by teachers as the students do theirs. Then discuss how some common problems were or were not solved. This practice reflects a "we're all in this together" feeling.

101–C *(Analyze-Organize/Audiotapes) "Musical Shares"*

To illustrate the need for continuity in compositions, show the same need in music. The sonata form is easy to analyze because its exposition, development, and recapitulation are so clearly evident. Careful listening to edited tapes will demonstrate the main theme of the sonata form and variations on that theme. Someone with a little musical ability (or get help from the music teacher) can trace many similarities between organization in music and in written composition.

102–C *(Experiment/Games) "Sack It to 'Em"*

After introducing just about any type of written composition, have students practice by bringing in an object in a paper sack. Each must introduce the object orally, involving the item as part of an anecdote, a joke, mini-mystery, series of questions, and so forth. The class is to guess from the involvement what the object is.

103–I,C *(Experiment/Mysteries) "A Quick Solution"*

Let each student create a "micro-mystery" such as these:
(1) The Johnson's daughter spent four years in the first grade. Why? (2) Donald McTavich's racer showed no tire wear at the Indy 500. Why? (3) A boy and his father are in a car accident.

The father is killed. In the hospital where the boy needs surgery, the doctor says, "I cannot operate on this boy because he is my son." Why?* Many other mysterious statements will come in. Collect several of the best and have students write several sentences or a short paragraph giving a brief explanation as to why each statement is possible.

104-C *(Experiment/Paragraphs) "Day to Day"*

An exercise that helps promote spontaneous written expression is a daily paragraph on whatever subject the student desires. This practice is an excellent extension of the daily sentence practice (idea 74). Improving sentences tends to improve paragraphs. Thus, improving paragraphs should improve a total composition. Writing without much attention to the grammar of the sentence serves to reduce the inhibitions of confronting a blank piece of paper. But it is only a first step toward improving composition and toward getting students to use what they already know about language.

105-C *(Organize/Paragraphs) "Short But Neat"*

To give frequent practice in succinct writing, place a single word—a verb, noun, or adjective—on a 3×5 or 5×7 card and distribute one card to each person. The student writes a short paragraph using the assigned word as the focal point. Cards are exchanged mainly to check on organization. Used once or twice weekly, this activity promotes growth in writing.

106-C *(Organize/Plans) "Just a Grocery List"*

Some teachers err by forcing young writers to prepare a topic or sentence outline (from Roman numerals to sub-subtopics) before putting pen to paper in a composition assignment. Complete outlining is excellent for getting the "meat" out of something already written—the reason most students do their outlines *after* they write—but outlining must be simple and quick or it alienates and makes writing an even more onerous task than it often is. Just a few key words and phrases—grocery list style—along the margin of the first page will usually give the needed organization.

107-I *(Interpret/Mixed Media) "Media at the Corner"*

To help students understand that knowledge in one communication area relates to other areas, have them write first on a given or self-selected situation or topic. Then they convey the

---

* Possible solutions: (1) The Johnson's daughter was a first-grade teacher; (2) The racer was never taken off the trailer; (3) The doctor was the boy's mother (Students' responses should be a bit longer.)

same information through another medium of their choice: painting, song, dance, dramatic interpretation, picture essay, or film, for instance.

POETRY

108–C *(Analyze/Models) "Compare the Pair"*

Open a discussion on how carefully a poet or author selects words. Prepare two copies of a short selection and place them side by side. One is the original; the other is a copy with key words changed to synonyms or words with other connotations. The problem is to decide which copy is the original and which is a poor substitute and to tell why.

109–I *(Compare/Models) "A Whataphor?"*

To evaluate the use of metaphor, students examine a poem such as Walt Whitman's "The Noiseless Patient Spider," in which a natural object and an incident become metaphors. They then write a short free-verse poem employing the same method. Before beginning, the students should state the objects and ideas being compared and tell how they are similar. For his poem, Whitman might have approached this assignment this way:

Things compared: Spider in a web and the isolation of man's soul.

Similarities: The spider throws out physical lines to make contact with outside elements in an effort to build a home and a supportive environment. Man "throws out" emotional attachments to build his life.

110–G *(Consolidate/Collections) "If, What Then?"*

As an introduction to writing poetry, challenge students with this group activity. The first student in each row writes something like this in iambic tetrameter: "My room is not the best to see." The second student (without being too concerned about a perfect sequences of ideas) extends the action in the same meter. The third student adds to the thought, and so on, until all in the row have contributed to the original idea. When each row's efforts are completed, the class will have developed several poems in the designated meter.

111–C, *(Experiment/Lists) "Poets Know It"*
G

After a study of poetry techniques, suggest that each class write a poem together. Begin by asking for natural, spontaneous responses to a word that will serve as the theme; for example, "darkness," "Mother," or "sorrow." The class members then write phrases, clauses, or sentences growing out of their reaction to the theme word. Collect and arrange these thoughts into a master list, possibly grouping similar ideas. Have the master list reproduced and distributed. Finally, announce to the class that they are to rework the list into a poem. If desirable, the students can work in groups. The entire project takes only three days at the minimum. The results are so amazing that awards might well be given for the best efforts.

112-C   *(Experiment/Models) "Best Foot Forward"*

To help themselves learn and identify meter, advance their listening skills, and increase awareness of different verse patterns, students write couplets to be read aloud. Each couplet should cover current subjects, be written in popular language and syntax, and should also employ a particular metrical foot (iambic, dactylic, trochaic, or anapestic). Samples from a class might look like these:

Iambic:
> *If we must save dear nature's sources,*
> *Then why not save us from these courses?*

Dactylic:
> *Graduates, graduates, all in a row,*
> *Happy and sad and not wanting to go.*

Trochaic:
> *Machines that vend and take our doughs,*
> *Will you just give me back my nose?*

Anapestic:
> *On a beach, on a date, he is tops in his class.*
> *In a course, with a book, he can barely just pass.*

113-I,C   *(Experiment/Poetry) "Poetricks"*

Each student locates a contemporary poem he or she especially likes. The individuals write their own poems, attempting to emulate the style of the poem each has chosen. Poems are coded with numbers and are duplicated for the class to read. Students vote for their favorite student-written poem. The student poet who receives the greatest number of votes is undoubtedly the budding poet and may possibly receive as a prize a book of poetry that the class "chipped in" to purchase.

3 Evaluation

ARGUMENTATION

114–G *(Compare/Discussions) "What Would You Do?"*

Using a popular, debatable issue, have students choose the pro or con side and write a composition stating their position. After sufficient writing time (one class period to several days), papers are handed in but not graded. Instead, the teacher reads them quickly to find two well-written papers—one pro and one con. These are duplicated in quantities so each student gets a set. The class is then divided into groups. Each group discusses the compositional merits of each paper as well as the argumentative qualities. In a later summation, a representative gives the consensus of his or her group.

DESCRIPTION

115–C *(Compare/Essays) "Casting a Look"*

After reading a play, students write a description of one character, giving physical and behavioral characteristics. Afterward, show a movie version of the play (e.g., James Mason in *Julius Caesar*). Such full-length films are available to schools for economical rental. The English department might sponsor an all-school showing or contact a local theater for a special matinee. Students then write an essay illustrating how their version of the play character (based on their reading of the play) differs from the movie interpretation.

116–I,C *(Extrapolate/Games) "What's It?"*

Through "Show and Tell" elementary teachers create interest among their students. A slight switch in this approach is the "What's It Box." Have each student bring a secret object to be placed in a box which is passed around the class. Students may shake the box and even reach through the hole to feel one object. Then each student writes a brief paper telling what one object might be. Later the objects can be displayed and students can pick out the one they described. This method increases powers of description and reveals how well students have learned the techniques.

117-I *(Extrapolate/Senses) "Sense-ative Descriptions"*

Students write a short paragraph employing one of the five senses that would not ordinarily be used to describe a topic. For example, a description of a ball game would normally tell the action of the game and the kinds of people seen. Instead, the topic could be described through smells only—the food, the crowd, the perfume of a girl nearby, the varnished floor, or new-mown grass. This activity tests ability to manipulate sensory experiences effectively.

118-C *(Judge/Games) "Monkeying Around"*

A switch in the usual personality sketch is to have a student write a description of another student (omitting the name or pronouns *he* or *she* and using *the subject* or *this person*). The character clues are stated in terms of an animal most representative of that student. The accuracy of the description is then tested by how quickly the class guesses the person being described.

119-G *(Restructure/Audiotapes) "Speaking Pen"*

Some students, though very articulate, are still unable to write well. For them, the teacher can emphasize the concept of "verbalizing on paper." Students in small groups tape a discussion wherein they describe an object the teacher has provided. They then listen to the tape and note the essential discussion points. Afterward, each student writes a short description based on these ideas, emphasizing clarity and organization. Time permitting, compositions can be read orally in groups for criticism. Finally, revisions are handed to the teacher for final evaluation and comments.

120-I,C *(Restructure/Notes) "Where Am I?"*

Each student is given a particular location and a specific object to write about, preferably located in the school, but it could be in a neighborhood library or a fast food restaurant, or even a roller rink. Students describe as best they can the object and the location without naming either. A few selections are read in class. A true mark of achievement in writing description is how quickly the class can guess the object and place.

EXPOSITION

121-I *(Extrapolate/Artwork) "Print Out"*

Obtain prints of the work of several famous artists. Pass them around the class, allowing each student to select the one that appears most interesting to him or her. Students then test their abilities to write an exposition from visual data. Something like Breughel's *School Children* could produce an exposition on poverty or on school life as the artist seemed to reflect these aspects. Papers could also contrast the artist's point of view with a student's.

122-I *(Extrapolate/Books) "Get to a Ghetto"*

Choose a current novel or nonfiction book that deals with life in a culture different from that of most students in your school. For example, a teacher in a middle- or upper-class school might choose Taylor's *Roll of Thunder, Hear My Cry* (Bantam) or Hinton's *The Outsiders* (Dell). An inner-city teacher could choose a book about people in more affluent surroundings: Bellow's *Seize the Day* (Avon) or Ney's *Ox: The Story of a Kid at the Top* (Bantam). Other books might describe Mexican Americans, Chinese Americans, or Indians, as found in LaFarge's *Laughing Boy* (New American Library). After the reading, students may describe in a piece of expository writing how the reality described in the book has affected their view of another culture. This activity tests ability to apply one set of data against another.

123-T *(Extrapolate/Essays) "Great Leveler"*

Students often complain that they could write better if they had good topics. Part-way into the semester, suggest they write about their teacher—you! They write what they like or dislike about your teaching, or they just describe you. To prevent stilted compositions, announce they will be graded not on what is said but *how* it is said. The problem of anonymity can be settled by class vote.

124-I *(Extrapolate/Essays) "Who Wrote Me?"*

To heighten awareness that an author's own character and personality can be revealed in his or her writing, students write a personal essay reacting to something they recently observed, read, heard, or felt. The papers are not signed, just a code or pseudonym is used. During the next class period the essays are shuffled so each student gets someone else's paper. The task is to read an essay and try to identify the writer. If the reader guesses the author, he or she must tell what traits revealed the writer.

125–I,C *(Extrapolate/Games)* *"Survival Game"*

Here is a well-known activity that is still good for evaluating ability to extrapolate data. Explain that nine people are stranded on an island because of some situation (which the students can suggest). Have each write on the subject: If you could save only five people, who would they be and why? Choices might be a navy lieutenant, thirteen-year-old girl or boy, famous doctor, fiancee, governor of a state, movie star, pastor (rabbi or priest), or president of a large motor company. The situation, of course, can be changed from an island to anywhere—even the last spaceship from a ravaged earth to a new planet. The variations are enormous and the discussions exciting.

126–C *(Judge/Authorities)* *"Crit-ticks"*

Students always like to evaluate what they have seen or heard. Test their ability to be critical. After a class has attended a play or seen a movie, let them write a short review based on what they have learned about writing such reviews. Observations should include even the smallest details of lighting or sound, as well as acting, story, characterization, direction, and so on. Perhaps start off by reading several reviews written by previous classes.

127–C *(Judge/Charts)* *"Eight to Rate"*

There are basically eight areas that students and teachers need to consider as they write. Expository writing undoubtedly draws on these eight more than any other type of composing:

1. Is the paper organized according to some plan?
2. Are the ideas developed effectively?
3. Are sentences complete and well-written?
4. Are words chosen precisely and effectively?
5. Have correct capitalization and punctuation been used?
6. Is the spelling correct?
7. Has correct manuscript form been used?
8. Is the overall impression effective?

These concerns might even be duplicated so that students can place them in a handy location for future reference.

128–G *(Judge/Demonstrations, Recordings) "A Spot for Writing"*

Using tape recorders, students prepare and record a brief announcement that "interrupts" a program in progress. Start out like this: "We interrupt the program in progress to bring you this important announcement." Follow with a one- or two-minute announcement on a disaster, a special announcement, or a plea for public cooperation to avoid a disaster. Such a piece of writing would be evaluated from tape. Stress content, correctness, succinctness, and total effect would be measured.

129–G *(Judge/Instructions) "Homing in on Composition"*

To test concise and explicit communication, have each student write a paragraph giving directions for getting home from school without the aid of a diagram or map. Then classmates check each other's work by tracing the route on a city map. If they don't get "lost," the paper must be effective, deserving a high evaluation.

130–G *(Judge/Instructions) "In a Jam"*

This exercise tests ability to write logically in an expository paragraph. All (or several) students write in correct order the instructions for making a peanut butter and jelly sandwich. The needed materials can be brought to class so some students can try another's instructions. If the writer has made a mistake in logical order, sandwiches will have peanut butter on the top or jelly dripping from the bottom or even spread on the hand. Of course, any number of other activities can be substituted for the sandwich idea; for example, tying shoe laces, bending paper clips, drawing pictures, or piling blocks. But food preparation works best since the props can be eaten.

131–I *(Judge/Movies) "Pick the Flick"*

As part of a unit on film as composition, have numerous published movie reviews available for study. After discussing such facets as purpose, technique, relationship of art to theme, quality of acting, and sensationalism, students will be able to see how different critics' opinions vary on the same point. Students will soon be ready to make their own judgments and movie reviews. Continue interest by reserving bulletin board section for reviews of films being shown in your town.

132–C *(Judge/Role Playing) "If I Could Be"*

Too often students write just because they have to. Without real meaning, topics are not written well, resulting in failing marks. Change the pace by suggesting they put themselves in the place of a famous person and write about a typical day. This may take some library research even if subjects are free choice. Later, papers can be read in class (or in groups) so they can be evaluated using a rating sheet as a guide.

133–I   *(Judge/Selves) "No-Prompt Impromptu"*

Ideas from a composition unit featuring expository writing may be presented in vain if students are evaluated and graded in the usual way. For a less competitive and more individualized approach, give each student an impromptu writing assignment. Each writes on a different topic found on a slip of paper drawn at random. No instructions are given since each student is to handle the assignment without being fettered by instructions and guidelines, except that the composition must be written within the class period. The results are evaluated based on the teacher's expectations for each writer. Topics should be those any student could handle adequately with general knowedge.

134–G   *(Judge/Talks) "Speak Easy"*

Divide the class into four or five groups. Each person in a group speaks on a given or selected topic that must have been researched and outlined, first for an oral then for a written report. Other members of the group take turns praising, evaluating, and criticizing the speaker. This procedure encourages responses from those who are too shy to speak before a large class. It also permits more speeches in a given time. The high noise level is not annoying within the group, just to the casual observer.

JOURNALISM

135–G   *(Restructure/Newspapers) "Start the Presses"*

As a follow-up and evaluation of a journalism unit—ideally including a field trip to a newspaper plant—students write a class newspaper, including school and community news. Divide the class into special-interest groups such as news, sports, amusements, fashions, editorials, cartoons, comics, and even advertising (if practical). Besides being good motivation, this approach really tests how well the principles of journalism have been taught and learned.

LETTER WRITING

136–I   *(Compare/Letters) "Better Letter Letter Grades"*

A student's composition progress can be measured less threateningly if he or she writes frequent letters to the teacher or to someone else (you would read these). Easier and more personal, this approach emphasizes a useful form of communication. Topics can be almost anything: reporting progress in perfecting an athletic skill, in building a model, in collecting hobby items, and others.

137-I *(Extrapolate/Newspapers) "Take a Letter"*

Encourage using classified ads as the basis for an actual letter applying for a summer job, making a personal inquiry, or ordering something. Assign a letter *before* study begins to evaluate ability to use such skills and to make inferences from given data. Students must write nearly perfect letters before any can be sent. Stress the four Cs of a business letter: Clarity, Conciseness, Correctness, and Courtesy.

MEDIA

138-C *(Compare-Judge/Periodicals) "Periodicalling"*

To help students evaluate knowledge of media in print, have them try some of these suggestions. (1) Clip newspaper stories on current events and judge content for who, what, where, when information. (2) Compare two different accounts of the same events reported in different newspapers. (3) Judge the *New York Times* to see why it is considered one of the best daily newspapers in the nation. (4) Compare writing in different newspapers to distinguish good writing from bad. (5) Judge the content, format, and emphasis of different magazines. (6) Display favorite magazine covers on the bulletin board and give reasons for choice. (7) Introduce some unfamiliar magazines to be judged and discussed.

139-I *(Judge/Cartoons) "See You in the Funnies"*

In a media or composition unit, look at the comic strip as a narrative form. Students cut out five or six newspaper comic strips, pasting each on a separate sheet of notebook paper. Then they answer questions such as: (1) What type of strip is it (adventure, mystery, humor, satire)? (2) Are the characters true to life? (3) What quality dialogue is used (standard English, dialect, idiom, child-talk)? (4) Is the strip complete in each episode or continued? (5) Who is the artist? Questions are answered on pages bearing the strips. If the class can handle it, they might summarize a strip they have followed for about two weeks, probably a continuing story. They can follow up this activity with another short paper evaluating their favorite strip and giving reasons for the choice.

140-C *(Judge/Periodicals) "Pulling a Switch"*

Often teachers duplicate copies of student writing for class criticism because students rarely hesitate to evaluate each other's work. But given a published article, they can usually find nothing wrong. They tend to believe all printed material is "sacred." To break this misconception, the teacher implies that a duplicated article from a newspaper or magazine is a student composition and asks the class to evaluate it. Afterward, they discover the article has actually been published. Besides helping to dispel the notion that printed material is always perfect, the activity also encourages students to watch for weaknesses and strengths in everything they read.

141-C *(Judge/Television) "Check the Tube"*

To determine if students understand concepts previously learned, let them write descriptions of their favorite television shows. Their papers can focus on one of several aspects: wholesomeness, character development, clarity of emotions, originality of humor, realism in plot and setting, objectivity (if a news commentator), uses of propaganda and stereotypes, or quality of advertising, depending on the type of program.

142-I *(Restructure/Radio, Television) "Spots on the Spot"*

To achieve a change of pace during a composition unit, students can challenge the commercials they hear daily on radio and television—particularly those they dislike. They can rewrite the spot to their liking. As they do so, they learn that commercials exemplify some of the best, most informative, precise writing that exists. The teacher could aid specific recall by seeing that the most popular selections are recorded. While students evaluate the commercials, the teacher can evaluate the student version for clarity among other concerns.

NARRATION

143-I *(Extrapolate/Pictures) "Sharing a Like"*

If student writers are to develop only one skill, it should be the capacity "to see." To check visual perception and written expression, students write dialogues between two or among several characters found in magazine ads. Subjects could be two women (or men) having their hair styled in a salon. Or it could be several citizens making their first trip to the moon when space travel becomes commonplace. To see if they can pursue a consistent point of view, have students select situations that can be drawn out over one or two pages of dialogue. Not only does this exercise prove whether or not students have learned to write and punctuate conversation, but it also shows how they can handle a creative writing assignment.

144–C *(Judge/Papers) "Being a Dictator"*

An elementary reading activity, the experience chart (students dictate a story which the teacher writes on large paper or the chalkboard), can be used as a secondary school composition activity. The class thinks up a plot, and various students offer sentences which the teacher writes on the chalkboard. Each sentence advances the story a bit. After the story is completed, the class criticizes the sentence structure and organization.

145–I *(Restructure/Movies) "Silents Please"*

Show a silent movie (e.g., Charlie Chaplin, Buster Keaton) lasting approximately twenty minutes. Ask students to write a dialogue for the story using their knowledge of the technique. Later it could be recorded for playback with the silent film. (See related idea 224.)

146–I *(Restructure/Tales) "Goldie's Clocks and the Three Mares"*

A narrative demands careful structure. Students can evaluate their knowledge of this technique by updating a fairy tale, making the characters fit their own interests and times. If the ages of the new characters differ from the original, the plot should be consistent with the characters' ages, but the original fairy tale plot should be followed, including any moral. The assignment calls for imagination and compliance with a given structure.

OVERVIEW

147–T *(Compare/Books) "Savings Book"*

When handing back well-written assignments, mark them "Type and Save." Near the close of the term, collect all such type-and-save narratives, poetry, essays, and so on, duplicate them, and compile enough booklets so each student gets one. Current booklets can be compared to the writing in booklets from a previous class.

148–I *(Compare/Charts) "Keeping Score"*

Each student keeps a personal chart of composition progress by posting the points earned through accuracy in specific evaluation areas. The following chart indicates how this may be done if, for instance, twelve points represented maximum performance in each of five qualities. Areas needing extra attention are clearly delineated. Best of all, this is a way to show success concretely. (Also see ideas 156 and 157.)

+ Points (12 maximum)

Topic	Grammar	Usage	Mechanics	Thought	Spelling	Grade
1. Description	9	2	3	2	11	C−
2. Personal Interview	7	9	4	4	10	C
3. Book Review	8	10	5	6	10	B
4. Personal Essay	6	5	6	8	12	C+
etc.						

149-I *(Compare/Talks) "Pro-File"*

Keep all written compositions in folders—along with other grades and evaluations. By comparing papers the teacher can note progress, which can serve as a talking point for individual writing conferences. The folder also helps justify semester grades. Next year's English teacher may also welcome a file on each student to better assess needs and to plan course content.

150-C *(Extrapolate/Audiotapes) "Write, Record, Listen"*

A tape recorder in the room is often a good way to cope with student apathy. After students write about something in today's society that distresses them, they record the composition for playback to the class. As each weakness in writing is noted, a class member raises his or her hand. The tape is stopped, criticism given, and, if necessary, the portion in question is replayed. This saves having to make duplicated copies for students to evaluate.

151–T *(Extrapolate/Lists) "Starting Out Write"*

The first day of class each student writes a short composition, a letter, or merely a list of all the things he or she has hated and/or liked about previous English classes. These responses are kept for future conferences or to plan future class work. The purpose, of course, is to make assignments more meaningful for the students.

152–G *(Extrapolate/Papers) "Seein' Is Believin'"*

Divide the class into groups of four or five and arrange desks accordingly. Students turn in an assigned theme and these are collected as a set from each group. Have each paper coded with a number instead of using names. Collect all sets of papers and redistribute them, making sure none are from the group that wrote them. Each member reads all the papers given to his or her group. Using the code number for identification, each student grades and makes comments, taking a separate sheet of paper for each composition. This procedure helps students see good techniques and recognize some mistakes they also make. The writer also finds out what others think of his or her writing—not just the teacher. Usually papers receive a more thorough analysis than if the teacher does all the evaluating. Those who hesitate to employ peer evaluation might do well to read articles that extoll peer tutoring. Students learn well from each other under proper guidance.

153–I *(Extrapolate/Papers) "Sounding Off"*

After writing a composition, students can catch obvious errors by reading their papers aloud before handing them in. Errors in agreement, sentence and paragraph order, usage, and weak sentence structure can be found more easily when they are heard. By reading their own work students sometimes miss too much. So the writer, while following along, may simply ask a friend to read. Another approach is reading into a tape recorder and then replaying the tape while following along on the paper with pencil poised and one hand on the stop control to allow for making on-the-spot changes.

154–T *(Extrapolate/Papers) "Yea, Team!"*

Cooperative writing assignments planned by teachers in different subject fields can be very profitable for all. For example, a history instructor may not feel qualified to correct the rhetoric of assigned papers. The English teacher down the hall is always looking for suitable topics for writing practice. The two teachers should work together on an assignment: the history teacher reading for content and effectiveness of gathering information, the English teacher evaluating sentence grammar, usage, and mechanics. Since both teachers work in areas of strength, neither is subordinate to the other. They can even assign separate grades, one for content and one for structure. (See also ideas 157 and 178.)

155–T   *(Extrapolate/Talks) "Conversable"*

One-to-one composition conferences require a pleasant location conducive to conversation, an unthreatened student, and an understanding teacher as the needed ingredients. Conference time can be obtained by making schedule changes that provide for extra library periods, free-reading days, and off-campus projects.

156–T   *(Identify/Charts) "G-Mut, the Writing Detective"*

G	M
U	T

Show the writer exactly where improvement is needed. Form and content are subdivided into grammar, usage, mechanics (including spelling), and thought. These are evaluated separately for assigned points. Not intended to supplant teacher comments, this technique can save considerable evaluation time. It could even be enhanced by using a "G-Mut form," which the student draws at the end of a paper before handing it in or which can be imprinted with a rubber stamp.

157–I   *(Identify/Charts) "Watch that Profile"*

When the teacher likes to note all composition errors, this idea will help students consolidate and interpret weaknesses that are difficult to digest when scattered throughout a paper. First, establish a vocabulary for labeling specific weaknesses (in any rhetoric book). To reduce written comment, devise some easily understood abbreviations (first letters or symbols—some are standard in the field) to mark in margins or near problems. Then hand out a Writer's Profile Form containing an alphabetical list of weaknesses, probably not more than twelve with easy-to-remember abbreviations. After each weakness item (in a string of graph-like boxes) the student fills in a section of graph, one for each weakness or error. When the form is filled, the several areas on which the student should concentrate for the next paper will usually be evident. If not—which is rare—the teacher should help decide.

The Writer's Profile
The Shape of Your Writing

Symbol	Weakness	Profile
(1) abs	abstract word	(1)
(2) mono	monotonous sentences	(2)
(3) ov	overloaded sentence	(3)
(4) om	overmodification	(4)
(5) ord	sentence order	(5)
(6) pdec	prepositional decay	(6)
	. . . and so on	

158-C *(Identify/Lists) "Book of Note"*

Too often students merely glance at composition grades and rarely look at the evaluations; the same mistakes then appear in the next paper. Two approaches will help improve the situation. First, students can keep a notebook with a section marked "comp errors." Here they list the types and frequencies of mechanical and grammatical errors. The object is to identify their major problems and to see if these are being eliminated through practice. A second approach is to write catchy, livelier comments so students will want to read them to chuckle, satisfy curiosity, and yes, even to learn.

159-I *(Identify/Lists) "Way to Go"*

To reduce the overwhelming comprehensive evaluation, try focusing on one or two aspects. Before beginning to write a composition, each student identifies at the top of his or her page the most serious writing problem uncovered in the last paper, as indicated by the teacher. This way the student is reminded what to improve and the teacher what to check. By being able to concentrate on one problem at a time, a writer is more apt to transfer learning from one paper to the next.

160-I *(Identify/Questions) "P.S., Teacher"*

After writing a paper, students often wish they could explain to the teacher where they ran into trouble, what they couldn't express as they would have liked, what they tried to research but couldn't, and many other problems. Invite students to attach an extra P.S. Sheet to their papers and to write freely about the problems they had in writing the paper. This helps the teacher understand why certain parts of the paper seem weaker and so on. Sometimes such explanations emerge as better writing than the paper itself. Thus, the P.S. Sheet gives additional writing experience painlessly.

161–I *(Judge/Audiotapes) "Speech Writing"*

Student writing is often unclear, not because the writer forgot a topic sentence or a supporting element, but because there was little or no relationship between ability in describing something orally and ability in writing effectively. The paragraph should develop like a conversation, simply and logically. The project could begin by tape recording some conversation, then transcribing it.

162–T *(Judge/Audiotapes) "Tapeographical Errors"*

Teachers frequently find there is not enough time to write all the needed comments on student themes. This idea cuts down on evaluation time but not on evaluation. Correct (or denote) grammar and mechanical errors as usual, but tape record comments about content. (Usually the two aspects must be considered separately anyway.) Give each student a five-minute cartridge tape, or mark on the paper the tape counter number where your comments begin among others on a longer tape. This procedure is quicker than writing lengthy comments and encourages a more thorough evaluation. Several listening stations can be provided around the room to facilitate feedback.

163–G *(Judge/Authorities) "Commit to Committee"*

Instead of each student proofreading his or her own composition, set up a proofreading committee or panel similar to a newspaper editing department. Sometimes the proofreaders can be subdivided into specialities such as spelling, punctuation, modification, and others. In that case, printed signs on their desks would help identify them. As usual, peer group opinion can often carry more weight than any other type.

164–T *(Judge/Charts) "What's in a Grade?"*

The Composition Criteria Chart (page 49) can be modified to make a profile by which to see lows and highs in the five areas: Thought, Harmony of Ideas, Esthetics, Mechanics, and Expression. The errors/weaknesses can be tallied after each area. This shows graphically where a student may be strong in "Thought," for example, but weak in "Mechanics." This might be enough incentive for trying to bring up weak areas.

Error Profile

Thought							
Harmony							
Esthetics							
Mechanics							
Expression							

165–C, G   *(Judge/Discussion) "Peering at Papers"*

Have students correct compositions using one of the following techniques: Duplicate papers for round-robin criticism, use projector for on-the-spot checking of a paper, or have students exchange papers and write a critique.

166–C, G,I,T   *(Judge/Lecture, Discussion) "Composition Competition"*

The workshop approach for improving composition writing provides a variety of techniques: lecture, individual and group projects, audio-visual demonstrations, gaming, and class participation. Before the workshop the teacher obtains a three- or four-page writing sample from each participant to determine writing needs and to make grouping decisions. All assignments need not be the same for all students.

The teacher then evaluates each sample, noting weaknesses beside the words and in the margins (see idea 157), editing (revising) the first page, and specifying on each writing sample one or two sentences which the writer will later place on an overhead transparency. (These transparencies are made by writing on plastic with felt pens or grease pencils.) Students will be told that the "before" or original sentence is placed first and is followed by the rewrite or "after" sample. The teacher also plans to divide the participants into six groups with approximately five students in each. Every group is to have a resource person who will later be a judge. Usually these are the students who submitted the best writing samples in the process described above.

Meanwhile, each participant has also prepared a brief paper from a common writing assignment and comes to the workshop with at least five copies to be distributed for discussion. When the participants report, the teacher makes an oral presentation on the common weaknesses uncovered in the original writing samples. Improvement techniques may be displayed on the chalkboard, slides, or transparencies using samples from past workshops.

Then a table competition is announced. Group members are to help each other rewrite the original sentence on the "before-after" transparencies, getting extra help from the resource person at each table.

After a sufficient time, the "before-after" transparencies are collected, their having been identified by table number and type of error (the abbreviation). A point system can be announced to award 0, 1, 2, or 3 points based on quality of the

Composition Criteria Chart

	Low	Middle	High
Thought			
Creativity	Weak ideas	Second-hand ideas	Original
Ideas	Not planned	Erratic clarity	Thought-out
Adaptability to type	Not original	Few examples or details	Uses examples, details
	Misses assign.		
Ability to follow dir.	Trite, silly	Somewhat related to topic	Related to topic
	Ambiguous	Not sincere	No padding
		Often padded	Sincere
Harmony (of ideas)			
Parag. org.	Very poor start	Weak start	Good start
Emphasis	Gets nowhere	Rambles often	Doesn't ramble
Parallelism	Random thoughts	Treats triviality	Point well made
Unity	No order	Conclusion: forced, awkward, absent	Logical organization
Coherence	No effective conclusion	Barely holds together	Well-balanced
Order	No unity or coherence	Often repeats	Unified, coherent
	Repetitious		
Esthetics			
Flavor	Uneducated statements	Impersonal	Comes from self
Style	No style	Lacks style	No airs
Attitude	Lacks suitable vocabulary	Unfairly biased	Definite style
Tone		Little feeling for topic	Takes sides fairly
Suitability of vocabulary	No feeling for topic	Broad generalities	Good feeling for topic
			Quite specific
Mechanics			
Punctuation	Many cap. and punc. errors	Many punc. errors	Observes standard forms
Capitalization	Erratic spelling	A few cap. errors	Few if any punc. or cap. errors
Spelling	Weak spelling	Some weak paragraph structure	Correct paragraphing
Paragraphing	Weak paragraph	Hard words mis-spelled	Accurate spelling
Format			
Expression			
Wording	Childish vocab.	Trite, hackneyed	Uses both common and uncommon words
Vocab. devel.	Substandard usage	Lifeless, simple structures	
Usage	Weak sentence structure	Some weak usage	Interesting struct.
Sent. structure	Tense switches	No experimentation	Good usage
Grammar	Poor agreement	Forced use of big words (sometimes wrong or ineffec-tive)	Accurate grammar
	Gropes for words		Clear, attractive
	Omits words		Fluent

rewrite. Transparencies are projected with the rewrite masked. After the weakness is fully identified and located in the "before" version, the rewrite is displayed. The teacher may be the sole judge or may rely on the resource people (now seated as a panel) to decide the number of points to be awarded, basing their decision on the class censensus after the rewrite is discussed. When each table has had an equal number of turns (up to four or five transparencies are available for each table), the table scores are totaled and compared.

For the next activity, the students continue to work in individual groups, with each group reading and discussing the common assignment papers and basing their ideas on the first workshop activity. As papers are being circulated within the group, each student secretly rates the five papers from his or her group on a scale of 5 (best) to 1 (worst). The paper with the highest cumulative rating (two if tied) is turned over to the six judges who will try to determine which of the six papers turned in (one from each group) is the best and the runner-up. The teacher's rating breaks any ties. Transparencies or class copies may be made of these for class discussion.

While the judges are making their choices, the teacher is conducting individual conferences with students about their original writing samples to help them understand how to alleviate the designated weaknesses. At the same time, the rest of the class can be rewriting their writing samples using the edited first page as a guide.

The grand finale of the workshop activity occurs when the runner-up common assignment paper (10 bonus points to that table group) and the winner (15 points) are revealed and discussed in that order. Prizes can be awarded to the winning table group: pizza treat, box of candy, or money, among others. The entire workshop can take several full days or two to three weeks of single class periods.

167–T   *(Judge/Lists) "Logical Call"*

So the students may see if a theme is well-organized, have them list or underline all the key words or ideas that reflect the point of each paragraph. Usually these will be subjects, verbs, and sometimes completers (complements). If they seem logical when read in order (without the rest of the sentence), chances are good the paper follows a logical progression. In fact, this emphasis on content should always precede structure and mechanics.

168–C   *(Judge/Models) "Outreach the Teach"*

Low-ability students are often encouraged to work harder when they can compete against the teacher. When giving an assignment, the teacher offers as an example a paper—not a perfect work but one including some obvious errors—that he or she wrote on the same assignment. The class is invited to find the errors and to discuss how the paper might have been better. Students can then be challenged to write a paper "better than the teacher's." Having to write the assignment assures the teacher that it is practical and points out possible trouble areas.

169-I   *(Judge/Papers) "Backward Words"*

This idea cuts down on one of the nastier jobs in evaluating themes—marking misspelled words. Before students hand in their final drafts, have them read their papers backwards. This forces attention to individual words that might be misspelled or typed incorrectly. Reading in reverse, students are not likely to brush over words as in regular proof- or copyreading, since they are not caught up in the message. Armed with dictionaries, students look up words for meaning and spelling, eliminating many errors the teacher would have to catch.

170-T   *(Judge/Papers) "Correctshuns"*

These four suggestions are useful to keep in mind when "correcting" themes:

> Comment but do not correct.
> Suggest ways to improve only one (or two) serious weakness(es).
> Check introduction and conclusion for effectiveness.
> Allow students to exchange papers for additional proofreading.

171-C,   *(Judge/Papers) "Future's Tense"*
G

Students generally are, or should be, very concerned about their futures. After some discussion, or even after a literary selection or two, have students compose their description of the ideal future city. They could illustrate with drawings or clippings. Evaluation might be done within groups. If five groups meet and choose the best paper in each, five model themes will be available for class evaluation and discussion. With these papers revised to perfection, they will be excellent models upon which to base future writing.

172-T   *(Judge/Papers) "Helping Hands"*

Peer pressure can be more effective than teacher-nagging when it comes to improving compositions. Also, students need to learn the value of criticism as well as improve their own abilities to be critical, and with this, peer evaluation helps. In one method, the teacher assigns a short composition. When the papers are complete, and with the class seated in rows, each student hands his or her paper to the person seated immediately behind; the student in the back seat takes his or hers to the front. Students make all grammatical and spelling corrections directly on the paper (perhaps with help from a guide-sheet as described in idea 164). Afterwards, they write comments about content, organization, novelty of expression, and coherence. Finally, they assign a letter grade (or two grades—one for structure and one for content). The teacher then collects the papers and evaluates the work of both the writer and the evaluator. The papers are then returned so effectiveness can be judged. Grades are changed if necessary.

173–T   *(Judge/Papers) "Neat Trick"*

Teachers often complain about not being able to read student writing. And, admitted or not, neatness often biases teacher evaluation. To encourage neatness, raise composition grades on some papers that are especially neat. After students get over the initial shock, tell them that occasionally you will give this extra credit for very neat papers.

174–I   *(Judge/Papers) "Pause that Refreshes"*

A long-time standard, this technique is often unused or un-stressed. After students write the first draft of a composition, they set it aside while they do some other work, such as studying some grammar. Later they will copyread their own papers in a new light and with greater objectivity. Mistakes will be more evident, and the students will be able to revise, using some of the new grammar they have learned.

175–T   *(Judge/Papers) "Peering Around"*

If time permits, experiment with this process and arrive at some eye-opening results. Locate a fairly good student paper. Make three copies of it and give the copies to three cooperative English teachers, asking them to evaluate each paper and assign a letter grade. Give them some criteria, such as the chart for idea 164. Even with this base, evaluations may vary considerably if results are typical. Grade the paper yourself to see how you compare with the other three. Meet with the other evaluators. Try to discover reasons for discrepancies. Find out what value judgments they made. It might be the first step in improving evaluation procedures.

176–G *(Judge/Papers) "Picking Prunes"*

Teachers frequently stress theme development and overlook the need to prune a paper of its superfluous elements. Students can learn to be more succinct this way. The next-to-final drafts of an assignment (writers' names removed) are exchanged, first with one student and then another. Reviewers are asked to strike out any words, phrases, or sentences that don't support the central issue. Since readers can be more objective, they will find much more padding than the writer. Twice (or more) reviewed, these copies are returned to the writer who will follow most of the acceptable suggestions when writing the final draft.

177–T *(Judge/Papers) "Seeing Red"*

Heard at a departmental meeting: "Throw out or give away your red pens. Fastened together on strings, they make good room dividers. Using them to evaluate student themes has only fearful results. Red stands for authority, blood, danger, trouble ahead, and Stop! Such a negative activity never builds rapport. Modest, inauspicious gray lead heals the paper that 'bleeds.' Think about it!"

178–T *(Judge/Papers) "Two for One"*

Some students have never had a successful experience in writing a composition. Teachers should try to do something about it, such as giving two grades instead of one. Above a separating line, place a letter grade (worth one-third the total) that reflects the format and structure (grammar, spelling, usage, and mechanics). Beneath the line place the grade for content and appropriateness to assignment (worth two-thirds the total grade). The content thus gets major emphasis as it should, for without anything to say the student doesn't have much to polish anyway. More important, the slow students get credit for their ideas even if they can't spell or punctuate. Remind students which grade is which by comparing the line to the deck of an ocean freighter. The heaviest part—the cargo (the content of theme)—is stored below deck. The superstructure (form) of the ship—how well it is decorated, painted, and polished—is above deck or above the line when a composition is assigned a grade.

179–I *(Restructure/Paragraphs) "On the Flip Side"*

In a combined literature and composition evaluation exercise, students rewrite paragraphs, aiming for opposite or vastly different affects by changing tragic scenes to comedy, or highly emotional writing to objective, cold descriptions. Besides assisting the student in checking on various composition techniques, this approach encourages a deeper study of both literature and composition.

POETRY

180–C *(Judge/Models) "Saw a Flaw"*

Near the end of a unit in which students have been studying poems and learning to write them, include several poems from published authors with some student-written poems—without telling the class, of course. Then have the class spend time judging all the poems as if they came from students. Besides seeing that even published authors have flaws in their work, students will discover ways to improve their own.

181–C *(Restructure/Models) "Corner on Poetry"*

To see if they understand the elements of poetry, students must try writing some. This activity may be approached either through the idea of form (sonnet, haîku, blank verse, and so on) or through the style of poets such as Bob Dylan or Langston Hughes, using their kind of imagery, meter, and subject matter. The student poetry is then read and discussed in an informal setting, as in the teacher's living room, at the school cafeteria with soft drinks, under the tree by the stream behind the school, or in any relaxing place. This added effort will heighten the feeling that poetry is something very special.

182–I *(Restructure/Music) "Lyrically Yours"*

Each student copies the lyrics of several popular songs. Some of these can be placed on overhead transparencies for study (and singing, of course). This is a good evaluative poetry writing exercise for slower groups. Songs are poems, yet many students do not realize this. Perhaps if they did, poetry would be more popular with youth than it frequently is.

4 Application

ARGUMENTATION

183–G *(Solve/Role Playing) "Hairy Harry"*

Involvement in group dynamics is an interesting, effective way to learn communication skills. A little practice in group problem solving and role playing would be beneficial to any class. Here is one model situation: "You are a forty-year-old parent of a seventeen-year-old son who wears his hair shoulder length. You must convince Harry to cut his hair." The class functions in three or four groups. Each group is permitted only one solution.

184–G *(Speak,Write/Critiques) "De Bait"*

Plan a panel discussion of a literary work such as *King Lear*. Arrange a debate so students can argue pro or con on well-defined topics about the play. Mimeograph some of Samuel Johnson's adverse critical judgments. Johnson felt the play taught an immoral lesson since good people like Cordelia and King Lear suffered, and he thought that only wicked characters should be shown suffering. Students might then defend or repudiate Johnson on these points. If the school is well-equipped, record or videotape the debate. Ask students to review their own discussions, preferably out of class, and to write a paper explaining who won the debate and why. The remainder of the class takes notes during the panel so they can write similar papers.

185–I *(Write/Journals) "Journalisms"*

Students bring a spiral notebook to class each day. The teacher writes a question on the board that will catch their attention. Each class member writes at least one paragraph to answer questions like "Do students have enough freedom in self-government at this school?" Books can be examined weekly to check progress. One teacher started by reading every day's assignment but later just read at random times, making comments but not correcting usage. If a weakness persisted, the teacher would write a comment indicating a section in the grammar book that might help remedy the error.

DESCRIPTION

186–I *(Write/Audiotapes) "Let Imagination Rain"*

Past experience conditions reactions to new stimuli more than one realizes. To illustrate, let the class listen to some familiar taped sound effects: a barking dog, siren, bell, small electric motor, or squeaking sound. Students then write paragraphs on three images they obtained from three sounds. These can be compared to show the variations among different students and to discuss why the differences occur.

187–C *(Write/Paragraphs) "Junkie Paragraph"*

 To obtain a descriptive paragraph from an unmotivated class, try bringing in a collection of assorted objects and spreading them out on a table. Be sure you have some thoughtful inclusions, keeping in mind the interests of the class. Then have the students write a complete and accurate description of one or more of the articles, distinguishing it from the others by shape, size, texture, color, and so forth. Read some of the descriptions to the class for discussion.

188–I *(Write/Paragraphs) "Martian Chronicle"*

For a challenging way to apply descriptive composition skills, students write short paragraphs to a visitor from another planet, precisely describing certain everyday objects and sensations: taste of sugar, smell of an onion, sight of a spoon, sound of a lowing cow, and so on.

189–I *(Write/Role Playing) "Be a Clock Watcher"*

Sometimes the best compositions grow out of the most far-fetched situations. Ask students to pretend they are a clock somewhere in the school. Have them describe what they see and hear. Or they could be a street light, a light bulb (being moved from lamp to lamp), a drop of water, a brick (on an historic building), or an antique candleholder. The possibilities are endless, the results exciting.

190–I *(Write/Topics) "Solve a Weighty Problem"*

Students can be motivated to write creatively by such topics as "Describe the opposite of a power pole," or "What is the heaviest object in the world and how could we weigh it?" By the perplexity of the topics, students are forced to think for themselves more than in the usual written assignments.

DRAMA

191–C *(Perform/Skits) "On the Air"*

The art of storytelling can be fun if the entire class participates. Students like to work on class projects such as short plays and radio skits. Some members can act out a selected story they have rewritten as a script. With the additional required behind-the-scenes work, such as selecting music, producing sound effects, costuming, and set designing, each student gets a chance for expression through interests and talents.

192–I *(Write/Role Playing) "Let's Pretend"*

To encourage the use of creativity and imagination, give assignments that promote role playing through writing. Try these: (1) Pretend you are Lady Macbeth and you keep a diary. Write the five entries just before you commit suicide. (2) A friend of yours has asked how he can better understand Edmond Rostand's *Cyrano de Bergerac*.

EXPOSITION

193–I *(Solve/Themes) "Letting Both Pen and Mind Wander"*

Instead of some of the usual "explain this," "compare that," and "contrast these" compositions, suggest students write something philosophical, to communicate abstract thoughts they often think about but have never tried to put on paper. In this way, the students reveal a lot about themselves and their thoughts while they are free to let their minds wander and develop as they struggle with various philosophical inconsistencies and paradoxes.

194–I,C *(Speak/Circulars) "Futuristic Vacation"*

Instead of the descriptive exposition "What I Did during My Summer Vacation," have students bring in maps, picture postcards, and brochures of places they visited during the summer. Let the students first discuss them and then write "Where I Would Like to Take My Next Vacation." Be prepared to find some students who did not do anything special. Since there probably will not be time for everyone to report, the demonstration portion of the assignment will be self-limiting.

195–I *(Speak/Library) "Kopy Kats"*

Each student selects an author to research for an oral report. This gathering of information helps the student understand what incidents in the author's life affected his or her writing. A planning conference with each student would be helpful in developing the final report. The exercise provides a variety of experiences: researcher, reporter, critic, writer, and student.

196-I   *(Write/Essays) "Gradual Take-Over"*

To penetrate the built-in defenses many students have against expressing their true feelings in major papers, give five-minute written assignments on simple topics: "My father always . . . ." "On Mondays I. . . ." "It disgusts me to. . . ." Saturate students with these ungraded papers almost daily for several weeks; stress freedom of expression instead of form. Then gradually slide into longer, more meaningful, graded assignments. No longer will students be so "pen-tied." The teacher also gets good insights about students.

197-I   *(Write/Essays) "My Ideal"*

Students usually admire and try to imitate someone. Perhaps they have read about someone with whom they would like to trade places. Suggest a short essay on the subject "If I Could Be Anybody. . . ."

198-I   *(Write/Essays) "Powerful Topic"*

Here is a composition topic that will always be current. "If you had the power for a day, how would you help the world?" Limits might be set on length or on ideas.

199-I   *(Write/Essays) "Snow Job"*

A successful essay topic must be relevant to each student's life. With this in mind, try some of the following: Wait for a blizzard—one of those days when cars and buses are stranded and when spring seems decades away. Then assign a personal essay called "Snow News Is Good News" or any clever title. To stimulate the thinking process, give a few sample sentences describing how you reacted to the unscheduled vacation—or if you live south of the snow belt, how a hurricane may have affected your life. Anxious moments about college admission, admission tests, term papers, athletics, girls, boys, and after-school employment can also become interesting essays. Students generally perform with extra effort if they can write about something important to themselves.

200-I   *(Write/Interviews) "Friendly Compositions"*

An interesting topic for the uninterested might be biographical sketches that students write about each other. Set up interviews between students; provide guidelines on types of questions to ask. Assign a short biographical sketch based on the interview. Urge that they include such items as the student's position among other siblings, a humorous childhood incident,

interests, ambitions, and likes and dislikes. Completed essays
are read aloud so that students can guess the subject of each
without being told the name. Play up interest by playing down
the errors. Also consider having students write their own auto-
biographical sketch, exchange papers anonymously, and guess
the identity of the author.

201-I *(Write/Letters) "Dear Gabby"*

A student's personal problems hold the key to subjects of real
interest. Concerns of any type are submitted in letter form as
if to an advice-giving columnist. Everyone then draws someone else's selection and writes an answer to it in the fashion of
"Dear Abby." Some of the best combinations can be duplicated
for closer observation.

202-I *(Write/Movies, Television) "Way to Get a Star"*

Sometimes what students watch on television or at the local
theater doesn't get enough attention at school, particularly in
composition applications. Students usually do well when writing descriptions of their favorite television or film character, or
when presenting an argument on why everyone should or
should not see a particular show or film.

203-I *(Write/Television) "Humor Us"*

Students are asked to watch their favorite TV comedy and
write a review giving the reasons for their choice. They can
illustrate their points by describing a particularly humorous
part. The papers can then be used for a discussion on humor
which, in turn, leads into humor found in the literature they
are studying.

204-I *(Write/Topics) "Artistrick"*

Looking for a different approach for a writing assignment?
Ask the students: "If you could create one of the world's great
paintings, literary works, musical compositions, or scientific
discoveries, which would you choose? Describe, then tell why
you would like to have been the creator." One student, for
example, wrote he would have liked to be talented like Rubens
so he could save a fortune by painting his own buxom nudes
rather than buying girly magazines. Facetious or not, the
paper explaining this in some detail was his best effort all year.

205-I *(Write/Topics) "Fur or Agin?"*

Give theme topics that require students to qualify and substantiate opinions. Allow a choice of topics that must be either
supported or refuted, topics about which students normally
have strong feelings: drivers' age limits, extending the school

year, integrating races and eliminating sexism in American schools and institutions, and many concerns about parental control and family responsibility. Other topics could deal with high school football games, pierced ears, pep rallies, voting and politics, student rights, and many more—just ask the class. The assignment calls forth enthusiasm but, at the same time, requires a certain objectivity not normally used in taking sides.

206–I *(Write/Topics) "Take-Off"*

Weekly, the teacher provides a takeoff point for "thought time." This takeoff point should be something that does not lend itself to a preconceived idea. For example, the teacher may hold up a battered golf shoe, or write a word on the board such as *timelessness*. Then the students spend a half hour writing down their thoughts on this subject. At the end of a six-week term they hand in a composition based on *one* of the takeoff points. The composition will be evaluated by the teacher, but it is up to the student to ponder over each weekly paper deciding which one to turn in.

JOURNALISM

207–C *(Construct/Magazines) "Maga-Scene"*

As an outgrowth of a journalism or media unit during which the class has completed a study of periodicals, create a classroom potpourri youth magazine. Divide the class into special interest groups: literature, sports, current events (even at school), science, advice columns, homemaking, puzzles, cartoons, jokes, word games, and letters to the editor. To divide the workload, everyone writes something and types it for spirit master or xerographic duplication. Then students add to their writing roles the tasks of being editor, co-editor, advertising manager, artists, layout people, copyreaders, and proofreaders. This magazine differs from the typical school literary magazine because it does not cater to the literary "geniuses." Seeing their names in print gives the "just average" writer the valuable encouragement rarely found in conventional composition approaches.

208–T *(Write/Magazines) "Free-lancing Freely"*

Next time you want to switch from the humdrum list of theme topics, try this: The editors of _____ magazine (whatever is popular and current) have asked you to write an article for a future issue, one featuring America's youth, their hopes, fears, interests, and attitudes toward themselves and American society. Thus, as a representative of this youth, give your views to the magazine's readers. For example, what can students do to conserve natural resources? (For an alternative assignment, one student can interview another on the same subject.)

209-I *(Write/Newspapers) "Start the Presses"*

After a concentrated study of newspapers, and following some news article or feature-writing assignments, let the class produce their own newspaper—even modeled after an actual publication such as the *Chicago Sun-Times*. Depending upon finances, the publishing methods may range from a simple dittoed, xeroxed, or mimeographed version to one produced in the school or community printshop. One class persuaded a newspaper publisher to let them put together a special insert section featuring the school. Whatever the medium, there will be much to do for everyone from the class artist to the zodiac expert. (Also see idea 135.)

210-G *(Write/Paragraphs) "Select Activity"*

Students apply knowledge of past composition studies. They divide into groups, each to concentrate on one type of written discourse. For example, one group devises a paragraph in the form of an editorial. Another writes a humorous paragraph like those on a newspaper feature page. The best approach is to have all students submit to their group a paragraph of their best writing. These are circulated to locate the best in the group.

211-I *(Write/Pictures) "Loud Report"*

Place magazine illustrations around the room that pose some form of confrontation activity. Students assume the role of reporter and write a news article as if the picture were to be used to illustrate the article.

LETTER WRITING

212-I *(Write/Letters) "Dear Napoleon"*

Letter writing exercises need not be boring. In this approach, students write imaginary letters to famous people of the past, telling them about life in the present. They must keep in mind the appropriateness of the subject matter to the recipient. Students are thus challenged to use only significant details—a good concern in any type of writing.

213-I *(Write/Letters) "Dear Peer"*

Junior high or middle school students find this an interesting way to begin a unit on letter writing. Each writes an informal letter telling about his or her interests, activities, personality, and so on, knowing only that a student of the opposite sex in another class will receive it. Students sign their names to the letters they write. In the second phase, each student receives a reply from the recipient of the letter. Then the first student writes a second letter including a little more about himself or herself and a short criticism of his or her correspondent's letter. This procedure continues for about three rounds. The first letter is then compared with the last to see if there are any changes in the letter-writing techniques.

214–I *(Write/Role Playing) "Mail Can't Fail"*

A simple letter-writing assignment can be much more interesting if students write under pseudonyms, perhaps assuming roles of contemporaries of literary characters recently studied. They first write a letter and later respond to a different letter drawn at random. Or roles can be drawn for each of two correspondents. Some successful letters of the past included these pairs: Hamlet and Ann Landers, Huckleberry Finn and Holden Caulfield, Mao Tse-tung and the Maharishi Mahesh Yogi, Joe Namath and Cassius (Mohammed Ali) Clay, Eldridge Cleaver and Alice Cooper, and Matt Dillon and Shane.

MEDIA

215–G *(Construct/Magazines, Projectors) "Mocking a Film"*

Filmmaking can be expensive, but here is a way to make a mock film economically and give writing practice, too. Students (small groups) decide on a theme and/or plot. They collect magazine illustrations, cartoons, photographs, or even drawings if needed. These are fastened securely to a roll of sturdy paper that fits the opaque projector table. Captions and tape-recorded background from a carefully written script can be added. The final product is threaded into the opaque projector and is either pulled or rolled through in unison with the tape narration and music.

216–I *(Write/Paragraphs) "Student Bestimonials"*

To add interest to what could be a rather routine media unit, suggest that each student write a short paragraph endorsing a favorite magazine. Select the best ones and type them to be posted with the student's picture (preferably in a hall display case). Besides adding a little life to a usually dull display area, the technique can be the preliminary to a magazine subscription drive to raise money for the school. In one tenth-grade class the best entries were actually sent to the magazine publishers, and one student's picture and "testimonial" were published in the magazine's house organ. Another student and her teacher were awarded a year's subscription to the magazine. This is additional evidence that more can be accomplished when writing for a purpose than writing for a grade.

NARRATION

217-I *(Perform/Role Playing) "On Being a Character"*

This idea works particularly well in middle school or junior high classes. Students think of a type of person—pilot, queen, congressperson, police officer, and so forth—they would like to be. Then they write and present a monologue of that person. Not only does this approach give students a feel for the monologue technique, but it also helps them understand the character.

218-C *(Perform/Role Playing) "Talk It Up"*

To synthesize skills in writing dialogue, students use the talk-show format and imagine conversations between strong personalities who are sometimes in conflict: the school principal and a student, Satan and a prominent evangelist preacher, a political conservative and a radical, a feminist and an antifeminist, or a hawk and a dove. The best of these products could also be presented live to the class, preferably extemporaneously.

219-G *(Speak/Interviews) "This Is Your Life"*

Narrative writing can be both easy and difficult. Choosing the right subject will make the task easier. A particularly motivating way to locate subjects is for students to interview each other. The one interviewed relates an incident from earlier life (tragic, humorous, anything). The interviewer then converts the incident to a narrative composition. Shared with the class, these papers will be interesting because the main characters are well-known to the class.

220-G,I *(Write/Books) "Book Makers"*

As a culminating activity in a story-writing unit, upper classes might write short stories or fairy tales, illustrating them if desired. This activity begins with reading and studying children's books. Individuals or groups choose plots and appropriate characters. Once written, stories can be duplicated and bound into books with student-designed covers. The completed books can be shared with younger children in the school system or given to children's hospitals.

221–G *(Write/Books) "Novel Way"*

Assign a plot or have the class choose one together. Then everyone writes a chapter of the novel. Assign specific areas or, if the plot allows (as does a biography), students may write whatever they want. The latter approach sometimes results in a humorous product which can stimulate discussion on integrating plots, character development, rising and falling action, and so on. The finished manuscript could be duplicated and stapled so that each class member gets a copy.

222–C *(Write/Games) "Added Attraction"*

With an especially creative class, try a progressive narrative. The teacher (or a student) starts it by writing the introductory paragraph. Each student takes a turn writing successive paragraphs directly related to the one just before. The subject must be broad enough to elicit responses from everyone. Since the finished composition will be on display, students should be specially aware of good writing skills. After several attempts, the class could select the most enjoyable or creative narrative.

223–I *(Write/Models) "Can You Top This?"*

A college student shares this idea. "One of the most successful and worthwhile high school assignments ever handed me concerned the short story. Having completed a unit on Poe, we were asked to write the beginning paragraphs of a short story of our own creation. The stories were to be written in the style of Poe but were to supply only the main characters and the beginning of the plot. They were then exchanged for completion. The results were fantastic. The assignment was effective in two major ways: (1) providing an excellent, individualized culminating activity for the unit, and (2) allowing the students to unconsciously express a great many personal feelings and emotions."

224–I *(Write/Movies) "To Be Continued"*

Use a filmed story to stimulate writing by stopping the film at a crucial point and having students complete the story by themselves. Some short animated films such as "Moonbird" and "The Hole" lend themselves to such an assignment. Other good short films include "An Occurrence at Owl Creek Bridge" and other Ambrose Bierce short stories: "Chickamauga" and "The Mockingbird."

225–I *(Write/Movies) "Sound Off"*

As a project for advanced writers, gather several short filmstrips or short five- or ten-minute movies, nature shorts, or cultural bits. Turn off the sound and show them to the class. Show films several times while students write their own script or narration. Then play the sound track and the film. This can be used in conjunction with narration or description, as well as preparation for writing their own scripts for film, videotape, or audiotape.

226–I   *(Write/Mysteries) "ABC Mystery"*

Most students love good mysteries. Here is a plan to encourage them to write their own. Each student places any person's name beginning with "A" on a slip of paper, a place that starts with "B" on another, and an object starting with "C" on the third. Scramble all slips and have each child pick one slip from each set. He or she may come up with "Albert," "Baltimore," and "car." Now that person must write a good short mystery incorporating these words as key ideas.

227–C,I   *(Write/Paragraphs) "Emote Chance"*

The great amount of material to be covered during a semester does not allow much time for creative writing. Paragraph assignments help take up the slack. Each student writes a narrative paragraph expressing an emotion—a reaction to some condition in his or her life, e.g., a catastrophe, a joy, a sadness. Later, hand out duplicated copies containing all the paragraphs. Spend at least one period discussing them. This activity can be coordinated with the study of short stories.

228–I   *(Write/Paragraphs) "Words to Write By"*

Write a series of words on the board such as: *boy, crying, train, bridge, water,* and *swim.* Each student writes one or more paragraphs incorporating these words into an idea or story. (See related idea number 233.)

229–I   *(Write/Pictures) "Cut Ups"*

Mount pictures and illustrated ads from magazines on colored construction paper, using a color that reflects the mood. Give one to each student to stimulate imagination in creating a short story. The picture can become the cover for the story.

230–I   *(Write/Puzzles) "Big Finish"*

Read the beginning of a short story orally in class—a detective story works well. Stop at an appropriate place so each student can write his or her own ending. Read some of these new endings aloud before the author's version is revealed, pointing out the need to maintain unity and credibility.

231–C   *(Write/Short Stories) "Noteworthy Idea"*

For the younger student, the "note in the bottle" gives rise to some very creative short stories. The teacher (or a student) brings in an interestingly shaped bottle and explains that there is a mysterious note inside and asks students to write a

story on how the note got there and what it says. The next day (or several days later), after some of the stories have been read, discussed, and offered as models, the bottle is opened and the note read. It, of course, says in rhyme or some other clever way that the bottle "has a meaning that is different to everyone."

232-I,C *(Write/Short Stories) "Your Own First Person"*

Each student writes a short story in which he or she is a character. It could be realistic or a fantasy. The important idea is that it be an exercise in self-awareness and an outlet for expression after a student looks at himself or herself seriously. The finished product would be enhanced by a montage or visual aid presentation.

233-I *(Write/Short Stories) "Interest a Human"*

Find a human interest picture in a magazine or newspaper. List five descriptive words or expressions that go with the picture. Then, using these words and the picture as motivation, write a story.

OVERVIEW

234-C *(Solve/Papers) "Communicate by Choice"*

Two often English teachers stress writing as though it is the only means of conveying a thought. Students who say they "can't write" often feel frustrated and consider themselves academic failures. Allow the students options in methods of communicating their term papers. Suggest alternative ways to solve the problem—cartooning, painting or drawing, writing poetry or a play, taking pictures, recording a tape, and other approaches.

235-I *(Write/Authorities) "Tale of Two Test Tubes"*

How do you motivate students whose interests lie in areas completely outside of English, e.g., math and physics? Show such students that learning how to write can benefit them regardless of field. When such students must write a paper on a class novel, let them pick their own related topic. Allow them to focus on the social, historical, or scientific background of the novel's period, depending on which area is of most interest. It is far better to receive a well-written paper on medicine in the late eighteenth century than a weakly written critique of *Silas Marner.*

236-I   *(Write/Bulletin Board) "Composition Competition"*

Many state or national writing competitions arise during the school year. Find out about as many of them as possible. List them on a bulletin board. Offer extra incentive to anyone who submits something for a contest, or give a class assignment from which the best products can be turned in as contest entries.

237-I   *(Write/Essays) "Familiar Writing"*

Students should learn to write confidently about people and situations that confront them daily. Assign a brief in-class essay written either humorously, ironically, or satirically but one that depicts a typical English class period. It may even be a character sketch of the teacher or another student. Read the essays in class, discussing their realistic qualities and appropriateness.

238-G   *(Write/Essays) "Write Group"*

Let the entire class participate in writing an essay on a popular topic. Divide the class into groups of four or five. Let them meet for two or three hours a week—possibly a half hour at a time—to decide their approach to their portion of the assigned topic. Then after the sections are completed, each group reads its contribution in the order of normal topic development. This approach can be varied by allowing each group to write the total topic and then comparing results. As a fringe benefit, working in groups helps the shy student overcome his or her problem.

239-I   *(Write/Journals) "Getting to Know You"*

The student journal remains an effective way to help remove writing inhibitions or to expand composition subjects. Sometimes a spiral notebook is used to collect a minimum number of weekly entries, as few as two or three so it won't be a chore. The journal concept encourages collecting ideas, observations, and opinions and makes students more aware of what is happening to them and to others. If students occasionally write something too personal, they should indicate this but should not use this as an excuse to avoid writing anything. Keep journals for a month or so. If the class is benefitting, continue. Naturally, the journals should not be corrected. Spot checks help evaluate the technique and assess the growth in expression and self-confidence. To increase student support, the teacher might also keep a journal to be shared.

240-I   *(Write/Papers) "Eradicating the Bugs"*

One way to solve the term paper problem is to urge students to write about issues that really concern them personally. Use topics such as "What's bugging you?" Urge them to write about something they think is very wrong in class, in school, or in society. They must give convincing reasons why the situation is wrong and then suggest ways to solve the problem. This should not only generate enthusiasm to write, but it should also force the students to reflect seriously on ways to improve their environment.

241–T   *(Write/Papers) "Pen Names"*

Invite students to use pseudonyms for their composition papers. This serves four purposes: (1) promotes impartial grading, (2) encourages creativity, (3) eliminates embarrassment, and (4) provides opportunity for fun in considering some particularly unusual names, e.g., Wilamina Shapespeer.

242–C   *(Write/Papers) "Wet Composition"*

Devote a class period to a surprise writing assignment to stimulate creativity. Bring in an object such as a half-filled glass of water. The class writes about it in any form, poetic to scientific. This results in a variety of themes ranging from the chemical aspects of water to space-age fiction.

243–I   *(Write/Paragraphs) "On the Head of a Pin"*

One student reported that the greatest composition exercise ever assigned her was when, as a seventh grader, she was asked to write one short paragraph on a single and very limited subject such as: "My Mother's Hair," "My Father's Nose," "The Color Red," or "A Cow's Horn." A classmate, she recalled, produced a brilliant piece entitled "The Varied Virtues of an Ordinary Straight Pin."

244–I,G   *(Write/Pictures) "Captured Captions"*

The bulletin board can help students locate good topics. Pictures of varied subjects are posted minus captions. Students, either individually or as a group project, write their own captions which can be humorous or serious and should lend themselves to much broader themes. Try these:

Picture: Cartoon of Snoopy hopping over croquet wickets.
Caption: "That reminds me. I did a *wicked* thing today."
Theme idea: Personal experience; world problem.
Picture: Full-color illustration of small forest.
Caption: "I think that I shall never see...."

Theme idea: Description of trees in various seasons; exposition on conserving natural resources; discussion of how trees help man.

245-G *(Write/Talks) "Quality, Not Quantity"*

For most people, it is easier to communicate a thought or an emotion by speaking than by writing. The teacher, therefore, should encourage frequent short summary-type paragraphs emanating from short talks. What one student has to say orally is copied (or recorded and then copied) by another student, then read and analyzed—and changed if necessary. How it is said is more important than how much is said. Once students have mastered the paragraph technique, they will be better equipped to write papers of any length. Some students would probably rather write diaries which are not read by others but which also help reduce writing inhibitions. (See also idea 239.)

246-I *(Write/Topics) "Pull, Not Push"*

Some students should not be pushed into class writing assignments but rather be given an independent project. They are more likely to motivate themselves under such conditions. They may write poetry, short stories, novels, skits, plays, or simply *copy* articles from books or magazines. Writing in a journal may also help. Most, even the very slow students, would prefer to rely on their own ingenuity and, thereby, find writing worthwhile, even fun.

247-I *(Write/Topics) "Way-Out Topics"*

To stimulate more imaginative writing, get away from stereotyped topics such as "My Favorite Pet," "What I Saw on the Way to School," "My Favorite Relative," ad nauseum. Offer these titles instead: "Green," "Black," "Square," "780," "Yes," "No," "Cube," "665-2698," "Time," "Friday," or "Can't." The list is endless. After the grumbling has subsided, ask students to sit quietly and think for five or ten minutes before writing. After several therapeutic sessions like this, imagination and creativity begin to emerge. Some students never get beyond the "green is the color of the grass" stage, but most results are excellent.

POETRY

248-I *(Write/Games) "Ballad-Ears"*

After a unit on the *Odyssey* or another epic, students convert the idea to a short ballad, applying their knowledge of that technique. Conduct a contest for the best ballad. Duplicate the entire set to each student receives the collection.

SYNTAX

249-C   *(Write/Sentences) "Pass Keys"*

Do you start simply enough when you assign compositions?
Sentences are also miniature compositions. Give two key words
such as *soldier moaned* or *brakes screeched*. Have students
write sentences telling where, how, and why the soldier
moaned or the brakes screeched.

250-C   *(Write/Sentences) "Sentence Sense"*

Try this as an early composition approach: Tell students to
write a sentence that will make a reader feel cold, hot, dirty, or
even nauseated. Or tell them to write a noisy sentence, or a
sweet sentence, or a slimy sentence. Of course, in all instances,
they cannot use the words *cold, hot, dirty, noisy, sweet* or
slimy. This activity allows free-rein outlets for previously
studied writing concepts.

Part Two

GRAMMAR/ LANGUAGE

5   Introduction

DIALECT

251–C   *(Discover/Lists) "Linguistic Insecurity"*

Distribute a list of familiar words that may be pronounced correctly at least two different ways. Alongside each word are the numbers 1 and 2. Inform the class that you will give two pronunciations of the listed words. Instruct students to circle the number of the pronunciation they believe is correct and then to check the one they would actually use. Words such as *tomato, aunt, either, vase, root,* and *route* are used. Then ask the class to count the number of discrepancies between the pronunciation they thought was correct and that which they like to use. Now tell the class that both pronunciations are correct. This exercise reveals the variety and flexibility of American regional and social dialects as well as the "prestige" often associated with certain pronunciations.

252–C   *(Listen/Audiotapes) "Where Y'all From?"*

With the assistance of other teachers and selected students who come from various parts of the nation or the world, tape record some passages being read in natural dialects. Such activity provides motivation for introducing ethnic and regional dialects. It also encourages acceptance of those who speak differently. If funds are available, purchase dialect records which the school librarian can locate.

253–T   *(Listen/Talk) "Add a Second Language"*

In a class where many students speak ethnic or regional dialects not accepted by society in general, the teacher's attitude and approaches toward acceptable spoken English are keys to one's teaching success or failure. Convincing students that learning to speak conventional English will help them in future job interviews and employment is not simple and sometimes not sufficient. Try to instill the idea that a nonstandard dialect is perfectly acceptable among family, friends, and in most informal occasions. At the same time suggest that standard English is a "second language"—the way to write and speak when formality is required or when there must be no chance for misinterpretation. Ask them to listen for language differences when popular radio and television announcers and even teachers are not on the job. Foreign language teachers could suggest ways to teach standard English as a second language.

254-C *(Observe/Demonstrations) "Why Can't I Be Sayin' Like How I Think?"*

Introduce language differences through copies of various dialects found in print. Include geographical, ethnic, professional, and popular vocabulary in your examples. Point out similarities and differences between the dialects and standard English. Let the students do a unit on dialects or present a skit to illustrate dialectical concerns.

LINGUISTICS

255-T *(Discover/Definitions) "A Noun Is a Noun Is a . . ."*

Instead of identifying nouns as "a word naming a person, place, thing, or idea," try this: Any word to which either *s* or *'s* can be added is a noun. Develop similar linguistic definitions for other parts of speech, particularly those that take various inflected endings. If you can't think of any, consult any modern grammar book.

256-C *(Discover/Instructions) "Words at Work"*

Naming parts of speech is not as important as asking "What work does this word do in the sentence?" Only four types of words are at work in any sentence: namers, tellers, connectors, and modifiers. Namers have three uses: subjects, appositives, and completers (direct objects and predicate nominatives). Tellers tell what the subject is doing: Jim *is walking*. Betty *skates*. Or the teller expresses a non-action or state of being: She *is* here. Modifiers describe the namers and tellers and are usually called adjectives and adverbs. Connectors link main sentence parts to extended modifiers (clauses and phrases) using subordinate conjunctions and prepositions. Coordinate conjunctions join sentences as well as namers, tellers, and modifiers. Thus, teach students how parts of speech function within the four categories.

257-C *(Discover/Mixed Media) "Great Grammarian Guru"*

Grammar often becomes boring if confined to a set of prescribed textbook rules and exercises. To help solve this problem, teach grammar in much the same way as chemistry. Let the students discover the rules themselves, pragmatically, by listening to the speech of their parents, friends, and teachers, and by examining the grammar used in newspapers and books. With proper direction, the students can uncover and eventually phrase all those rules from the text. Moreover, they will be much more likely to use rules they make for themselves than those of the Great Mystery Grammarian.

258-T *(Discover/Self) "Built-in Grammar Systems"*

Here are several reminders that experienced teachers generally suggest to those preparing to teach grammar: (1) Most essentials of a linguistic system are learned by native speakers before adolescence. (2) Except for certain structures more common to writing than to speech, the average teen-ager uses all the major grammatical resources in day-to-day conversation. (3) Most grammar vocabulary is a convenience enabling people to talk about and improve oral and written speech.

259-C *(Discover/Sentences) "Quin Ud Fungle Srip?"*

To introduce structure, make up nonsense sentences such as, "Ni twindle punged frackly." Ask basic questions about the sentence such as: What is the subject? What is the verb? How can you tell? Have students suggest word substitutions to make a meaningful sentence. This illustrates that in every sentence the same elements are relatively constant, both in position and in inflected endings.

260-C *(Listen/Paragraphs) "Whatzit Say?"*

Introduce punctuation by dictating a mispunctuated or unpunctuated paragraph. Many will be unable to take the dictation because of the inherent problem of incorrect or no voice modulation. Finally, hand out a duplicated copy of what was read. Discuss its punctuation with the class; compare with their own.

261-C *(Listen/Talk) "Pause that Inflexes"*

Instead of memorizing all those rules, students can learn punctuation by intonation patterns. Reading poetry aloud is excellent practice for this. By voice inflection students can determine what punctuation is needed, where, and why. Raising the voice at sentence endings signals a question mark; lowering, a period; extra force, the exclamation mark; and a pause, a comma.

262–C   *(Listen/Talk, Lists) "A Plus"*

Students listen to the teacher reading sentences—some conventional English sentences, some not so conventional but otherwise correct, and finally some that are not correct. Students number their papers for each sentence and then mark after the number a + or 0, depending upon how they conceive (or feel) the acceptability of the sentence. Chances are very good that most students will get the sentences correct. Discuss why. Then discuss why these same students might have difficulty writing the same sentences.

263–C   *(Observe/Models) "Patterns for Saying"*

If students can learn five simple, basic sentence patterns, they can easily move to transformations of them. They do so whenever they speak. The following skeletons can be repatterned and fleshed out through the various forms of modification. (Different linguists will have varying labels for these patterns.)

I. Subject / Verb (S / V)
II. Subject / Verb + Direct Object (S / V + DO)
III. Subject / Verb + Indirect Object + Direct Object
(S / V + IO + DO)
IV. Subject / Verb + Predicate Nominative (S / V + PN)
V. Subject / Verb + Predicate Adjective (S / V + PA)

Provide a chart with these formulas pictured. Add some illustrative sentences as reference when students write. Refer to the chart when similar sentences occur in the literature.

264–C   *(Observe/Television) "TV Test Pattern"*

Except for face-to-face communication, television is the most abundant source of linguistic experiences for today's student. For an introduction to the social and economic values of standard English, students can observe the differences between the speech patterns of various television characters while simultaneously noting corresponding differences in their professions, status, and dress.

265–C   *(Read/Books) "Sensible Nonsense"*

Use Lewis Carroll's "Jabberwocky" to illustrate built-in language signals—a structuralist idea. Although the words are nonsensical, their positions and inflected endings indicate the part of speech and the function they serve. Students can also create their own nonsense stories in the manner of Carroll.

MECHANICS

266–T   *(Observe/Cartoons, Displays) "Visual Ed"*

A way to vitalize grammar, especially for middle school students, is to personify, illustrate, or animate essential elements. For example, bring in cartoons illustrating punctuation. Prepare posters or skits that show a comma as "a snake that causes us to pause"; a question mark as "a fat person whose diet we question"; an exclamation point as "a hypodermic syringe—ouch!" Mobiles, slogans, and graffiti can provide other mnemonic devices to gain the students' interests and to motivate their own creative displays.

267–C, T   *(Observe/Instructions) "Mechanical Problems"*

Integrate grammar study and composition. When a composition assignment reveals a wide misunderstanding of some mechanical device, teach that aspect when it can be most effective—not in isolation.

268–C   *(Read/Models) "Write or Wrong"*

Dramatize the importance of punctuation for a correct interpretation of a sentence by placing on the chalkboard models that illustrate the point. For example: "He lost his wife not only his wealth." (He lost his wife not, only his wealth.)

OVERVIEW

269–T   *(Discover/Papers) "Write Start"*

The best motivation to study grammar is for students to see the need in their own writing. At the beginning of the term, assign a simple composition. From that, inventory the kinds of grammatical and language errors made. Stress these during the year instead of the typical bookish approach. The study of grammar evolves most naturally out of composition.

270–I   *(Discover/Newspapers) "A Line on Headlines"*

Students find words in headlines that can be used as verbs or nouns (depending upon context). Then they write a headline that places the word in its opposite use, pasting the original headline next to the newly created one.

271–I   *(Discover/Tutoring) "Teach Me and I'll Teach You"*

Students can learn effectively from other students. Put this theory into practice by allowing each student to be a specialist in one grammatical or mechanical area. When writing their own papers, or analyzing other people's, students consult with the "specialist" who deals in his or her specific problem. Learning from peers is often more lasting than receiving information from the teacher.

272-T *(Listen/Discussions) "Your Turn"*

If you hear groans when a grammar unit or lesson is announced, tell the students it's their turn to give you their ideas and suggestions for new and interesting ways to approach the subject. Devote some time discussing these ideas. Encourage devising games or adapting existing games. Some of the best classroom approaches have come from the students themselves. Thirty-five minds working are bound to think up more ideas than one.

273-C, *(Listen/Papers) "Play It by Ear"*
G

Teach grammar like composition—by sound. Pair off the class. One student reads another's paper aloud and stops when something sounds incorrect to either. If sentences sound "right," no correction is needed. Constant stress on perfection stifles the desire to write or speak in class. Another version of this same idea is for the teacher to read a passage aloud. Students listen and write what they hear, including punctuation and spelling. As writing and speaking become more natural in the classroom and less traumatic, students will learn "correct English" when they are ready but only when they discover the need.

274-C *(Observe/Skits) "Grammar Upstage"*

For those having difficulty learning parts of speech and their functions, diagramming sentences and memorizing rules usually do not work. Make it fun! Devise a short skit illustrating what can happen if certain parts of speech are omitted, overused, or improperly used. A job interview that goes awry is a popular choice. Each student participates by being involved with the grammatical principle that is most difficult for him or her.

275-T *(Read/Books) "Bridge the Gap"*

Today's English teacher keeps asking what grammar to teach: traditional, structural, transformational-generative, or no grammar. For many, the latter seems to be the way out of the confusion. Their rationale, they say, is grammar does not seem to improve students' written or oral language. Recent research, however, has brought forth encouragement through the transformational-generative technique of sentence combining. Too involved for detailing here, sentence combining provides a series of models and formulas for combining simple thoughts (kernel sentences) into more sophisticated forms. Compound sentence structures, modifying phrases and clauses, and other forms of imbedding are encouraged.

For some teachers, sentence combining is the answer; for others, it's getting students to write simple, declarative sentences. Neither the former or latter approaches can be implemented, however, without some teacher preparation. Classroom grammar problems will be settled only by reading and selecting from among the alternatives offered. Check the bibliography in this book.

276–C   *(Read/Books) "Filling 'Wholes' "*

The teacher writes on the chalkboard some key words that are omitted from a story the teacher is reading to the class. Where a word has been omitted, the teacher pauses while students take turns telling which word on the board should fit into the "blank." This helps establish how certain words repeatedly work together in sentences. All types of words from the story should be used.

277–T   *(Read/Books) "Mini-Text; Maxi-Use"*

At the beginning of the year, create a booklet or programmed self-progress, branched text that succinctly presents the grammatical strengths and weaknesses common to students at your grade level. Rely mainly upon student writing: sentences, paragraphs, and whole compositions. Stress positive samples of student writing along with a few poor ones for comparison. If the booklets are three-hole punched, they can be placed in the students' looseleaf binders. An occasional illustration or cartoon slipped into the booklet will help break up the pages interestingly. One class's literary magazine could even become another class's "text."

278–C   *(Read/Books) "The More the Better"*

Instead of a single set of grammar books, provide texts from various publishers. Students will enjoy comparing notes on how different authors approach similar problems and use different models. Healthy debates will ensue at times, but grammar lessons assigned en masse out of the same book will hardly be missed.

279–T   *(Read/Books) "Theory of Evolution"*

In dealing with grammar, students appreciate a nonprescriptive approach. If possible, the teacher and students should do some prior reading in linguistics. Then the following ideas will seem reasonable: (1) Different grammatical structures are appropriate to different situations. (2) A particular grammatical structure is not condemned as long as it gets across the meaning. (3) Words and syntax must be considered and evaluated with a specific situation and audience in mind. (4) The effect of words upon a listener or reader is probably the most important concern in communication. (5) Language and, therefore, grammar constantly change and evolve. (6) People should not be judged negatively because their speech patterns and dialects differ from the standard. (7) Language teaching is a science, not a system of prescribed rules for memorization.

280–C *(Read/Handouts) "Ten Illustrated Tips"*

One teacher submits this list of Do's and Do Not's to introduce a few grammatical principles.

1. Use commas only, when needed.
2. Don't use no double negatives.
3. Prepositions are not to end sentences with.
4. Keep your ᵂᵒʳᵏ neat and tidy.
5. Never abbrev.
6. Pronouns must agree with its antecedents.
7. Verbs has to agree with their subjects.
8. Use commas to separate words in a series parenthetical expressions introductory clauses and the like.
9. Examine your work carefully to make sure you have not out any words.
10. While a transcendent vocabulary is laudable, one must nonetheless maintain unceasing surveillance against such loquacious, effusive, voluble verbiage that the calculated objective of the communique emerges ensconced in nebulousness and obfuscation.

281–I *(Read/Models) "Writing Recipes"*

Provide a "recipe box" showing applications of each grammatical principle to be taught. Then when students have writing problems, they can refer to the appropriate card and quickly find several easy-to-follow samples. This collection can be garnered from student writing. Whenever the teacher notes a good sample sentence, he or she provides an index card on which the student can print the model to be used in the file.

282–C *(Read/Paragraphs) "Real-World English"*

At least a few students think good English is just the teacher's infatuation and it "doesn't count" in out-of-class situations. After teaching paragraph structure, from a source the student needs or respects, duplicate four paragraphs for analysis, three with forced, obvious lapses in unity and organization, and one paragraph which, while well-structured, has glaring errors in spelling, punctuation, and grammar. Ask the students to pick out the one that is best structured. The chances are good most students will notice the obvious errors in the last paragraph and reject it for that reason, not realizing that its organization and content are best of the four. When they realize how small items like spelling, punctuation, usage, and grammar can weaken even the best presentation of ideas, they will also realize the reason for the English teacher's concern.

283–T *(Read/Poems) "Better to Be Anonymous?"*

Traditionalist grammarians will enjoy seeing this old poem in print and will perhaps use it for teaching parts of speech. Teachers with a more linguistic bent might try to rewrite the poem to meet their labeling preferences.

Couplets on Grammar

Three little words you often see
Are articles—a, an, and the.

A noun's a name of anything,
As school, or garden, hoop, or swing.

Adjectives tell the kind of noun,
As great, small, pretty, white, or brown.

Instead of nouns the pronouns stand:
I think; she sings; you frown; my hand.

Verbs tell of something to be done:
To read, count, sing, laugh, jump, or run.

How things are done the adverbs tell,
As slowly, quickly, ill, or well.

Conjunctions join the words together,
As man and woman, wind and weather.

The preposition stands before
A noun, as in or through the door.

The interjection shows surprise,
as "Oh, how pretty! Ah, how wise!"

The whole are called nine parts of speech,
Which reading, writing, speaking teach.

284–C *(Research/Bulletin Boards) "Can Labels? Yes"*

For a mass media or grammar unit bulletin board, students bring in labels from different products found in their homes. These are displayed to show one area of communication that is frequently overlooked. Surprisingly, some have never read the lists of ingredients on products they eat regularly. It is a concern because certain products are being charged as injurious to health.

285-G *(Research/Mixed Media) "Career Care"*

Combine career development with learning grammar and language skills. Collect a variety of published materials from all occupations. Divide the class (by special interests perhaps) into groups to study occupational vocabularies, kinds of subjects written about, sentence structures, special formats, and so on. Include published materials from at least five areas: commercial, governmental, informational, recreational, and social.

SEMANTICS

286-C *(Discover/Discussion) "What's in a Word?"*

A good question for class discussion is: Why is it that a noun never has exactly the same meaning any time it is repeated? It would be wise for the teacher to ponder this one carefully before asking the class. A clue, of course, is another question: Who or what gives meaning to words?

287-I *(Research/Mixed Media) "Linguistic Pollution"*

Through a little individual research, students can learn how society uses language to mold thoughts and sometimes to distort information. One type of this linguistic "doublespeak" is euphemism—uplifting certain vocations or moderating unpleasant topics. To introduce euphemisms and doublespeak (doubletalk), have students search newspapers, magazines, and other resources for words and expressions to add to this list:

Common Terms	*Euphemisms*
hairdresser	beautician
undertaker	mortician
ghetto	inner city
garbage man	sanitation engineer
guard	security officer
slum clearance	urban renewal

SPELLING

288-T *(Discover/Tests) "Spelling Out Spelling Procedures"*

Give pretests before teaching any spelling words. This will help determine the words that need emphasizing and the letter combinations that are most troublesome. Students who can pass a pretest should receive more challenging lists. The following steps can help anyone learn to spell better:

1. Study only a few words at a time.
2. See the word used in a sentence so the full meaning is understood.
3. Pronounce each word aloud.
4. Study each part of the word: syllables, prefixes, suffixes, and any special letter combinations.
5. Apply appropriate phonetic principles.
6. Copy the word carefully.
7. Write the word from memory.
8. Allow several days to pass; then try rewriting each word from memory.
9. Restudy any troublesome words.
10. Take a posttest on the words studied in the above manner to see which need more work. (To reinforce learning that has already taken place, the words from previous lessons should be included. Also, the words under study should be used in conversation and writing as frequently as possible.)

289–T *(Read/Sentences) "Casting a Spell"*

As each word being introduced is dictated, students write it down, spelling it two or three different ways, in a free association manner. They are then permitted to circle the one spelling they consider most accurate. This way the teacher can locate problems that can be anticipated for certain words. The inherent problems can then provide the focus for future study.

290–I *(Research/Models) "Loungeray Dept"*

Introduce the need for accurate spelling by asking students to search the business community for misspelled words on signs, particularly hand-lettered messages. Sources are relatively easy to find.

SYNTAX

291–C *(Discover/Sentences) "Chalk One Up"*

Instead of using a prepared text, teach language skills with on-the-spot sentences the class and teacher make up together. For example, the teacher places a sample sentence on the board illustrating an awkward dangling modifier. Example: "This is a book about a little girl whose mother died and had no relatives to stay with." Without any explanation, the class is asked why the sentence is misleading. Ask students for other examples, giving them a chance to write a few on paper. Eventually define the rule of misplaced modifiers. A class secretary records the sentences placed on the board, and at the end of the lesson they are placed on handouts for use as models. If this inductive procedure for exploring grammar were followed periodically, the class would soon compose their own grammar workbook.

292–C *(Discover/Sentences) "Compound It"*

Complex and compound sentences can be introduced by using sets of three related simple sentences printed on tag board strips. Students combine them on paper, adding or subtracting words as needed and then discuss the effect.

293–C *(Listen/Audiotapes) "Sounds of Syntax"*

The class listens to a tape of the teacher (or someone else) reading a paragraph from a student's paper, as originally written. Then they hear the same paragraph, rewritten according to the rules of good grammar. Students should follow along using mimeographed copies of both versions of the paragraph. From this, the teacher launches a discussion of why the second version sounds better. This *auditory* and *visual* discrimination exercise enhances learning.

294–I *(Read/Models) "Four Ways Better"*

Students reluctant to vary their sentences may not realize the many ways to do so. Show these problem writers several related simple sentences and models illustrating ways to combine or change them: transformation of pattern (passive to active, for instance); inversion (questions to statements); expansion (modifiers); and substitution (dependent clause for an independent then subordinated with another sentence). Just have students remember the acronym TIES (first letter of each variation). "This idea TIES in with better writing."

295–I *(Read/Newspapers, Magazines) "Space Age"*

Newspapers and magazines contain much advertising copy and even cartoon captions that do not use complete sentences. Have students bring in samples that illustrate ways rules of good rhetoric are being "fractured." Then they can discuss why (or why not) these "faults" add effectiveness. They may even discover how blank space can carry meaning.

USAGE

296–C *(Discover/Books) "New and Used Slanguage"*

A discussion of current and historical slang provides a beginning study of how language changes and how it reflects the conditions of a society in a particular era. Novels are good sources for slang.

297-T *(Discover/Discussions) "Errorless Ways"*

Ordinarily, the teacher does not interrupt a student's contribution in oral discussion to point out a grammatical error since this may destroy the activity's purpose. But with good student-teacher rapport, a student who consistently says "This here," "You know," "and stuff" may be willing to have the class suggest corrections the moment a weak or faulty expression is used. With enough such occurrences, these students may begin correcting themselves, eventually eliminating the error.

298-T *(Discover/Handouts) "What Art This?"*

Pick any appropriate sentence or short passage. To show how language changes, phrase the sample as it might have appeared in biblical times, then in other eras of history. Tracing this development on a handout will help students understand how language has come to us over the centuries.

299-C *(Read/Poems, Dictionaries) "Germinating Words"*

Introduce students to the *Oxford English Dictionary* through poetry study. Students look up all the key words found in a short poem. Many different connotations and variations in meaning will emerge from this study.

300-C *(Research/Lists) " 'Ow's Your Hinglish?"*

An interesting approach to introducing the nature of language and dialect is to point out vocabulary differences between British and American English. Give the students a list of British nouns (such as the following) and ask them to give or, if necessary, discover the American equivalents:

British	American
braces	suspenders
biscuit	cookie
chemist	druggist
lift	elevator
stores	groceries
treacle	molasses
draughts	checkers
bonnet	automobile hood
flickers	movies
telly	TV (television)
lorry	truck

bank raider	bank robber
parking pitch	parking place
dustman	garbage collector
post	mail
portfolio	briefcase
queue	line
tube	subway
tram	streetcar

Students will see that usage is not rigidly standardized but, rather, a matter of location and family history.

301-C *(Research/Mixed Media) "Foreign Slanguage"*

Taking a tip from those who teach English as a foreign language, discuss slang as needed at times for concise expression. Explain the universality of slang. Compare slang expressions in some foreign languages to American slang. Recordings, student publications, current novels, and magazines are good sources.

302-G *(Research/Mixed Media) "It's Not Groovy Anymore"*

Demonstrate the short life-span of slang and illustrate the danger of using it in formal writing. Divide the class into groups of three or four to research slang jargon from the past. Assign specific time periods for each group (five years ago, ten, fifteen). Old movie magazines, school yearbooks, and interviews with parents are good resources. After compiling a list of slang terms, each group discusses lists for sharing with the class. Be ready for some laughs.

VOCABULARY

303-C *(Discover/Dictionary) "Insight to Sight Words"*

Knowing the source and original meaning of a word often helps in understanding the word's present meaning and correct use. The dictionary becomes an indispensable tool for the reading or language student once he or she understands the functions and uses of etymology. Demonstrate how to trace the origin and development of a word by interpreting the abbreviations and symbols used in the dictionary. Then illustrate how the meaning of a word may be revealed by noting its derivation. For example, flor- flower, floral, florid; ora- oration, oracle. Prepare several lessons exploring the etymology of words. As the dictionary becomes more meaningful and useful, reading and language skills should improve.

304–C *(Discover/Games) "Word Exchange"*

Hold a "new word" exchange. Students exchange 3 × 5 cards on which they have written a vocabulary word they have recently learned. When students receive cards, they try to identify the new word and use it in a sentence without looking at the meaning on the back. Each student who does so successfully gets a point for each word. The highest total of points determines the winner.

305–I *(Discover/Sentences, Paragraphs) "Adopt-a-Word"*

When beginning to teach composition to younger students, try to give them the feel for a word and its meaning. Ask students to select a word that they will have to work with until the next paper. They will have to join it to other words, make it into a sentence, add related sentences, and finally construct a paragraph. Building a finished paragraph by this gradual process will increase understanding of the importance of words and provide a better knowledge of how a composition grows. For example, the word might be *cults*. After writing a few sentences bordering on definitions and gradually expanding them until they develop an informational paragraph, the students, curiosity aroused, could hardly be prevented from writing an entire report on, say, religious cults.

306–I *(Discover/Tutoring) "PTA/Peer Tutoring Approach"*

Vocabulary learning is more enjoyable if students teach one another. Each student selects several words to teach, using pictures, records, collages, and the like for reinforcement. After one student has taught a set, partners switch roles.

307–I,C *(Discover/Tutoring) "Word-a-Day"*

Students should assemble their personal word-definition list from words they encounter in reading. Each day throughout the semester one or two students present a new word. They write each word on the board, read a sentence or the context in which the word was found, define the word, and explain its derivation. Vocabulary quizzes may be given using a student-assembled list of words presented during the week.

308–T *(Read/Chalkboard, Words) "Chalk Up a Few"*

If any new terms or words are going to be used during the lesson, write them on the board while the students are still getting into their seats. Discuss the words briefly. Besides being a good way for students to acquire new words, this approach eliminates having to clarify new words in the middle of a lecture or discussion.

309–I   *(Read/Dictionaries) "Not a Miss Match"*

Challenge the students' interest in vocabulary study by giving
them a list of words without definitions. Distribute a separate
sheet containing the definitions. Students match the clues and
words (numbers and letters). Given a week to do this, they
must check various sources to make sure they have correct
matches. This process can build into timed or untimed contests
for individuals or teams. One ultimate requirement is to be
able to paraphrase a definition of any word when asked.

310–I   *(Read/Dictionaries) "Words in the News"*

To increase vocabulary and motivate slow learners, pick a
weekly topic based on student interests, e.g., cars, grooming
hints, or sports, and have them bring in current magazine or
newspaper articles dealing with that topic. From their sources
compile a list of names such as these for the auto topic:
Cougar, Gremlin, Maverick, Wildcat. Each student must find a
dictionary definition of one word and write an explanation of
why that particular word is appropriate for a car.

311–C   *(Research/Bulletin Boards, Words) "Three for the Book"*

Each day post three vocabulary words on a Vocab Section of
the bulletin board. Students copy them as a continuing list in
their notebooks. They must be prepared to define and use them
correctly in sentences on request at any time. A brief weekly
quiz on the fifteen new words will help keep the slackers on
their toes.

312–G   *(Research/Dictionaries, Discussions) "Quintet Query"*

Divide the class into groups of about five students each. Give
each group a list of words to be defined. Each group must
research their own definitions and use their words in common
sentences to show that they know meanings. Allow two days
for the research. On the third and fourth days, each group presents a fifteen-minute oral presentation (even a panel) to reveal
what they have discovered about the words on their lists.

313–G   *(Research/Lists) "Synonymously Speaking"*

The growth of our system of language hardly knows any
bounds. We can illustrate this by pointing out that Roget's
Thesaurus lists more than 175 synonyms for money, such as:
kale, shekels, wherewithal, wampum, jack, chips, gingerbread,
and wad. Students will enjoy an exercise listing all the words
for some very familiar terms. Turn it into a contest. See, for
example, who can come up with the most synonyms for *said*
without looking in the *Thesaurus*. There are clearly 75 to 100.

314-C *(Research/Lists) "Operation Cooperation"*

INTEREST VOCABULARY

SEX MUSIC ART SPORTS

Rather than assign vocabulary lists, let groups devise lists. Each group should contain students with similar interests so the vocabulary study will be profitable, e.g., science buffs, mechanical experts, or literary types. Valuable terms and concepts can be learned if each member finds, defines, and uses the words correctly and trades information with other group members.

315-I *(Research/Lists) "What's New?"*

To learn the importance of vocabulary development, students obtain file cards or a small spiral notebook for jotting down new words they encounter in reading or listening. Periodically collect the cards or notebooks to create a class vocabulary list. This helps assure that new words arise from actual experiences. Also provide opportunities to use these words in sentences.

316-I *(Research/Mixed Media) "Wordy Class"*

Increased exposure to mass media, particularly periodicals, broadens vocabulary. Each day students find and cut out one paragraph containing an unknown word. They paste the paragraph in a notebook, above the newly found definition which they have looked up. After several weeks when the notebooks are completed, the class might enjoy sharing their knowledge by comparing lists and sources. Possibly the most frequently appearing words can be placed on a master list for some formal or informal testing later.

WORDS

317-C *(Discover/Games) "Reacting Adverbally"*

This game can be used to introduce the value of vivid language in writing. One student leaves the room. While he or she is gone, the class decides on an adverb which the student must guess, for example, *angrily*. When the student has returned and asks questions about the word, the class answers in the manner the adverb denoted, in this case, angrily. This continues until the student guesses the word. Then the turn is passed on. Naturally, the most difficult of all the adverbs to portray is *naturally*.

318–C   *(Discover/Games) "Whozit?"*

Introducing adjectives and their best use need not be dull.
Describe a person in class (or an object) by beginning with one
general adjective such as *big*. Then list more descriptive adjectives, moving slowly from abstract to concrete until someone
in the class guesses who or what is being described.

319–T   *(Observe/Artwork) "Real Abstract"*

Comments that frequently appear
on evaluated compositions are
"Unclear" or "Be Specific!" A
clear writer recognizes abstract
words and realizes they often
need more explanation than concrete words. Art can help illustrate the difference between abstract and concrete language
more vividly than the ladder of
abstraction. Students view two
paintings, one abstract and one
realistic. The ensuing discussion
helps formulate ideas on what is concrete or abstract and how art
and language express ideas.

320–C   *(Discover/Paragraphs) "Reaching Extremes"*

Write a paragraph describing a walk or some other activity
using no adjectives or adverbs. Then write two more paragraphs, one using as many descriptive words as possible and
another with a judicious number. Distribute copies of all three
paragraphs and discuss the most effective and the reasons
why.

321–C   *(Discover/Poems) "Diamonds In the Rough"*

Writing diamante (diamond) poetry helps students understand
word functions. A diamante verse contains seven lines and
sixteen words; it is a contrast poem showing how two things
or concepts differ:

line 1 a noun (the subject)
line 2 two adjectives describing line 1
line 3 three participles describing line 1
line 4 four nouns (2 related to line 1; 2 related to line 7)
line 5 three participles describing line 7
line 6 two adjectives describing line 7
line 7 a noun opposite (or nearly opposite) to the one in line 1

Rain
Cold, wet
Freezing, driving, drenching
Umbrellas, raincoats, beach, sunglasses
Warming, relaxing, soothing
Golden, bright
Sunshine

With a little imagination, other parts of speech could be included, e.g., verbs.

322-I   *(Research/Dictionaries) "Turn on the Rajio"*

Many words used in foreign countries are strictly American words only slightly modified. For example, in a Japanese-American dictionary there are such shared words as *rajio* for radio, *inki* for ink, and *hankachi* for handkerchief. Students list as many of these words as possible from foreign language dictionaries. Besides being fun, the exercise helps students realize how widespread the English language has become.

6 Deliberation

DIALECT

323-C *(Analyze/Models)* *"Soul Searching"*

After an introductory study of dialect, ask students to bring in examples of the following: regional variations (language differences in various geographical areas of the United States); social dialects (language based on social status); and functional or temporal (changes that conform to the formality or informality of the occasion). Samples may be found in the media, films, and folk songs. For added challenge, suggest folk etymology (vocabulary changes due to prolonged use).

LINGUISTICS

324-C *(Analyze/Discussion)* *"So, What's the Difference?"*

To emphasize differences between oral and written English, two students describe the plot of a short story. One reads the plot summary he or she has written, the other gives a summary aloud. The class then analyzes the obvious differences (structure, sentence variety, organization, or formality) between the two presentations.

325-T *(Analyze/Sentences)* *"Two Plus Two"*

Most teachers are familiar with traditional sentence diagramming often used as a tool to explain how words in a sentence relate. Linguists theorize that diagrams force words out of their natural order and serve to confuse students. They suggest the immediate constituent approach to sentence diagramming: the idea that each part of a sentence can be divided into two parts. Each part can be additionally divided by two until only single words remain:

Several rude people in the audience/laughed very loudly.
Several rude people/in the audience · laughed/very loudly.
Several/rude people · in/the audience · laughed · very/loudly.
Several · rude/people · in · the/audience · laughed · very · loudly.
Several · rude · people · in · the · audience · laughed · very · loudly.

Sentence analysis proceeds with discussions of each cut and how the structures function in the sentence. For example, the first cut yields the complete subject and the predicate. The functions of the additional cuts, although they should be obvious, can be highlighted by colors or various forms of brackets.

326–C *(Experiment/Chalkboard, Sentences) "Born Linguists"*

In learning the parts of speech, native speakers can rely on their own use of language. Write a sample sentence on the chalkboard: The athlete _____ well. Each student supplies a word for the blank. The result will be a long list of verbs (except for a few errors). Do the same for other sentence parts. Students prefer implementing their innate knowledge of language as opposed to memorizing grammar rules.

327–T *(Experiment/Sentences) "Strrrretch"*

If exercises in workbooks or texts seem too short, have students make up additional sentences to be handled as the directions state. This not only gives additional grammar practice, but it also provides sentence-writing experiences.

328–C, *(Organize/Chalkboard, Sentences) "Participatory Sentences"*
G

Various views are expressed about modern or traditional sentence diagramming—some not so complimentary. Perhaps more can be learned by this approach. First, students become acquainted with the five (some teachers use six with a passive of S-V) basic sentence structures upon which all English sentences are built. (See idea 263.) Then form five (or six) groups of students who become specialists on that particular sentence structure. Each group must identify the basic pattern in an oral presentation, show the pattern reflected in a sentence, and offer about three or four similar sentences with different key words and modifiers for variations on the pattern. These can be placed on the chalkboard or on overhead transparencies.

MECHANICS

329–C *(Analyze/Poems) "Punctuation Cummings and Goings"*

Students read and discuss several poems by E. E. Cummings, who omits conventional punctuation. Talk about the effect on the reader. The class will gain a greater appreciation for studying punctuation.

330-C *(Experiment/Paragraphs) "No Nonsense Punctuation"*

In a punctuation unit, the students need to understand why they must know the rules. Frequently, paragraphs without punctuation or capitalization are given for practice. An interesting variation is a passage containing nonsense words. Students fill in the needed punctuation marks according to their knowledge of standard sentence patterns and vocal inflection. Vigorous discussion about changes of meaning through different punctuation patterns is a healthy sign.

OVERVIEW

331-C *(Analyze/Chalkboard, Sentences) "Clearly Unclear"*

Although students may not know all the rules of grammar, they do know what they can or can't understand. Write some ambiguous sentences on the chalkboard. The class analyzes each for word choice, word order, and modification. They can also make up their own grammar rules based on the samples.

332-C *(Analyze/Magazines) "Discussing the Issue"*

Obtain an issue of *Hot Rod, Seventeen,* or any other magazine for adolescents. Remove one or several short articles, retype them, and deliberately make strategic grammar mistakes in the process. Duplicate or project copies for each student. Correct the examples in class as a demonstration exercise. When students are unsure of an answer, the teacher does not supply it. They must consult the original printed article and explain the discrepancies themselves.

333-I *(Analyze/Mixed Media, Sentences) "Media Messages"*

Grammar can be made more relevant by examining sentences in newspapers, magazines, and speeches for differences and similarities in structure and style. Analyze various news articles reporting the same incident to see how the information can be stated different ways. By their very nature, sentences out of the media create student interest in a way that conventional materials cannot.

334-C *(Analyze/Newspapers) "Quantity Not Quality"*

Have students count the various parts of speech used in headlines or articles on the front page of the newspaper. Compare front-page counts among different leading newspapers. See, for example, if some publishers use more modifiers than others. Many other "accounting" analyses can be done to help characterize publishing philosophies.

335-C *(Experiment/Cartoons) "Balloon Talk"*

For variety, instead of continuously assigning exercises from a grammar text, have students identify grammatical principles in their favorite comic strips. Balloon talk is usually grammatical. From balloons, students select or identify subject, verb, and completer (when present), adding to these any other sentence parts being studied at the time. In place of comic strips, panel cartoons can be used.

336-I *(Experiment/Cartoons) "Funny Papers"*

Students can practice sentence control by converting selected comic strips into brief narratives. The students must tell the story of their comic strip by using narration with dialogue as well as using description where needed. Here is how a student might begin:

Snoopy and Woodstock walked slowly across the yard. Woodstock mumbled in his usual unintelligible way, but Snoopy understood and replied, "You could be an eagle. Why not?" He sat on a log and looked into the sky.
        Woodstock answered, "*ʌᵛᵻᵴⱴᵴᵻⱴᵴᵻ·ᵻ.*" Then he sat down beside Snoopy . . . (etc.).

337-I *(Experiment/Mixed Media) "Grammar Search"*

When students have some knowledge of basic grammatical concepts, allow them to prove how many they can find in printed messages on matchbook covers, cereal boxes, giant highway billboards, and the like. They must note the source as well as the concept when they report.

338-C *(Restructure/Models) "Fill 'Er Up"*

The teacher writes on the board one kernel sentence such as "I saw animals." Students volunteer words and groups of words that can be added as modifiers. Perhaps the entire board will be filled. This does not mean, of course, that the best sentences are the longest.

SEMANTICS

339-C *(Consolidate/Bulletin Boards) "Semantics Antics"*

After introducing clarity in communication, design a bulletin board around such ambiguities as: (1) A married son sent his mother a telegram reading, "Twins arrived tonight. More to come." (2) A puzzled boy with a fishing pole stood by a stream where a sign was posted: "Fine for fishing." Students are encouraged to locate other double meaning or ambiguous statements in magazines and newspapers. They can also locate illustrations such as one for "Flying airplanes can be dangerous." Discuss ways to correct the faults.

340–C *(Consolidate/Demonstration) "Back to Blocks"*

Place two desks back to back in front of the classroom. On each, place an identical supply of multishaped children's blocks. A student occupies each desk while the class observes. The student on the right assembles a simple structure using the blocks on his or her desk. Then that student tries to communicate the design so that the partner behind him or her can assemble a duplicate structure. The first student or sender must be precise, but the receiver is allowed to ask questions, especially to find out whether the order is reversed. This activity emphasizes the need for clarity in language.

341–C *(Consolidate/Lists) "Loaded List"*

Start the class thinking about the importance of referents by having them compile a list of words that usually have no referents and denote abstract concepts—words such as *big business, prosperity, free world, democracy* and many others that are found in speeches and periodicals. Additionally, discuss why these are sometimes called "loaded terms."

SPELLING

342–T *(Consolidate/Models) "My Pal, the Principal"*

Mnemonic devices as memory aids can help improve spelling. Here are some association ideas. Make up some others.

all right	*All* right is better than *all* wrong.
parallel	*All* railroad tracks run par*all*el.
principal	The princi*pal* is our *pal*.
separate	Each *rat* will *rate* a sepa*rat*e cage

343–T *(Experiment/Lists) "Spelling Step by Step"*

Suggest that students learn lists of spelling words not simply by writing each word five or ten times but also by studying it carefully, analyzing it syllable by syllable, affix by affix, and writing it in sentences.

SYNTAX

344–T *(Analyze/Sentences) "Compose vs. Decompose"*

Teach sentence structure by providing models of good sentences rather than so many poor ones. If visual impact is important to learning, students should be getting positive experiences.

345–C *(Analyze/Sentences) "Winning Context-ant"*

Distribute a duplicated sheet with several sentence pairs, each set employing a word that sounds the same in both sentences. Ask the class to identify the homonym or homophone (see below) by using the clue in parentheses and by examining the context of the sample sentences. Then have them correct any that are wrong, as in the second set.

(witch, which)
1. This book, (relative pronoun) I read last night, gave me nightmares.
2. For Halloween she was a (noun) on a broomstick.

(would, wood)
3. She went to the (auxilliary verb) shed to get firewood.
4. Every evening Uncle Louie (adjective) smoke his water pipe.

The exercise draws on knowledge of grammar, word definitions, and syntax.

346–C *(Analyze/Skits) "Living Language"*

Role play correct sentence structure by letting each student represent a part of speech (approximately 40 percent verbs, 30 percent nouns, 10 percent adjectives, 10 percent adverbs, a few determiners and some prepositions). Each one holds a small poster on which the name of a part of speech is printed. Secretly the student chooses a word that might be used as the designated part of speech and prints it on a large note pad attached to the reverse side of the poster. With any short sentence in mind, a volunteer chooses and lines up students bearing the appropriate parts of speech, arranging them in correct syntactical order. The student then reads the sentence he or she had in mind. Finally, as a humorous finish, each student in the lineup shows his or her own word for the part of speech by turning the poster around. This results in some very unusual and comical sentences, but it does teach syntax.

347–C,I *(Consolidate/Definitions) "Whatsa Sentence?"*

Do students know what a sentence really is? For a quick impromptu exercise, ask them to define a sentence. The variety of responses will be interesting. Finally the class and teacher agree on a definition.

Here is a possible definition. Is it a good one? "A sentence is an uninterrupted utterance that lies between silence and a terminal upward or downward voice pitch and, whether stated or implied, contains a subject and a message about that subject." Perhaps that's a bit exaggerated, but it's better than "A sentence expresses a complete thought."

348-C *(Consolidate/Magazine Pictures) "Snip of a Tip"*

This idea could be used for a younger class. Cut out magazine pictures, one for each student. Class members write at least one sentence about the picture using a noun with two adjectives, one verb, and one adverb—or any other combinations to gain needed practice. Sentences are read aloud while corresponding pictures are held up for viewing by the class.

349-I *(Experiment/Audiotape) "Off the Record"*

Use the tape recorder to aid sentence development in this extemporaneous approach. As each student goes to the microphone, he or she is handed a card on which four words are printed. The student must use them in a sentence that conveys a complete idea. The student has one minute to produce a sentence on paper before reading it for immediate playback. Through this type of analysis, the student quickly sees written and oral language interact.

350-I *(Experiment/Audiotape) "Sound Writing"*

 Each student writes a paragraph on a given topic and then reads the paragraph aloud while recording it on tape. After playing it back and listening to weaknesses, which seem to be magnified by recording, the student rewrites the paragraph, records and listens again, repeating the process until satisfied.

351-I *(Experiment/Paragraphs) "Topic Quartette"*

After studying the four types of sentences (declarative, imperative, exclamatory, interrogative), students write paragraphs using each of the four sentence types. Other experiments can include the four sentence patterns (simple, compound, complex, compound-complex). This will provide more viable models for discussion than most textbooks.

352-C *(Experiment/Sentences) "Feeling Sklurophy?"*

Encourage the class to create new words. With each new word they write a complete definition and use it in a sentence. The meaning of the word, of course, should be made clear through the context of the sentence, its position in relation to other words, or by inflected endings. This exercise is a good introduction to etymology and syntax.

353–T   *(Experiment/Sentences) "Resourceful Sentence Source"*

Student-originated sentences provide a valuable source of exercise material when studying syntactical structure. Dictate a list of ten key words. Ask students to write a sentence using each key word as the subject or main idea. Then when you need to develop practice exercises or tests, you'll have a good supply of student-written sentences on hand. Five classes of thirty-five students will create a pool of 1,750 from which to select.

354–C   *(Organize/Sentences) "Know the Combination"*

Redundant words and phrases often characterize student writing. Practice in combining short sentences will help pupils recognize and eliminate this problem. Give sentence kernels such as the following and ask students to combine them into one good sentence. For this pair, suggest including a prepositional phrase:

Detroit is an industrial city.
Detroit is located in Michigan.

With the imbedded prepositional phrase, the sentence might read:

Detroit is an industrial city in Michigan.

Other kernel sentences can be offered along with signals for other types of combining: compound sentences, various compound structures, subordinate clauses, and verbal modifiers.

355–C   *(Organize/Sentences) "Something Different"*

Show students how to vary their sentence structure by placing each subject in a different position from the original. Stress that the order must sound pleasant and natural. For this practice let students rewrite about a dozen such sentences.

356–C   *(Restructure/Books Sentences) "Being Stylish"*

Compare passages from such authors as Conrad, Faulkner, Hemingway, and Steinbeck. Study the syntax that is characteristic of each. Predominant patterns can be identified and frequencies compared. For practice, students rewrite the passages by using different grammatical structures. This exercise not only reinforces the compositional aspects of grammar, but it also enhances literary perception.

USAGE

357–C *(Analyze/Models) "Just Write for the Audience"*

Provide two writing examples about the same incident. One might be in pedantic prose style, the other appropriate to a newspaper. Discuss differences in usage and diction. Analyze how the writer fulfills his or her intentions for a particular audience.

358–C *(Analyze/Models) "Letter Rip"*

The teacher provides a duplicated letter written in childish sentences. Students rewrite as they see the need. Discuss the revision later, perhaps taking the best one and comparing a transparency of it with one for the original.

359–I *(Analyze/Talk) "Listen and List"*

Urge students to listen critically to the language found in their daily lives and to list those examples for discussion. Suggest various sources: in class, to or from school, around the dinner table, on the telephone, or even at the hair stylist's where conversation usually runs rampant. One special division might be trite expressions or overused sayings: "eats like a horse," "barrel of laughs," "hard as nails," or "flatter than a pancake." Discuss other possible sources. Also discuss the importance or unimportance of such expressions in conversation. What do they reflect about the user? Suggest that students attempt to write original, creative replacements. Other sources of language peculiarities might include differences in pronunciation, partial sentences, number of topic changes in a specific time span, slang, appropriateness for occasion, and tallies of typical topics heard within a time frame.

360–G *(Experiment/Lists) "Remodeling Old Clichés"*

To learn more about clichés, small groups make up lists of clichés and try to determine the source of the original and its intent. Then they write it in a different way. For example, "nose to the grindstone" means "to work hard." Which is more effective? Why? What is a better saying, more current and descriptive?

361–C *(Experiment/Papers) "Say It Again"*

Suggest that the class write two versions of the same event. In the first version they write in colloquialisms and in the second, formal English. This exercise helps illustrate that both forms are effective in the proper situation: colloquialisms for everyday communication and formal English for an unseen, relatively well-educated audience.

362–G *(Experiment/Role Playing) "Comedy of Errors"*

Have the class think about situations in which a working knowledge of good grammar would be beneficial (interviewing for a job, introducing people, entertaining the boss, or making court appearances, for instances). Divide the class into groups of three or four to role play situations illustrating use of good and bad grammar in any social activity. Allow members to speculate on the simulations. This approach emphasizes the importance of good English in everyday situations.

363–I *(Restructure/Paragraphs) "To Be or Tain't So"*

You art had it !

When reading a play by an Elizabethan playwright, assign each student a pertinent passage to be rewritten using the vocabulary common today. This will increase knowledge of how and why language changes.

364–C *(Organize/Dictionaries) "Id-tionary"*

Let students compile a dictionary of the specialized vocabulary and idioms they use. This attempt to define fresh and vigorous expression dramatizes the continual changes in vocabulary and helps the teacher understand the rather private language of the students.

VOCABULARY

365–C *(Analyze/Talk) "Watch Yer Pronounciation!"*

Aside from vocabulary tests, students often have little motivation for developing vocabulary. To keep the class alert, intentionally misspell, misuse, or mispronounce "big" words, inviting students to make corrections.

366–C *(Consolidate/Bulletin Board, Pictures, Words) "Picturesque Words"*

Motivating students to learn the meanings and use of new words can be difficult. An enjoyable way to learn vocabulary is through picture association. Devote a portion of the bulletin board to lists of words (coded) on one half and pictures (similarly coded) representing the words on the other side. The idea is to match the words with the correct pictures. For example, the word *corpulent* could be matched with a picture of an extremely obese person.

367-C *(Consolidate/Puzzles) "What's that Again?"*

Kindle enthusiasm for vocabulary development by having students rephrase famous quotations. With the help of a dictionary or thesaurus, "One small step for man; one giant step for mankind" becomes "A micromotor ambulatory progression for a featherless biped; a macromotor ambulatory progression for featherless bipeds."

368-I *(Experiment/Dictionary) "Used Words"*

A word becomes part of an individual's vocabulary only if it is used frequently after the initial contact. Suggested dictionary practices are: (1) Find an antonym for the word and compare the meanings. (2) Ask a question using the word. (3) Supply another form of the word (synonym). (4) Use the word in a sentence.

369-T *(Experiment/Games) "Monday List; Friday Test"*

Many students regard vocabulary building as dull, tiresome memorization. And even if they work hard at memorization, all they receive is a dull test on Friday. Suggest that each person study a few words for fifteen minutes a day. Then to assess achievement on Friday—or any day—use a crossword puzzle, a fill-in passage, flash cards, anagrams, dictionary hunt, "baseball" or "football" game, Scrabble, or other word games. Use a different approach each week. For additional ideas, see Games in the Index.

370-T *(Experiment/Games) "Well-Stocked Larder"*

For vocabulary studies, keep a box or preferably a file drawer stocked with motivation tips: original or collected crossword puzzles, word games, and exercises. Offer these, affixed in folders for easy filing, as challenges for students who find time for additional practice.

WORDS

371-C *(Analyze/Newspapers) "Ads Wanted"*

Prepare classified ads using too many words. Have the class cut down the ad without losing the important information.

372-C *(Analyze/Paragraphs, Games) "Prune Verbiage Like Foliage"*

To become familiar with the key words—the message-bearing words—in sentences, students are instructed to obliterate the modifiers in paragraph sentences by drawing lines through the adjectives, adverbs, modifying phrases, and clauses. The remaining words should be subjects, verbs, and completers. When read together, these words carry the main idea, reading like a telegram. Play a game with this approach. See which team can "send the most economical telegram (rewritten paragraph)" at two dollars a word. Stress the cost of excess verbiage. Later, students can analyze the value of the deleted material to the message.

373-C *(Analyze/Paragraphs) "Rough-in a Diamond"*

Have students write "diamond paragraphs" consisting of seven sentences using these types and in this order: simple, compound, complex, compound-complex, complex, compound, and simple. This provides practice in sentence variety through subordinate and coordinate conjunctions—important words in the composing act.

374-C *(Analyze/Sentences) "Like It or Not"*

Instead of asking students to demonstrate grammar knowedge by labeling and defining terms, give one sentence in which the subject or verb is underlined. Then introduce a second similar sentence in which students must choose the word which is like or accomplishes the same purpose as the underlined word in the first sentence. This method, if used consistently, teaches word function concepts without students having to memorize grammatical terms.

375-C *(Consolidate/Chalkboard, Sentences) "Oral Moral"*

After teaching the parts of speech, write any subject and verb on the chalkboard. Then ask students for an adjective, adverb, preposition, and so on, to form a simple sentence. Example: "Dog barked" is written on the chalkboard; then this type of exchange follows between teacher (T) and class (C):

T: Adverb?   C: The
C: Suddenly   *T: Adjective?*
T: Article?   C: Big

T:	*Oh, you can do better than that!*	C:	Truck
		T:	*Preposition?*
C:	Enormous	C:	At
T:	*Another adjective?*	*T:*	*Article?*
C:	Red	C:	The
T:	*Preposition?*	*T:*	*What next?*
C:	In	C:	Noun (or Object).
T:	*Article?*	*T:*	*Give one.*
C:	The	C:	Policeman
T:	*Noun (or Object)?*		

Resulting sentence: "Suddenly the enormous, red dog in the truck barked at the policeman." (An interesting related discussion could uncover an imaginative reason for the sentence.) This technique can also be used for teaching compound and complex sentences, but in this case expand each sentence by having the students offer the entire clauses and phrases.

376–C *(Consolidate/Chalkboard, Sentences) "Fun Free-For-All"*

To arouse interest in a grammar lesson, have a little fun with the parts of speech. Construct sentences on the chalkboard by calling for words from different students. When each student gives a word, he or she identifies its function in the model sentence. While learning a lesson in grammar, students can create some very absurd, humorous, sentences.

377–G *(Experiment/Bulletin Board) "Board with Words"*

During a unit on parts of speech, groups of students create bulletin board displays clearly depicting the parts of speech in use. Displays may be original posters, pictures, cartoons with captions, or collage or montage paste-ups with appropriate titles and inscriptions. Since displays remain over extended periods of time, the chance to drive home a grammatical concept is enhanced.

378–C *(Experiment/Lists) "Driving Differently"*

An interesting way to practice using verb tenses is to select two words such as *I* and *drive.* Students list as many variations as possible using only the two words and the additional words required by a change of tense.

379–C *(Experiment/Mixed Media) "Fill-in Assignment"*

Skillful use of the parts of speech is required for this exercise. Students bring in news articles or short stories from magazines. Working in pairs, one obliterates key words throughout the article. He or she asks the other student to think of a noun, adjective, verb, or whatever is needed to fill in the blanks. Any word can be used as long as it fits the sentence pattern. Compare the originals with the rewrites. Some of the funnier versions can be saved to share with the class.

380–C *(Experiment/Movies) "Moving Grammar Lesson"*

Show the class two or three short ten-minute sports films illustrating actions. Keep the sound low. Students then write every verb (and adverb, if desired) they can associate with the action as it occurs. This list can serve as the basis for a paragraph on motion or may be incorporated into a short vocabulary lesson.

381–I *(Experiment/Sentences) "Modification Vacation"*

To avoid the routine of traditional grammar lessons on modification, give students a "map" to follow with directions to fill in the blanks with the needed information.

Time—The speaker arrived _____.
Space—The building is _____.
How something is done—The mouse moved _____.

382–C *(Organize/Games) "Telling Storease"*

The purpose of this game is to reinforce the learning of a particular part of speech, in this case a verb. Each student in succession tells a portion of a story built around a familiar experience. Each player adds one sentence and must use a different verb each time to score. Sentences continue until a satisfactory story ending is reached.

7 Evaluation

DIALECT

383–C *(Extrapolate/Books) "Tain't Proper"*

How successfully students can locate regional vocabulary can be readily determined by having them scan the writings of Faulkner, Twain, Huxley, Lardner, Steinbeck, Hughes, and others. Each student examines one portion in detail, picking out examples of dialect, coined words, and other terms unusual to his or her own speech. This approach leads to further evaluative discussions on how, where, and why certain words are used.

LINGUISTICS

384–G *(Judge/Chalkboard, Lists) "Gluk"*

As a sort of break, evaluate how a typical conversation sounds between two persons. Spoken conversation connects words. Students soon realize that spoken words do not appear as they do on the printed page. Have students suggest printed words for this conversation:

Hiyajack!	Sordalite.
Lobud.	Wauoozin?
Benearlong?	Lottaworms.
Cupalours.	Fishnonahboddum?
Kitchaneny?	Rydonnaboddum.
Gottafew.	Igottago.
Kindrdey?	Seeyaroun.
Carpanbass.	Takidezy.
Ennasiztuem?	Gluk!
Cuppalapounds.	
Hittinard?	(Source unknown)

Have some fun; let students write some of their own.

MECHANICS

385–I *(Restructure/Paragraphs) "Guided Tour"*

Select a brief writing sample calling for a variety of punctuation marks. Type and duplicate the passage, omitting all punctuation and capitalization. At the bottom of the page, however, place a checklist covering what has been omitted. This list might read:

Beginning/End	*Internal*
Capital letters: 30	Commas: 15
Periods: 27	Semicolons: 2
Question marks: 2	Colons: 1
Exclamation marks: 1	Dashes: 1
Quotation marks: 6 sets	Hyphens: 2

The student must return all the marks of punctuation to their proper places and capitalize as needed. They can keep track of their progress by tallying on the list. In this exercise, if the students know they must use a certain number of semicolons, for instance, they will be forced to carefully consider the rules governing their use.

OVERVIEW

386-I   *(Identify/Plans) "Grammar Contact Contract"*

After some form of diagnosis or assessment, have students prepare written contracts stating what each must learn to improve and use language skills more effectively. This employs accountability in the classroom since the students state specifically what they want (need) to learn and, by accepting the contract, the teacher indicates what will be taught.

387-C   *(Identify/Problems) "The Big Three"*

Here is a useful test approach to see if a student comprehends important sentence elements and how they are used. Advise the student to set down three column heads at the top of a sheet of paper: *Element, Use,* and *Relationship*. Then present at least ten sentences with a word or several key phrases underlined. The student places the underlined word(s) in the first column and then fills in the other two columns appropriately. For example:

The *hungry* boy was waiting for his lunch.

Element	*Use*	*Relationship*
hungry	adjective	modifies boy

The test also works with linguistic terminology.

388-T   *(Identify/Problems) "Start at the Start"*

Some teachers forget that students do not learn to express themselves well in a total composition through osmosis, but that there is a series of important learning steps needed to reach such a level. Students who have difficulty reading and writing words or putting them into recognizable thought units cannot deal with sentences, paragraphs, and total composition. Therefore, they should not be frustrated into defeat by requirements to write a total composition. No one writes at a higher skill level than present ability to read or deal with grammar. Thus, it is important to determine where students are in language development before starting an instructional program. A few diagnostic tests or writing samples will establish a starting point.

389–T   *(Judge/Papers) "Figure It Out"*

Instead of identifying errors and correcting them, simply underline and let the students make the correction: spelling, punctuation, agreement, parallel problem, wrong word, tense switch, etc.

390–G   *(Judge/Papers) "Grammar Is Not Dead"*

Divide the class into small groups to exchange and judge papers (based on recently learned grammatical principles). For variety, use an overhead projector. In addition, an anonymous theme or sentences collected from several themes may be projected and then corrected by the class. Students can learn effectively from one another. Allow each student (or group) to become specialists in one grammatical or mechanical area. When evaluating their own papers, students consult with the "specialists" who deal with their specific problems.

391–I   *(Judge/Papers) "Read-a-long"*

For students who have a consistent writing problem in grammar or punctuation, such as incomplete sentences or comma faults, read a weak portion of their papers aloud to them during individual conferences. Listening to these mistakes, the students will readily become aware of the need for improvement and will probably try the same procedure for the next paper.

392–T   *(Restructure/Games) "Adapt or Adopt"*

Reviews or evaluations of whether or not students have learned need not be dull. Just about any TV game or competitive sport can be turned into a classroom activity. Let groups adopt their favorite game shows to classroom use—with questions and all.

393-I *(Restructure/Puzzles) "Ruleword Puzzle"*

Students can study grammatical rules by completing a crossword puzzle. To answer, complete the blanks and reveal the rule. A much better learning incentive than simply reading the rules, this game forces the student to think.

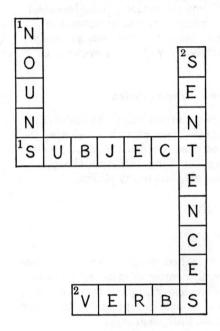

Across

1. The ____ is who or what the sentence is about.

2. ____ appear in the predicate and tell what action is taking place.

Down

1. ____ are words that name the subject.

2. ____ have both a subject and predicate.

When a puzzle is completed, have the students prepare a summary statement:

Nouns usually name the *subject* of *sentences* but *verbs* never do this.

394-I *(Restructure/Sentences) "Grammar Is Looking Up"*

Combine grammar study with all written work. Code major weaknesses to match practices in the textbook. When papers are returned, students look up each grammatical weakness, work on the exercises as needed, then place rewritten portions on a special sheet to be returned to the teacher along with the original. A simple checkoff system handled by a room cadet will assure that all work has been accomplished. From time to time, in conferences, students explain how they overcome certain writing weaknesses.

SEMANTICS

395–I   *(Extrapolate/Lists) "Down the Up Ladder"*

Limiting the subject to their own interests, students draw the classic ladder of abstraction with the top rungs being in the "clouds of abstraction." An athlete might develop a ladder beginning with "person" at the top, progressing to a well-grounded "Westfield's Quarterback, Al Smith." A student with an interest in the medical field might design a ladder with the top rung labeled "instrument" and the bottom, "stainless steel hemostat." Besides improving knowledge and awareness of abstractions, this encourages students to write more precisely. Ladder displays on the bulletin board will create even more interest.

396–C   *(Judge/Magazines, Newspapers) "Type Casting"*

Examine magazine and newspapers (particularly the advertisements) to see how often they stereotype through the words used to characterize people and describe ideas: reticent, precise, preceptive, vital, chic, sporting, beguiling, talkative, sharp, quick-witted, energetic, shrewd, sly, and many others.

SPELLING

397–C   *(Compare/Lists) "Misspelt Werds"*

Divide a list of commonly misspelled words into four separate lists. In each list have a varying number of incorrectly spelled words. Let the students study the lists and place them in the order of least errors, e.g., in the sample groups below, list I has the most errors, list III the least. Sample groups:

I	*II*	*III*	*IV*
rassberry	suround	stinginess	cordinate
knowlidge	parallel	similar	thorough
tradgedy	sufficate	Massachusetts	spectacle
summersalt	reinforce	doubt	psycology
envelop	bisness	trapeeze	surprise

398–C   *(Judge/Games) "Bee a Good Teacher"*

The old-fashioned spelling bee is still a good activity, and it promotes participation. If spelling isn't the goal, try a grammar or literature bee. Such activities are especially useful when the class is restless.

399–C   *(Judge/Games) "Nu Words"*

With the class divided into several teams, students have a day or so to examine product names and advertising to find deliberately misspelled words, e.g., blu, krisp, lo, mony, nu, kool, kleen, vu, and so on. Students list the "found spelling" and write the correctly spelled version opposite. The team with the longest list wins, of course. This could begin an interesting study: how advertisers or businesses may be contributing to a more laissez faire attitude toward spelling and grammar in general.

400–C *(Judge/Games) "Spell-Down Switch"*

This version of the popular spelling contest helps the poor speller more than the usual form. Set up like the conventional spell-down, this approach allows everyone to remain on the team, but each incorrect word counts as one mark against the team. Each time a word is misspelled, it is written correctly on the chalkboard. The entire class then pronounces it several times emphasizing the syllables. The word is then erased and is repeated later in the contest.

401–C *(Restructure/Games) "Up Front"*

Here is a game for assessing the spelling skills of middle or junior high pupils. Give each class member a small placard with a lower case letter on it. One student comes to the front of the room and is given five minutes to form words by combining his or her letter with the letters various students are holding. (It may be wise to assign students several of the same vowels and frequently used consonants.) When the timekeeper calls "Start," the participant picks out the letters he or she wants. Those students come forward and place their cards on the chalk rail as directed. This continues until the time is up. At the end of the class period, whoever made the most correctly spelled words is the winner.

402–C *(Restructure/Games) "Scramble a Few"*

Learning new spelling words becomes more interesting when they are presented in different forms. Scramble the letters of each word for the students to reassemble. Also try hiding the words in vertical, horizontal, or diagonal lines of random letters formed into a rectangle as in the popular word-finding puzzle. Students must know how to spell, find, and encircle the hidden words. Even though a list is given of words to locate, the student is forced to look at single letters and combinations rather than to look at a word superficially.

403–C *(Restructure/Games) "That Puzzles Me"*

When spelling and vocabulary can be feasibly integrated (all vocabulary words do not necessarily have to be spelled), try a "game test." To pass the test, students complete a crossword puzzle and succeed in getting at least 75 percent of the words correctly spelled and correctly defined.

SYNTAX

404–I *(Extrapolate/Papers) "Improved with Age"*

The students rewrite compositions they originally wrote for an earlier assignment. In so doing, they follow instructions and suggestions attached to that assignment. Both the old and new copies are then handed to the teacher who evaluates the *degree* of improvement.

405–C *(Extrapolate/Sentences) "Charting the Way"*

See if your class can recognize good sentence structure and parts of speech through patterns and word inflections. Have them form sentences by substituting real words for nonsense words.

	Adjective	*Noun*	*Verb*		*Noun*
The	frilby	sard	dowked	the	lod
The	hungry	bird	swallowed	the	worm.

Make this activity into a game by asking for: (1) the most "almost real" sentences, (2) the most unusual sentences, and (3) the most imaginative adjectives, nouns, and verbs. Some of the best sentences can be used as future composition topics. Other sentences with errors provide models for proofreading.

406–T *(Judge/Sentences, Paragraphs) "Bare Sentences"*

One way to determine whether or not a composition communicates the message intended is to pare down the verbiage to the bare essentials. Simple subjects, verbs, and complements carry the message of any sentence. After students have written a composition, they write on another sheet of paper: *Skeleton Sentences.* For each subject in the original copy they write only the simple subject, the verb (and helpers), and complements, if any. If the skeleton sentence does not convey a basic message, the original may have some emphasis problems. These weaknesses occur when students hide main ideas in dependent clauses and modifying prepositional phrases. Sentences that are questionable are then revised. (See related idea 372.)

407–C   *(Judge/Songs) "Hop on Bop"*

Analyze the sentence structure of published popular songs and decide if each is written in the most effective way or if it should be reworded. The objective is to get the full impact and meaning in a minimum number of words. Some results will take away from the lyrics. Discuss whether grammar should be sacrificed for effect in art and entertainment.

408–C   *(Restructure/Games) "Gramplify"*

Understand grammar with a game called Gramplify. First, make flash cards for the different parts of speech and punctuation. Then have the students build sentences in the following manner: Distribute cards to the entire class. Call on one student to go to the front and hold up a card. If the card contains a noun, a student with a verb usually follows in typical sentence order. The students use their own judgment as to what part of speech is next. Have the class be alert for errors and correct them as the sentence develops. Because so many sentence variations can be made, the process is both fun and instructional.

409–C   *(Restructure/Games) "Grummy"*

This card game helps assess knowledge of sentence structure. Make a deck of cards containing words that can be subjects, predicates, adjectives, conjunctions, objects, and prepositions. The total number of cards is optional. The object of the game is to make one complete sentence with as many words as possible by discarding and picking. The more words the sentence contains, the higher the score. Members of the class can formulate their own rules; writing them would be good practice.

410–C   *(Restructure/Games) "Sentence Building"*

Play a game called Sentence Builders. The instructor asks the first two students to give the simple subject and verb of what could be a sentence. Each student in turn (on a team perhaps) must add a word or phrase, each time repeating the entire sentence. If someone adds something that destroys sentence unity, he or she is disqualified. Set a time limit so that the sentence does not become too unwieldy. More capable students can name the type of grammatical construction they are adding before saying the words.

411–I   *(Restructure/Paragraphs) "Scramble Two"*

Ask the students to rewrite two paragraphs that have been intentionally poorly written. One paragraph may exhibit faulty sentence structure and misuse of the parts of speech. Another may be characterized by ambiguous meaning, improper emphasis, and weak word choice. This exercise will help pinpoint the strengths and weaknesses of student writers when their revisions are compared with the originals.

412-I *(Restructure/Sentences) "Hole in One"*

Knowledge of sentence syntax (or many other areas) can be evaluated through a simple self-instructional learning "machine." Use index cards with a question written on one half and three possible answers on the other half. Holes are punched next to the answers. The student places the point of a pencil through the hole next to the chosen answer. The card is turned over. If a star appears next to the pencil point, the answer is correct. Other holes might have statements as to why the answer is wrong. Students can help the teacher prepare these learning "machines."

USAGE

413-G *(Compare/Models) "Find the Worstest"*

By individual and group efforts, students collect and study examples of incorrect usage found in books, everyday contacts, and in the media. Through group discussion each sample is revised until it is in its most effective form. Both the original and revised versions are then presented to the entire class for evaluating the degree and type of improvement.

414-C *(Extrapolate/Lists) "Making It Clear"*

Have students graph their repeated grammatical errors. This allows them to clearly see the problems that persist and those that are gradually disappearing. (See related idea 157.)

415-C *(Identify/Games) "Picky, Picky"*

To determine knowledge of grammar principles, initiate a long-term game in which the students try to catch each other's oral or written usage problems. One way is to form small groups. Have them engage in occasional oral discussions or paper exchanges on self-selected or assigned topics. (Though the noise level may be high, things are being accomplished.) Collect errors on slips of paper. A contest manager can be appointed to gather and tabulate the errors, and list the students who committed them and on what occasion. After a set length of time, perhaps two weeks, the student with the least weaknesses gets some recognition along with the student who catches the most mistakes.

416-I *(Judge/Essays) "Up for Inspection"*

Whether or not a student has a working knowledge of the principles of grammar can be revealed by letting the students critically review and correct someone else's essay. Each student should be ready to justify corrections. It is easier to see weaknesses in someone else's writing than in one's own. Finally, the teacher may assess the work of the writer and the reviewer.

417-T *(Judge/Journals) "Proof in the 'Putting' "*

Student journals have many uses, not the least of which is to determine language improvement. For example, journals can show if a study of effective modifiers (or any grammatical aspect) has carried over. Of course, they also show what needs more work. This fact need not be announced (so that student writing remains relaxed). The approach can be used to assess any learning in language improvement, since whatever is applied naturally dipicts true learning.

VOCABULARY

418-C *(Compare/Games) "Dictionary—A Game?"*

Check familiarity with dictionaries (*Roget's Thesaurus of the English Language in Dictionary Form, Funk and Wagnall's Standard Handbook of Synonyms, Antonyms and Prepositions* (Fernald), and *Webster's Dictionary of Synonyms*). Create games that employ these aids. In one approach, two opposing team participants each guess a word definition. Several impartial judges look up the word to discover which participant's meaning is closest to the real meaning.

419-C *(Extrapolate/Games) "Beat the Clock"*

This is a good game for low verbal, middle or junior high level students. Here quantity is more important than quality. Use a stopwatch for best results. Give time intervals (thirty seconds to one minute) in which to write as many words as possible in a given category—adjectives, kinds of animals, or famous people, to name a few. Or pair up the students to say them aloud to each other. Each partner keeps score. A cumulative record of scores each week will show improvement.

420-C   *(Extrapolate/Games) "It's a Mystery"*

Convert the process of vocabulary assessment into a game.
Give the class a short list of new words to define and use in
sentences. On the following day, recognize the student who
uses one of the words—the "mystery word"—in the proper context of the discussion. Although students know the particular
list of words, only the teacher knows which one is the mystery
word.

421-C   *(Identify/Games) "Bowl 'em Over"*

Test vocabulary background by forming the class into teams
who choose a college to represent—any college from Yale to
Podunk Junior College. Then each team is given a definition
for which they must supply the word, or vice versa. Working in
teams gives the students the incentive to learn new vocabulary.
Scoring, of course, is by points for correct answers.

422-G   *(Identify/Games) "Concentrate on Concentration"*

Number one side of thirty index cards with large-sized numbers 1 through 30. Using manuscript form (not block or capital
letters), list fifteen selected words, one on each blank side (two
sets of the same words). Two players set up the cards in six
rows, five cards per row. The numbers are arranged consecu-
tively. One student turns over two cards. If they match, the
student leaves them face up and scores a point if he or she can
pronounce them, two if he or she can define them, three if he
or she can look away and rewrite the word, and five points if
he or she can write the word in a sentence. When two cards do
not match, the student places them face down again and relin-
quishes to an opponent who proceeds in the same manner.
Game continues until all cards face upward. The player with
the most points wins that round. This game helps improve
memory, spelling, and vocabulary.

423-C   *(Identify/Games) "Define a Fine Word"*

To give practice in using new words and to check on understanding, divide the class into two teams. The captain of Team
One chooses a word from a list being studied and calls on the
first member of Team Two to use the word in a sentence. The
Team Two captain then chooses a word for the other team,
and the teams continue to alternate. Each word must be used
correctly within thirty seconds. The same sentence may not be
used twice. One student serves as timekeeper and another as
scorekeeper. The teacher is umpire and decides whether or not
the word is used correctly. The team with the highest number
of right answers wins.

424–C   *(Identify/Games) "Defining Bee"*

Instead of the typical spelling bee, hold a word-defining bee. One person gives a definition of a word, then the teams try to guess the word. An extra point is given if the word is spelled correctly. (Requiring students to correctly spell all words they can read and understand can be a defeating exercise. Few people are able to spell all the words they can read.)

425–C   *(Identify/Games) "Let the Hunt Begin"*

Hold a word scavenger hunt. Select a set of words that appear in ten different articles from current periodicals. The words chosen should challenge the mental abilities of the students but should not be beyond their capabilities to understand. The teacher lists the articles by magazine title, date, and page numbers, and then prepares a list of definitions: "A word that means a sudden forcible overthrow of a government." When the lists of articles and the definitions are distributed, the hunt begins. It may last any desired length of time, with different rewards. (Some articles should be distractors but worth reading).

426–C   *(Identify/Games) "Password Word Game"*

To evaluate vocabulary development, play "Password." Words should be on various levels of difficulty and emanate primarily from previous studies. Print two copies of each word on small cards. The teacher or a student, as master of ceremonies, gives one card to a member of each two-person team. This member tries to elicit the word from his or her partner by issuing clues, usually synonyms. There is a timekeeper for each round of one or two minutes. Each word starts at ten points, and each time an incorrect guess is made, one point is lost. The first pair to get twenty-five points wins the game. Play the game a few times each week until all members of the class have participated. The second card reveals the word to the other team.

427–C   *(Identify/Games) "Stump of Approval"*

Students make a list of words and definitions they don't understand in their reading assignments. At the end of the week, they play "Stump the Class." A student reads a word from his or her list. Volunteers from the class try to define it for one point. If none can, the questioner gets a point after defining the word.

428–C,   *(Identify/Games) "Triple Threat"*
G

An associations test could be used as the basis for a vocabulary game. The object is to find a word that unites three other words such as *day, load, master*. The answer is *pay* (payday, payload, and paymaster). Some others:

man	dog	word	_____	(watch)
work	land	sick	_____	(home)
eat	work	sleep	_____	(over)
fare	lock	dance	_____	(war)
long	fall	mare	_____	(night)

Divide the class into two teams. Each produces ten or fifteen of these triads. The lists are put on the board for each opposing team to identify. The team that completes its list first wins.

429–C   *(Identify/Games) "Wild, Wild Weird-One"*

To discover if students are learning the vocabulary, play a game based on the onetime classic, "Hangman." Pick a list of words that should be known. For each word, place a series of short blank spaces on the chalkboard, one for each letter. Ask each game participant to guess the word that fits a blank in a sample sentence, or he or she may ask questions to get clues. For each wrong answer, another class member adds a part of a monster (left to one's imagination): first the head, then the trunk, followed by the legs, arms, and the rest of the body, one at a time. If the monster is completed before the word is supplied, the participant loses the point. To help in the word building, include one or two letters for the longer words.

430–C   *(Identify/Sentences) "No Losers"*

Every student brings in a new word each day, knows its meaning, and can use it in sentences. The class tries to guess the meaning of the new word from the way it is used in several sentences the student makes up. If no one guesses correctly, the meaning is revealed. These words can be filed on index cards. At the end of a designated period, the class might be asked to write a short paper using some of the new words. The teacher may purposely use the words while teaching. The entire process allows the teacher to evaluate vocabulary skills.

431–G   *(Judge/Sentences) "Mean Words"*

Check vocabulary knowledge by having the students place words new to them (introduced in the day's lesson) into sentences. Divide the class into groups. Each member of a group must use his or her new word in an interesting sentence, and the sentence must somehow relate logically to the previous person's sentence. Some could be recorded for playback to the class.

WORDS

432-I *(Extrapolate/Models) "Combination Composition"*

Combine grammar with composition. Through assignments in written description, have the students apply knowledge of modifiers. Beginning with simple one-word modifiers, students write how they feel about a situation or describe a set of objects or pictures. Their work will soon prove whether or not they know the basic important grammatical concepts of a sentence. The same situation, objects, or pictures can be used again when the students write more sophisticated modifiers; phrases and dependent clauses. The fact that they have already written many sentences from the same stimuli will increase their written output.

433-C *(Extrapolate/Papers) "Big Combo"*

Evaluate the class's knowledge of the parts of speech while they are practicing composition skills. Students write a short composition beginning each sentence with a different part of speech, labeling each in parentheses. Besides providing sentence variety, this practice helps assess knowledge of grammar.

434-C *(Identify/Games) "Homing in on Homonyms"*

This simple game will amuse students and reveal if they know homonyms. Two students are asked to choose two homonyms, e.g., *bore* and *boar,* which the rest of the class must try to guess. Each student gives clues about his or her homonym saying, for example, "I am a personality." The other might say, "I am an animal." The two presenters must continue giving clues (sometimes in pantomime) until the words are guessed. Scoring, if desired, can be based on the length of time the two can continue giving clues without tipping off the class. The couple lasting longest wins. (The teacher may find it necessary to supply a list of homonyms to speed the action.)

435-I *(Identify/Papers) "Join the Evolution"*

After studying how our language originated and evolved, assign a noun to students. Ask them to write a one-page paper on the word, giving its origin, evolution, current usage, and related points. This exercise will disclose the writer's knowledge and understanding of etymology.

436–C *(Identify/Paragraphs)* *"Novel Approach"*

The teacher gives each class member a duplicated copy of a short descriptive passage from a novel or short story, preferably one being studied in literature. Each student takes a turn reading a sentence aloud, first as it appears originally and then without adjectives and adverbs. Ask the students if they can see the value of modifiers as the contrasts are compared. This demonstrates that modifiers are important to amplify the key words even though they can be removed without destroying the basic message.

437–C *(Identify/Sentences)* *"Those Blankety Blanks"*

Hand out a list of sentences, each with several key words removed. Students fill in blanks with suitable words, based on context and pattern, and identify the sentence parts.

438–C *(Restructure/Games)* *"Acronymania"*

One participant or team member must choose a noun and print it vertically on the chalkboard. The other members of the team must place an adjective horizontally, one for each letter. The adjective may begin with the letter or, for an easier version, include the letter anywhere. For example, using the nouns of equal length like *child* or *house* might result in these objectives:

C uddly   c H eerful

H appy   c O ld

I rritated   ha U nted

L aughing   un S ightly

D rooling   E mpty

Teams take turns. The rounds are timed for fairness, and points are based on how many adjectives are completed within the time limit, usually one point for each.

439–I *(Restructure/Sentences)* *"Try an Additive"*

Have students add interesting adjective and adverb prepositional phrases to very simple sentences. After writing the assignment, the class should read their sentences aloud to prove they can use modifying phrases to expand and clarify the basic idea of a sentence. Sentence samples to expand: The sun rises. Silence falls. Charles leaves.

8 Application

OVERVIEW

440-I *(Construct/Mixed Media) "Between the Words"*

Words are only one medium of communication and can be skillfully juxtaposed with other forms such as art, dance, films, and music to develop interesting perspectives on ways to create a message. Assign the problem of developing a project that combines visuals and words. Preparing a motion picture script or writing a movie review, for example, requires thoughtful consideration and use of all communication skills.

441-C *(Write/Newspaper) "Start the Presses"*

Correcting and proofreading help improve language skills. Students can check each other's writing. Facilitate this motivational approach through a class newspaper project. The paper would chronicle happenings in and around the school. In compiling articles, students will need to read the articles carefully, putting into practice their knowledge of spelling, vocabulary, sentence structure, punctuation, and so on.

442-I *(Write/Papers) "Experience Grammar"*

Find ways to relate language study with student experience. Have students write fifty to one hundred sentences about themselves, not in any sequence, just random thoughts. Include in this assignment some required grammatical applications such as asking that eight to ten sentences contain a predicate adjective describing the writer's personality, or that at least five sentences begin with a prepositional phrase such as "At home I am usually...." To help an evaluator locate these grammatical principles, suggest they be underlined and labeled.

443-I   *(Write/Papers) "Short Circuit Grammar"*

To integrate grammar and literary skills, assign the writing of
a short story. Part of the final evaluation would be based on
correct use of grammar and mechanics. Another aspect would
require narration in standard English and dialogue in dialect
or informal speech.

SYNTAX

444-I   *(Write/Paragraphs) "In the Eye of the Beholder"*

Each student is given a series of objects or illustrations to describe (one paragraph for each). Lists of verbs, nouns, and
modifiers may also be supplied. This exercise presents an opportunity to apply knowledge of description and paragraph
organization.

USAGE

445-I   *(Write/Books) "Expression Collection"*

In a three-ring notebook, each student keeps a "dictionary" of
once-popular sayings or expressions. Each sheet—one word to
a sheet—includes the expression, its meaning, when or where
it may have originated, and an illustration of its use. Students
are expected to do some research and then discuss their lists.
Room and hall displays combined with appropriate illustrations will generate interest in language and how it changes.

446-I   *(Write/Papers) "Slanguage"*

Invite written compositions that employ slang expressions.
English purists object to this corruption of the English language and lose sight of the value of slang in a youth's (anyone's) world. Many times a slang word or phrase expresses a
nuance of meaning for which there is no substitute. The class
can engage in an indepth study of slang, even picking out instances where famous authors or speakers have used slang to
add color, humor, or emphasis.

VOCABULARY

447-I   *(Write/Lists) "Be a Word Dog"*

After a vocabulary study, students compile a list of words adopted and adapted for our contemporary vocabulary from: (1) foreign expressions, (2) clothing and household items, (3) scientific and professional jargon, (4) multi-ethnic sources, (5) religions, (6) slang, (7) sports, and (8) the theater. Have students define each word briefly and illustrate some with pictures or drawings. Share and discuss information.

WORDS

448-I   *(Construct/Pictures) "Eye-Catchers"*

Follow up a word study unit by launching a media search for dynamic, attention-getting words. Encourage students to look for words being used effectively by news reporters, advertisers, and writers to attract an audience and in some way to move that audience emotionally. As they read newspapers and magazines, then, students can clip the effective words (with accompanying illustrations if available) or just copy them for use later. Then, on a sheet of poster board, each student prepares a montage of both pictures and words, clearly depicting the word choices. Lines of contrasting cellophane tape or paper strips can be affixed to connect each word to an appropriate illustration. Words recopied rather than clipped can be drawn on small strips of contrasting construction paper. Later, the student could write a brief paper justifying the choice of these particular words and telling what, if anything, was learned from this project.

449-I   *(Write/Lists) "Facing Up"*

Most people can think of adjectives like *happy, pretty, sad,* or *smiling* to describe a face. For more interest, authors use synonyms for these words. Have students prepare lists of words that could be used to describe "face" other than simple, obvious ones. Finally, ask the students to write a short paper using as the central idea the word they like best to modify "face."

450–T   *(Write, Speak, Solve, Perform, Construct/All Vehicles)*
"All Mixed Up"

Perhaps the best idea offered in this section is to suggest that grammar and language are best studied as an integral part of all communication, not as separate entities.

Part Three

LITERATURE

9 Introduction

DRAMA

451–T   *(Discover/Demonstrations) "Backing a Play"*

Drama study can be much more interesting with proper groundwork. Choice of plays is the first concern. They must have good plots and plenty of action for today's television-nurtured youngsters. The background of the play should be discussed before the reading begins. Along with discussion and some lecture, bring in appropriate media (music, pictures, and playbills of professional productions) to accompany presentations.

452–C   *(Discover/Discussions) "What's in a Name?"*

Greater insights into literary characters can be obtained by examining their names. Some writers use names that denote special meanings which may or may not be significant for characterization. Some names are chosen because the sound reflects the character, others because the name alludes to a personal characteristic. For example, Willy Loman in *Death of a Salesman* may well be described by some student as "low man on the totem pole"—a "has-been" in society. Students discuss names of characters in both drama and fiction for allusions, derivations, and meanings. They will soon realize that selecting names is as much of a craft as plot development.

453–T   *(Discover/Inventories) "Variety Shows"*

Before teaching Shakespeare to high school students find out which other of his plays the students have read. Most likely it will be a tragedy such as *Julius Caesar* or *Macbeth*. If so, this time choose one of Shakespeare's comedies or historical plays like *Richard III* or *Henry IV*. His plays covered too many aspects of life to neglect any one.

454–T *(Discover/Models) "Learn the Lexicon"*

The problem many students have with understanding Shakespeare is relating what is said to how it is said. Instead of making the lexicon—the special vocabulary of the age—become an unavoidable drudgery, go through a linguistic set of drills to aid recognition of certain speech patterns. In addition to the exercises, explain what the words and expressions meant in Elizabethan times. Interject peculiar themes and patterns commonly used by Shakespeare. From here, students read the play with greater enjoyment and better understanding.

455–C *(Discover/Models) "Noting Nothing Changes"*

When studying any period in literature, whether Greek, Elizabethan, or Modern, the class examines one play from each period, noting the similarities and differences. For example, one thread running through all the plays might be the one characterizing the "flavor" of the times. Excerpts from Sheridan or Molière can capture the comedy of Restoration period manners. These can be compared with preceding and later social customs.

456–C *(Listen/Records) "Romeo and Julie Go West"*

Study *Romeo and Juliet* and *West Side Story* together. Compare the modern-day version with that of Shakespeare and discuss the social conditions that may have brought about both plays. Classical music may also be introduced through the sound track of *West Side Story* and then Tchaikovsky's *Romeo and Juliet*. Besides simply listening to the easily discernible themes and lilting melodies, compare Maria and Tony's musical themes with those of Romeo and Juliet.

457–C *(Listen/Role Playing) "It's a Draw"*

Having students read a play aloud is usually a good way to interest the class in drama. Most of the dramatic effect, however, is lost because students may be self-conscious or unprepared. For better reading, students can draw for parts the day before the play is read in class. With a chance to study the characters and practice their roles, students will do a better job in presenting the characters they drew.

458–C *(Observe/Field Trips) "Trip Tip"*

Inevitably, during some part of the school year a great movie or play will be presented in your community or within driving distance. If it relates in any way to material being studied, organize a theater party as an introductory or culminating activity. Besides generating class interest, such an event will be a new experience for some. It also provides a chance for a teacher to display some personal qualities not easily revealed in the classroom.

459-C   *(Observe/Role Playing) "Off and On the Record"*

Obtain a recording of the assigned play or poem to aid students in reading aloud with proper intonation. In the case of drama, it is interesting to compare an actor's interpretation of a role with the class's. Some students may want to engage in some mime, mouthing the words along with the record while performing the appropriate actions.

460-T   *(Research/Authorities) "Philosophically Speaking"*

Since the Greeks first introduced dialogue into their religious rites, drama has been considered an accurate key to people's thought processes in any age. An indispensable aid to understanding the true meaning of a play is to have an historical and philosophical perspective of the era. To assure that no student misses this background, teachers must accumulate the necessary information explaining why drama over the years took the form it has. A team of English teachers could prepare a helpful companion text for the plays being studied by combining explanations of events with notes on the pressures of a class philosophy that strongly influenced the authors. For instance, a brief summary of the Irish Revolution—not only battles but also the effect of the prevailing Lockean philosophy of the people—would make the plays of Synge and O'Casey more interesting to study and more rewarding to the uninformed observer.

HUMANITIES

461-T   *(Discover/Demonstrations) "Constant Struggle"*

Demonstrate the persistence of common themes that occur in the various media. Man's struggle to organize and understand his experiences can be shown in a multimedia approach to a particular theme. This diversity of expression, for example, can approach the odyssey theme through various forms of lyric poetry (Homer's *Odyssey*), modern poetry ("Telemachos Remembered"), and modern prose (*Ulysses,* James Joyce). Add to these some famous works of music and art.

462-C   *(Observe/Slides) "Safe on a Slide"*

Often, relating the literature of an age to art and architecture can be very frustrating because illustrations are lacking or hard to find. Sometimes pictures in art books are passed around the class. A better approach is to use slides. First obtain a simple photo copy stand and a 35mm camera (single lens reflex is best) with close-up lens. Then photograph pictures from books and magazines to be made into slides. These may be accompanied by narration, music, or both. If used for an individual class on a limited basis, such reproductions will not lead to copyright problems. If there is a question regarding copyright, send a permissions letter to the publisher.

463-T   *(Research/Books) "Killing Two Birds with One Library"*

Unless a program of unified studies is being followed in a school, the English department and the social studies department should attempt a coordinated program. Studying a book such as Upton Sinclair's *The Jungle* is a good start. Or if the Civil War is the subject of the social studies class, Harriet Beecher Stowe's *Uncle Tom's Cabin* or Stephen Crane's *The Red Badge of Courage* could be used in English. In a study of the post-World War I era, such classics as Frederick Allen's informal history *Only Yesterday* or Fitzgerald's *The Great Gatsby* would be excellent. By this method the class is not only studying literature and poetry but is learning more about an era and the people in it.

MEDIA

464-T   *(Discover/Discussions) "Light Side of the Dark Ages"*

Students often think literature is something in thick, dust-covered volumes. They would enjoy a long-time classic more if they saw it not as something that is dead but as a very live form of entertainment reflecting the times. Discuss how people's ideas of having fun (being entertained) have changed over the years. Using TV and films along with contemporary literary works and then "progressing backward" in time will help make the point.

465-T   *(Discover/Television) "Electronic Boom Boon"*

As television becomes more and more a part of every student's life, teachers are capitalizing on the medium as a study aid. Reserve one unit a semester for studying television genres such as the detective story, the family situation comedy, or the western. These forms can be traced to early literary works: Arthur Conan Doyle (detective), Clarence Day (family situation),

Louisa May Alcott ("soap operas"), and James Fenimore Cooper (western). This experience can serve as an entree to literature.

466-T *(Observe/Bulletin Board, Mixed Media) "Not Bored with Board"*

Initiate a unit on satire by placing on the bulletin board examples of parody, irony, satire, and others from everyday conversation and the mass media. These can be either quotes, paintings, photographs, caricatures, cartoons, or whatever fits. Such concrete examples help clarify the often difficult literary devices.

467-T *(Observe/Movies) "Open Your Film Cans to Frame Number ..."*

Movies are frequently mentioned as a way to implement a study of literature, but how about studying the movie for its own sake? An interesting unit might combine film viewing with readings from any current film "anthology." If the students are aware of various film techniques, such as camera angle, panning, cutting, montage, superimposed images, dissolves, or cuts, they will approach discussions on character development, plot structure, and theme more enthusiastically. Later, cinemagraphic development can be compared or contrasted with the literary method. When interest has grown, begin a Film Society, charge dues, and rent films.

468-C *(Observe/Movies, Slides) "Tic-Tac-Toe the Mark"*

Using audio-visual equipment can be a waste of time if the students use the darkened room as an opportunity to sleep or carry on conversations. Movies and slides can restore enthusiasm and vitality, but students must get more than enjoyment out of a film. So provide viewing guides that can be used to

How does Jarvis	act	feel	think
When he flies a plane?			
When he lands a plane?			
When he is grounded by bad weather?			

teach content without preventing the watching of the presentation. One easy-to-follow guide is the tic-tac-toe graph, pictured in sample form here. Write the questions alongside as in the diagram. If large writing areas are provided, even in subdued light the class can take notes while watching the film.

469–C *(Read/Magazines) "Tonal Qualities"*

A bad magazine article can teach more about tone than a week of essays on the subject. Get something that the students readily agree is bad. Have them tell why. Their very good reasons will be enough on which to build at least one good lesson on tone in literature.

NOVELS

470–C *(Discover/Discussions) "Choice Cuts"*

Unless the novels for class study are prescribed (hopefully, with so many from which to choose, there is a choice), have the class suggest a novel on which to spend some alloted time. Students who have read certain titles could do a selling job by reading choice cuts from the book. The class would then vote for the selection that intrigued them. If such wide-open choices are not possible, the teacher can limit the choices to several on a prepared list, using the same "sales pitch" approach, however, handled by several students who read the books and established a preference.

471–G *(Discover/Discussions) "Five Times Five"*

Did you ever wish that the class could cover more than a single common-study novel in a report card period? It can be done. A seventh-grade accelerated class, for example, was divided into five equal groups, each assigned one of five books. Each group decided how to present their book to the class. A panel approach, for example, might have one student handling the plot, another the characters, and so on. For instance, a group taking *Oliver Twist* might assign the historical times of the novel to one student; Dickens' life to another student, and to still another, the social problems of the times. A different but similar approach would be to have the groups study and report various aspects of a single novel.

472–C *(Discover/Discussions) "Titles Only Skin Deep"*

Make a list of interesting titles of novels, plays, and critical works that the students may have heard about but not read, e.g., *Death of a Salesman, Lord of the Flies, The Return of the Native,* and so on. Ask the class to guess the possible content from the titles. The variety of opinions will interest students to find out what the books are really about.

473-T *(Discover/Pictures) "Simple Symbols"*

The abstract concept of symbolization is often difficult for a student to comprehend. A number of devices can be used. The world is full of readily understandable symbols such as flags, coins, paper money, the holy cross, the star of David, the eagle, and even Santa Claus. Don't forget the status symbols either. Mount these samples or prepare slides. Students discover that interpreting symbols is easy. They do it every day.

474-C *(Discover/Talk) "Sound and Sense"*

Oral interpretation, a long-time speech department or forensic activity, offers a valuable approach for appreciating and understanding literature. Volunteers select particularly emotional pieces to present in class. From this experience the student discovers both the importance of the oral sense and the literary understanding. The entire class, unhindered by print, can empathize with the shared experience.

475-C *(Listen/Authorities) "Live and in Full Color"*

To help students realize that writers are ordinary, creative people just like themselves, bring to class a local author who has written a book similar to one currently being studied. (A famous, published author would be ideal but probably too expensive.) Urge the author to express how the book came to be written and to answer student questions. If an author is not readily available, choose a capable student, teacher, or parent to study the life of the author thoroughly enough to role play a guest author. Several actors, such as Hal Holbrook portraying Mark Twain, have made recordings and films that can be purchased or rented.

476-C *(Observe/Bulletin Board) "Feeling Down"*

An artist in class can develop cutout sketches of each character in a novel the class is reading. Mount the sketches on the bulletin board. As the story goes along, and characters interact, the characters are moved accordingly. The class can easily see character involvement and movement as each incident unfolds. This helps clear up some of the complexities between plot and characters and groups of characters.

477-C *(Observe/Displays, Pictures) "Scenes Heard"*

Students sometimes fail to understand novels because they are not able to visualize the characters or settings. Consequently, the action and, thus, the plot mean very little. Use pictures, diagrams, drawings, and even costumed actors to clarify the abstract. For *A Tale of Two Cities,* for example, someone could draw a floor plan of the prison or find a picture of the carriages used in the opening scene. For a novel like *The Deerslayer,* a student could dress in a frontiersman's costume. If many characters must be herded into a very small space such as a cell, use masking tape on the classroom floor to mark off an area of corresponding size. Crowd students into that area so they can better imagine the conditions. Make a point of telling students why authors purposely give vague settings and characterization. The rather obscure setting in *The Bridge of San Luis Rey* helps give the novel a more universal appeal than a specific setting would provide. Audiences can more readily identify with indefinite description by filling in their own details from past experience.

478–C   *(Observe/Movies, Pictures) "Flicker of Interest"*

Very few classic films are available for classroom use. One that is used frequently and is, indeed, a classic is "Nanook of the North." This sixty-minute silent, black and white film made in the early 1920s can be the motivation for that budding writer in your class. The goal or underlying message is that the novelist should write so convincingly that just as you become enwrapped by this film you will be enveloped by the pages of the book. The film can be rented; try Pyramid Films, Box 1048, Santa Monica, CA 90406.

479–T   *(Read/Books) "Out with Overkill"*

A novel's appeal and enjoyment can be killed by overteaching. A good book practically teaches itself. Before discovering the hard way how much analysis the class can accept and appreciate, let them enjoy the book first; then find out what else the book has to offer.

480–C   *(Read/Books) "Reading Religiously"*

Although prayer and religious holidays are things of the past in many schools, few can criticize using the Bible as a way to study both classic and contemporary literature and to gain insights into that literature. Biblical stories and parables form the basic themes for many novels, both famous and unknown.

In Genesis, the beginning of the Bible, is the theme that establishes the plot conflict in many pieces of literature: eating the forbidden fruit, with "fruit" taking on many meanings. Obvious influences of the crucifixion story are found in *The Scarlet Letter, Red Badge of Courage, Moby Dick, The Old Man and the Sea,* and in many others. Similarly, but certainly not synonymously, key myths and fables from ancient mythology can be found in literature. A glimpse of these devices before a book is read can add much interest. (Also see idea 505.)

481-T *(Read/Tales) "Short Tales and Long"*

A fascinating literary device that keeps recurring and can be readily studied is that of fantasy and fairy tale. Recall how often fairies and the fantastic happen in *Beowulf, Canterbury Tales, The Faerie Queene, Gulliver's Travels, Midsummer Night's Dream, Paradise Lost, Romeo and Juliet,* and *The Tempest.* Besides reading articles and books by authorities on fantasies and fairy tales, study the tales themselves for devices, plot structure, and themes that strongly resemble those in novels.

482-T *(Research/Authorities) "A Real Dig"*

Some students find it easier to read a novel if given a historical background. Instead of a term paper or lecture approach, expose the class to the history of an era by locating old newspaper articles, editorials, criticisms, movies, and recordings. Try to relate this background to our current social and political trends—even inviting a speaker to prove that some pieces of literature have set a foundation for recent events, e.g., Swift's "The Drapier Papers" and the era of religious quarrels in Ireland.

483-T *(Research/Authorities) "This Is Their Life"*

An entire course could focus on the different ways of life in the United States as represented in fiction such as *Grapes of Wrath, The Jungle, Main Street, Native Son, Not Without Laughing,* and *Tobacco Road.* Symbolism, style, craftsmanship, and all the usual facets of literature study might be purposely played down. The student instead learns the customs, moral values, and the sociopsychological structures of people with a different life style. This course, a kind of sociology of fiction, would help the student recognize the differences among people and at the same time become more tolerant—a desirable goal for English or any subject.

484-T *(Research/Mixed Media) "Looking Glass Class"*

A profound and interesting literature study can be based on the all-time children's favorite *Alice in Wonderland*. Numerous journal articles have been written on the social implications and symbolisms in this novel. Besides this resource, library vertical files often contain ready supplies of bulletin board illustrations of *Alice*. There is also at least one filmed version of this great classic.

485-C, G *(Research/Libraries) "Devised Devices"*

Authors frequently use special literary devices that occur over and over. Examples include the tower imagery, which can be traced through Hawthorne's works, and the water imagery found in Hemingway's works. Have students research an author to see what images are frequently repeated as characteristic of the author's work.

OVERVIEW

486-T *(Discover/Books) "Going, Going, Gone!"*

Many of the most entertaining and informative books cannot be covered in an English class because of lack of time or funds. Set aside the first five minutes of class each day for an "auction" of one or two books from the instructor's personal collection or from used book sales. First, students are introduced to the books. If they wish to read one, they bid for it. In an above-average class, highest bidder is whoever offers to read the book in the least amount of time. In an average or heterogeneous class, bidding may be by tokens which the teacher converts to party treats at the semester's end. The more bids, of course, the more food will be available. Students may "purchase" only one book at a time. Upon its return, the book may be reauctioned if there are any bidders. This procedure effectively introduces students to a wide array of authors and subjects. Sharing the plan with parents is recommended.

487-T *(Discover/Discussion) "Current of Current Events"*

By keeping abreast of current events a teacher can increase student interest in literature. Book lists and discussions are then developed to coincide with world happenings. This makes reading more meaningful to each student, particularly for those who see little value in it.

488-T *(Discover/Discussion) "Start Young"*

Begin a study of literature with current themes and modern writers. Students usually know more about the new authors, so they will contribute more freely in discussion. Determine similarities and differences between the modern authors and earlier ones to be studied. Then, when the earlier writers are studied in depth, students soon understand that authors write primarily about the same subjects but in their own times.

489-I *(Discover/Displays) "Share and Share Alike"*

Many students would read more if they were able to read books on subjects they enjoy. Since teachers usually don't have time to assign specific books to individuals, the class might match the right books with the right people. One approach is for students to write advertisements touting books they have read and to then share these comments with the rest of the class. Since students know each other and their personal tastes, peer suggestion is probably the best "sales pitch" a book can have. This also helps the teacher check on reading progress. (See related idea 34 on determining class interests.)

490-T *(Discover/Inventories) "Clues from Kids"*

The first day of class ask each student for a list of five books (or some other quantity) that he or she might like to read. Chances are, if each turns in a substantial list, certain books will appear repeatedly. Reading groups can then be set up around these popular selections. The books can be related to literature themes or genre being studied by the entire class.

491-T *(Discover/Lists) "Best of the West"*

For added motivation in literature classes, post the current best seller list. (This list can be expanded by adding past best sellers.) In another version, make up a list of English or American titles that have been best sellers in much earlier days. Or allow students to compose their own "Top Ten" or "Fabulous Forty" book lists. These are, surprisingly, often very well-conceived.

492-T *(Discover/Plans) "Basic Black"*

If your school has not yet established a course in Black Studies, you can easily plan a unit of your own with such works as *All God's Dangers,* Rosengarten (Avon); *The Autobiography of Miss Jane Pittman,* Gaines (Bantam); *Black Like Me,* Griffin (NAL: New American Library); *Black Voices,* Chapman

(NAL); *The Confessions of Nat Turner,* Styron (NAL); *Go Tell It on the Mountain,* Baldwin (Dell); *Invisible Man,* Ellison (Random House); *Native Son,* Wright (Harper & Row); *Roots,* Haley (Dell); *Song of Solomon,* Morrison (NAL); and *A Woman Called Moses,* Heidish (Bantam). Also include selected poems by such black poets as Paul Dunbar, James Weldon Johnson, Gwendolyn Brooks, Nikki Giovanni, and Langston Hughes. Use an inductive approach first, relating the literature to individual experiences. Then advance to a more abstract level such as comparing philosophies. Even try a multiethnic approach to include literature from other minorities such as Indian and Hispanic.

493–T   *(Discover/Self) "On Being Yourself"*

Emphasize how important it is to be aware of effect on self when reading a piece of literature. All good art creates a feeling or reaction in the reader or viewer. Knowing this increases enjoyment of any art form. Since some children need some guidelines for this, study a few different art forms and trace their artistic similarities. (Also see idea 531.)

494–T   *(Listen/Authorities) "Resource-full Classes"*

More than ever before, schools are using community resources to supplement instruction. Speakers are often available gratis. Many parents have skills and knowledge on certain subjects being covered in class. A farmer or a lawyer certainly can give more useful information on farming and law than the average teacher. This applies to English also. If a play is being studied, a local actor or actress who once acted in that play could discuss it in class. Parents may have slides of places visited in England or in Mark Twain land—Hannibal, Missouri. A lecture by such a person would give both students and teacher a change. Urge the school to send out a resource speaker questionnaire.

495–T   *(Listen/Books) "Read It and Weep"*

Literature has a beauty that many teachers fail to point out—sound. Many authors create certain moods and feelings that come alive only when their works are read aloud. If the teacher doesn't care to read, student volunteers can be used or original tapes played so as to share the sounds of literature.

496-T *(Listen/Lectures) "Put that Down"*

In some high schools the pure lecture technique in English classes is not used enough to prepare students for its more frequent use later, particularly in college. Occasional lectures can be effective to give introductory information or background of a poet, author, or literary period. Students should be required to take notes on these lectures to learn the procedure for picking out key ideas. Later, college-type blue book exams might be given to evaluate information gained from the lectures. This gives students practice answering essay questions, a skill in succinct writing that has many fringe benefits in and out of education.

497-I *(Read/Books) "Call a Sub"*

Instead of requiring everyone to read the same novel, poem, or short story, give them a choice of reading thematically similar works; for example, *A Portrait of the Artist as a Young Man* instead of *David Copperfield,* or *Dover Beach* instead of *Ozymandias.* Include research on the authors and the locale of the work.

498-I *(Read/Books) "Ethnic Pick"*

After discovering and discussing the many nationalities and races represented in the class, have students read at least one book (fiction or nonfiction) featuring characters—even situations—that parallel their own family backgrounds. This introduction can lead into many interesting, related activities as students share experiences.

499-T *(Read/Books) "Get the Point?"*

All students need the experience of reading a book to meet a personal need. These needs vary, student to student, day to day. To encourage individual reading, eliminate the required book list in favor of a free-choice approach. Display a chart listing students' names and titles of all books they read. Students record their own books on the chart. Each book is assigned weighted points by type: two points for easy reading (fiction, romance, or "hot rod" stories); five points for medium-hard (biographies, autobiographies); and ten points for difficult (lengthy fiction, nonfiction in a historical vein). Students are "rewarded" according to the number of points they earn.

500-I *(Read/Books) "Read—It's Free"*

As they often claim, many students actually do not have time for reading on their own. Homework for other classes, part-time work, athletics, and socializing consume what free time they have outside the classroom. As a valuable service to students, regularly allow generous amounts of class time and permit each student to read according to individual interests and ability levels.

501–T   *(Read/Books) "Spacing Out"*

Junior high students are interested in adventure and the unusual. To arouse reading interest in slower students, provide them with something they will want to read: good science fiction, detective stories, mysteries, and tales of the supernatural. Include some of these in the classroom library so they will be available for those who are not ready for reading the classics. Order these high-interest books from paperback book clubs or traveling library collections.

502–T   *(Read/Books) "Time to Browse"*

In communities where sources of reading matter are limited, sell the better periodicals and paperbacks at a school bookstore. If the operation is a nonprofit venture, prices can be reduced significantly. This is a convenient way for the teacher to order and assign a class novel. The reading and buying habits formed are likely to have carry-over value. Perhaps a bookstore such as this could be set up and staffed by the student council as a service project.

503–T   *(Read/Book Reports) "Paperback Backing"*

Arrange a display of paperbacks contributed by both teacher and students. The contributor writes a description and evaluation of each book on a 3 × 5 card and places it in a book pocket. This will help others select books that meet their interests. (Also see idea 863.)

504–C   *(Read/Handouts) "Coming on Live"*

Way to get your lumps

When studying any type of literature, supply students with information on the writer's life. Since literature usually reflects the author's life experiences, the class will be interested in facts such as these: Alexander Pope, in pain most of his life, was a 4'6" hunchback; Jonathan Swift was so energetic that if the weather kept him indoors, he ran up and down his deanery stairs; Samuel Johnson once threw a glass of lemonade out the window because a waiter who gave him a lump of sugar had dirty fingers. Through such anecdotes students come to realize that writers are human and that their humanity affects what they write.

505-T   *(Read/Myths) "A Hit or a Myth"*

After reading a few myths, have students search the world around them for sources that ovbiously draw from mythology: commercials, sports, general entertainment, heroes, and dreams, just to name a few. The mythology examples are numerous: Jolly Green Giant, any "prince charming," Superman, great statesmen and women, the Olympic games, and Charles Atlas, to list several.

506-I,G *(Research, Discussion) "Theme Teams"*

World literature can be effectively studied through a thematic approach. Groups (or individuals) could be introduced to three or four themes in Western literature and a similar number in Eastern literature. An obvious advantage of the thematic approach is that students can become so knowledgeable in one area that they want to trace their new-found interests through many types of literature.

POETRY

507-C   *(Discover/Discussions) "Activated Poetry"*

For a group of juniors or seniors who seem to favor the activist approach to life, present a unit on the revolutionary ideas of the Romantic poets. For example, Blake shows church condemnation and government regimentation ("Holy Thursday" and "The Human Abstract.") Shelley gives a brilliant analogy between revolution and the changes of autumn in "Ode to West Wind." Students will be surprised to discover that many of their so-called *new* causes have been dealt with in earlier times.

508-G   *(Discover/Discussions) "Diverse Verse"*

Use a great variety of verse so individual students are not excluded from participation by being included in "mass-think" exercises. A grab-bag of titles will provide a variety of poetry to read, explicate, paraphrase, love, or despise—not in isolation but in small groups, each having drawn the same poem. This procedure allows for a bit of competition through community opinion and, luckily, counter-opinion.

509-T   *(Discover/Discussions) "Poetry: Three Deep"*

In teaching poetry to high school students, discuss a poem on three levels: *surface, subsoil,* and *in-depth.* The *surface* level of a poem is its direct translation—the story line. The term *sub-soil* has psychological connotations. It suggests something beneath the conscious, roots piercing downward, or the base of the iceberg below the waterline. The term *in-depth* also has psychological implications, suggesting the deepest soil beneath the oak's taproot or the water below the iceberg. But the term *in-depth* also connotes darkness which can, in turn, suggest something evil or, paradoxically, something holy as in the phrase, "dark night of the soul." This conscious division of a poem helps students understand that poetry is often written with several different meanings in mind. This formula can be applied successfully to a poem like Robert Frost's "The Road Not Taken."

510-T *(Discover/Discussion) "Textbook Writers, Take Note"*

Often, too much time is devoted to teaching and discussing the mechanical or technical aspects of poetry, such as meter, rhyme, or metaphor. To help students learn and remember these important devices is a troublesome problem. Thus, to leave more time for the experiential and inferential levels of poetry (see idea 707), English department members should get together, decide on the basic poetry for each grade level, and prepare a parallel study handbook bringing in poetic structure as it becomes useful to create a mood or build an idea.

511-C *(Discover/Discussion) "To Each His Own"*

Before moving into a more formalized study of poetry, promote and hold class interest by giving students a choice of the poets and poems on which they can concentrate. Some class periods may be used as library days, others for discussion, comparing likes, dislikes, types, elements, and problems. As an eventual follow-through, the end-of-the-unit test should also be unstructured to allow each student to demonstrate in his or her own way what was learned.

512-C *(Discover/Discussion) "Typical Typo"*

This exercise focuses on the questions of if, how, and why typography is part of poetry. Pass out a sample with two sentences on it, each written to emphasize the typography (poems of E. E. Cummings illustrate this technique). Take one of the sentences out of a prose selection, the other from an actual poem. Students decide which is poetry and discuss the questions above, after which they practice writing some visually expressive lines of their own.

513–T   *(Discover/Field Trips) "Poetry Renaissance"*

One way to stimulate the enjoyment of poetry is to get out of the formal classroom. A number of alternatives are available: group poetry readings after school in a relaxed environment, attendance at a lecture by a visiting poet, or a good program of poetry reading on radio or television. The essential component is to try to recapture that feeling of camaraderie that people once experienced through the medium of poetry.

514–T   *(Discover/Lists) "Prove It"*

The announcement of a poetry unit often results in a chorus of groans. One way to handle this problem is to ask each student who dislikes poetry to list all the reasons for feeling this way. If desired, ask the others to list reasons they like poetry. These lists are used by the teacher to compile a master list of the most frequently mentioned reasons and to find poems that refute each negative reaction. This collection is read aloud and/or placed in a notebook for future poetry haters.

515–T   *(Discover/Talks) "Off to a Good Start"*

Before beginning to study poetry, many teachers feel compelled to defend poetry because they assume most students hate it. Instead of taking the defensive, teachers might take a more positive approach. One way is to organize a discussion on "Why a study of poetry is of value," or use the same topic for a paper. A teacher with a bent for drama may encourage students to dramatize a poem either through choral reading or by rewriting it as a play. Poems such as "The Highwayman" or "The Pied Piper of Hamelin" can serve as starters. Some lines may need some changing; others need to be added, but soon the poem can live—with sound effects and even scenery.

516–C   *(Listen/Audiotapes) "Teaming with Poets"*

Introduce surrealistic poetry, which borders on stream-of-consciousness, by the following method: Assign the name of one of three parts of speech (adjective, noun, and verb) in that order to each student. Each child says a word for his or her part of speech—any word that comes to mind. One student tapes as the activity moves along. Replaying the tape results in a form of surrealistic poetry. (Bring in a surrealistic painting to compare with the poetry.) Often the results are really very good if each response genuinely influences the next one. At any rate, by observing the disastrous results of haphazard choices, students realize that precise word selection is important in writing poetry.

517-C *(Listen/Music)* *"Notes about Lyrics"*

Employ a careful study of lyrics from popular songs, past and present, to introduce and illustrate poetry. Ballads like "Barbara Allen," "John Henry," "Ode to Billie Joe," and "Frankie and Johnnie," are good choices. The fact that almost everything that has happened in the past happens today in some form or another comes clear when the older ballads are compared with those of the modern-day balladeer. Students usually put aside negative reactions toward poetry when they realize the songs they like are really poems set to music.

518-C *(Listen/Recordings)* *"Now Hear This"*

Locate recordings of professional announcers and actors reading poetry, perhaps poets reading their own works. Besides making poems easier to understand, this auditory approach makes poetry come alive by attaching it to human emotion rather than words on paper.

519-C *(Listen/Recordings)* *"Sing Us a Poem"*

When introducing rhythm, have students choose a particular poem they will read accompanied by musical instruments. If live music is unavailable, the reading can be backed by appropriate recorded music. Listening carefully to the tempo, crescendos, and decrescendos of the music, the reader can better attribute proper vocal inflection, intensity, pitch, and rhythm to the poetry. Setting the poetry to music gives an empathic feeling that cannot be obtained any other.

520-C *(Listen/Mixed Media, Recordings)* *"Sound Al'round"*

While teaching various elements of poetry, introduce ideas with which students are already familiar. Poetic sound combinations and repetitions are used in slogans created by advertisers to attract attention. Locate and record some of the popular slogans with their alliterations and rhymes: "It takes a licking and keeps on ticking," "Better than butter," "Brighten a barbecue," "Built better not cheaper," "The best wrap around." Look for onomatopoeia as in "Snap,

Crackle, Pop" and "Pop, pop; fizz, fizz" and the rhyme of "Fun in the sun." Encourage students to search for many such samples to contribute to a "Found Poetry" unit.

521-T   *(Observe/Displays) "Stop, Look, Listen Poetry"*

Poetry can be more dramatic and more fun if read aloud within an appropriate environment. Create a mood by using a colored spotlight. When certain poems suggest softness and romanticism, bathe the room in soft blue light. When the heat of the battle comes along in epic poetry, try a red floodlight. Project slides of appropriate magazine illustrations on light-colored walls, a movie screen, or a bedsheet for backgrounds. Add some appropriate music, too. Few can ignore the impact of the multimedia presentation.

522-T   *(Observe/Plans) "Wide-Open Choice"*

Just as you might approach the novel historically, socially, psychologically, emotionally, didactically, or even analytically, so might you teach poetry. Certain poems, as do novels, lend themselves to specific approaches.

523-C   *(Observe/Slides) "Seeing Is Believing"*

To illustrate a poet's use of imagery, metaphor, or simile, show some appropriate slides on the subject. For instance, if the class has difficulty understanding Emily Dickinson's "I'll Tell You How the Sun Rose," show slides of sunrises and sunsets while reading it. This helps students visualize and appreciate the poet's word-picture.

524-T   *(Read/Models) "Made in Japan"*

The Japanese verse form haiku has become popular in America during the past few years because of its appeal to all age groups. This form can be introduced in classrooms as early as grade school and can be continued through high school and beyond. An interesting approach for high school is to include the haiku in a study of an American poet such as Robert Frost. Frost poems such as "Design," "Dust of Snow," "Nothing Gold Can Stay," and "Spring Pools" use complex juxtapositions. One is unnatural whiteness and the natural life-death cycle. Both are reflected in this original haiku:

Bedded patient, dead
Still, white in a sun-drenched gown,
Grasping sheets of white.

Thus, the student gains both a clearer understanding of Frost's images and the single-impact haiku. (See idea 42.)

SHORT STORY

525–C   *(Listen/Recordings) "Sounding Off"*

When reading a short story orally in class—especially descriptive passages, have some students provide a background of appropriate sound effects, live or on tape. Record distributors often have sound effects albums. A good introductory selection is John Steinbeck's "Flight"— Pepe's escape into the mountains.

526–C   *(Research/Libraries, Role Playing) "Full Immersion"*

This activity is recommended for middle or junior high students when studying short stories about ethnic groups. After some library research on social customs, particularly special foods, have a banquet featuring the authentic foods and styles of cooking. Whether the cooking is done in school or at home, the point will be made strongly that American society is truly pluralistic. Some classes have even donned costumes for the occasion. The history behind the characteristic menus also makes an interesting study.

VOCABULARY

527–C   *(Discover/Chalkboard, Words) "Take It from Lit"*

Difficult vocabulary in literature—obscure or archaic phrases, allusions, and new words—should be clarified before the reading begins. At the start of each lesson, place a few of the day's difficult words on the board. For full enjoyment of a poem or other work, discuss and define these stumbling blocks. But spend only a short time on this phase, since the main reason for reading literature is not the vocabulary study.

10 Deliberation

DRAMA

528-T *(Analyze/Discussion) "Shakespearean Sin"*

Sometimes, in teaching Shakespeare, we find ourselves concentrating too much on the plot and obvious action. Instead, we need to delve into Shakespeare's genius and analyze the deep beauty and meaning of his plays. Such discussions, quite naturally, will enhance interest and understanding of the past as well as the present and future of our society.

529-C *(Experiment/Field Trips) "Orchestra or Loge?"*

While doing a theater unit, plan a field trip to see a community or civic theater production of an appropriate play. Possibly a special matinee performance can be offered to combined English classes. Make arrangements for the cast and/or stage manager or director to speak to the class after the performance. Perhaps this could include a costume, prop, or make-up demonstration and an opportunity for the students to ask questions.

530-G *(Interpret/Role Playing) "Living Arts"*

Have groups present key themes or character studies from a play, novel, or short story. Students pose in tableau-like positions which symbolize the way these characters relate to each other. For example, one group might portray the prevailing theme in *A Raisin in the Sun* by joining hands and forming a circle facing stoically outward, away from a frustrated student placed in the middle. Another couple might portray Hester Prynne *(The Scarlet Letter)* standing tall above a genuflecting Dimmesdale. Add a bit of competition through a contest in which students guess the play or key scenes within a play through these tableaus or simple charades.

HUMANITIES

531–T   *(Analyze/Artwork) "Literature in 3-D"*

Review the methods for analyzing the visual arts and music
and then have students apply the same principles to literature.
One approach, emphasizing line, form, and space, is to show
how each work of art incorporates design, differences, and
dominance (the 3-D theory): design through repetition, differences through contrasts and variations, dominance through a
device such as prevailing colors, forms, or themes that hold
the work together to give it purpose. The effective use of all
three aspects differentiate between any art and good art.

532–T   *(Consolidate/Instruction) "Multi-Lit"*

Encourage reading that parallels current studies in other subject fields. For example, every period of history has had its
writers who reflect the age. Many books are based in lands
being studied in geography. Civics classes consider many
themes found in novels and short stories. Foreign language
classes can quite naturally tie in with world literature. Science
courses can introduce a host of biographies, novels, and short
stories. To accomplish this goal ask other subject matter teachers to forward their future plans, allowing time to research titles
and sources. Then allow students to make free choices that
will eventually help them consolidate these seemingly diver-
gent but actually very similar sources.

NOVELS

533–I   *(Analyze/Books) "Mirroring the Images"*

Following a discussion of the concept of imagery in literature,
provide activities that will encourage students to look for repeated images in a novel, e.g., water imagery in Hemingway.
A good starting point would be a study of the author's life to
provide a possible clue to the strong images. The teacher can
help students in developing this study of imagery by providing
lists of strong image words. Such an approach provides some
relief to the usual ways of analyzing a piece of literature.

534–C   *(Analyze/Discussion) "Parallel-o-Greats"*

This game involves character analysis. Start with a group discussion and proceed to a deeper exercise of individual thought
and research. Taking one character at a time, work up a list of
a half-dozen one-word character traits. Then for *each* trait decide what famous person in history or entertainment might
epitomize this trait. From here, move to a guessing game by

merely leaving out the character's name; list just his or her
traits and name the famous people who epitomize each trait.
For example, one personality trait of Odysseus is being crafty
or cunning, which might be compared with someone like
James Bond, Dick Tracy, or a famous militarist in recent
history.

535–I   *(Analyze/Notes) "Psych 'em Out"*

Students are often asked to
write character sketches for
novels or short stories they
are reading. To create a
deeper interest in such an
activity, present this exercise. Each student becomes a
"psychoanalyst." As the
story proceeds, the student
writes ongoing observations about a main character and then,
through analysis, draws some conclusions about the individual's
personality that were not brought out in the text.

536–C   *(Discover/Discussion) "A Novel Approach"*

This idea works best if the assigned novel has not yet been
read. For one of the primary characters, list behavioral traits,
appearance, attitudes, and so on, and state briefly the character's relevance to the novel. Then the class considers what type
of person the character is and how he or she will probably act
within the novel. With this preliminary discussion, the students should be anxious to start reading the novel to find out
if they are correct.

537–C   *(Experiment/Tales) "Twice-Told Tales"*

After introducing various narrative styles, have students imitate writings of well-known authors. They may select, for example, a popular fairy tale, myth, or a newspaper article on a
news event and retell it, for instance, as Chaucer, Melville,
Hemingway, Joyce, or even writers of the Bible might write it.
This exercise helps illustrate that style is a personal literary
attribute and serves as a sort of trademark of that author's
work. Style is characterized by preferred sentence length and
structures, modification techniques, and description (type and
amount). One interesting study is to compare styles of authors
handling such commonplace events as people walking and the
sun rising or setting.

538–I   *(Interpret/Cartoons) "Comical Characters"*

Practice how an author creates a character. The class reads a
comic book and on paper they decide the main character as

completely as possible using material from the comic book to support contentions. Have the students discuss the complexity of these characters in relation to what they think makes a real or great literary character. Many similarities exist between character development in the comics and good literature.

539-I *(Interpret/Papers) "Calling All Careers"*

Capitalize on the need to bring more career education into the classroom by taking an inventory of the students' career interests and combining this information with the need to read. After students have decided what their life ambitions might be, they will read at least three novels in which the main characters are also engaged in the same career. Then each student writes a paper drawing the parallels between knowledge of the career and the books' versions, concluding with an interpretation of what such a career may be like.

540-I *(Interpret/Papers) "Who's Who?"*

Lengthy novels often contain so many characters that it is difficult to remember them. Selected students or volunteers could read ahead, each writing a brief description of one particular character, including appearance, speech habits, moral traits, and eccentricities, as well as the character's function in the novel. When each new character is first introduced, the paper may be read orally and discussed. These thumbnail sketches, which can be illustrated and placed on the bulletin board, serve to crystallize characters so they will be recognized as the plot unfolds. Whenever anyone has a question concerning a character, the student who researched the character is called upon as a resource.

541-G *(Interpret/Paragraphs) "Subbing"*

To help everyone keep track of what is going on in a long novel, write a plot outline on the chalkboard showing the main plot and various subplots. Then divide the class into groups, assigning each one of the subplots. As each subplot occurs in the study, ask the group to summarize it in one paragraph and then read it to the class. Discussions can occur when time permits to consider how the subplots relate to the main story line.

542-C *(Organize/Games) "Who, What, When, Where, Why—and How!"*

This simple game helps develop the concept of plot. Place five members on a team, one member for each of the five Ws: who, what, when, where, and why. Students first establish a few characters and a simple plot. On signal, one team member writes a word or sentence answering "who," then folds over his or her response and hands the paper to the next person on the team who then writes a "what" to go with the "who," etc. A story will develop for each team and is read aloud immediately. In awarding points for teams, the class uses some criteria: Does the story have a plot? Does it make sense? Is it complete?

OVERVIEW

543-C *(Analyze/Games) "Four for Metaphor"*

When studying a novel or play that has many characters, such as Galsworthy's *The Man of Property* (forerunner of *The Forsyte Saga*), students may find it difficult to understand and recall the aspects of each personality. To better explain the characters' actions and importance, try a game of "Metaphors." A team of three or four students leaves the room briefly while the rest of the class chooses one fictional character for the team to guess. Returning, the small group suggests a category from a selection decided earlier, such as favorite color, clothes, transportation, furniture, or books. Volunteers give clues that fit the category and would most likely represent the character in question, e.g., the type of clothing the character would probably wear to a party. Someone writes these suggestions on the board to aid recall. If the character has not been guessed by the time limit, the name is given. Discussion to clarify may follow. Teams can participate in timed competition.

544-C *(Interpret/Books) "Going My Way?"*

When teaching literary criticism, keep in mind the following notions. There is no single "right" method to handle literary approaches or to uncover all the significant truths of a work. Although scrutinizing various literary theories is a useful philosophical activity, the full understanding of literature does not always depend on such theorizing. Try to have students construct their own sets of valid, simple statements to clarify the nature and quality of a work and thereby increase appreciation.

545-I *(Interpret/Books) "Stitch in Time"*

Use proverbs to bring out the theme of a book or story. Encourage students to either find a proverb or write their own describing what was said in a work under study. This helps reduce themes to a sentence rather than forcing the all-too-common paragraph or report. To illustrate themes and interacting sub-themes, more than one proverb may be found, or one major proverb and several related. For example, Frost's repeated line in "Stopping by Woods"—"And miles to go before I sleep"— will evoke several interesting explanations.

546-T *(Organize/Talk) "Enjoying by Joining"*

Start an English Club composed of students whose interest in literature is reflected in their scholastic achievement. At the beginning of the fall semester hold a social meeting with a short program aimed at encouraging membership. Club members elect officers and plan programs focusing on dramatic presentations, readings by guest poets, debates, lectures by visiting authors, the production of an original play, or a language arts exhibit for the entire student body. The club could also help promote use of the school library.

POETRY

547-T *(Analyze/Discussion) "Meritorious Poetry"*

Time and again when students analyze poetry and prose they are subtly coerced to agree that a poem or play is good because it is by Carl Sandburg, Bob Dylan, or someone equally famous. It is easy, then, for students to think literature is good only if it is written by a well-known author. This idea makes it more difficult for new writers and poets to be read and accepted. Teach students what true poetry is and what makes good poetry. Then bring good poems to class regardless of who wrote them. Encourage students to bring in little-known poems they feel are worthy. Discuss these poems for content, not ever mentioning the poet's name.

548-C *(Analyze/Discussion) "Poets Who Know It"*

The teacher reads aloud two contrasting poems without comment. The class discusses the subject of each poem, the authors' attitudes, likenesses and differences, the sound of each poem and the relation of sound to tone, and the tone in each and how it is achieved. With the students themselves providing the answers, they will soon realize that they really do know something about poetry.

549-C *(Analyze/Models) "Air and Compare"*

Analyze the effect of poetry upon the listener by duplicating some song lyrics and several poems. See if students can tell which are which. Delete a stanza of a poem, or substitute either words or entire stanzas. How quickly do students note a change in effect? Then ask different students to read a short poem aloud to show its dramatic quality and prove that the effect varies with each reader. (Each time a poem is read, others reading the same poem should be out of hearing range.)

550-C *(Experiment/Chalkboard) "Chalk One Up for Poetry"*

To better understand how a poem is created, the class will write a poem and post it on the chalkboard. First, list poetic devices as reminders—alliteration, meter, metaphor, and rhyme. Then the class chooses the topic and suggests content. Even if the poem isn't too good, it helps develop a working understanding of poetry.

551-C *(Analyze/Music) "Class-ick Hit"*

Students become very interested in poetry when it is current. Before delving into the classics, duplicate songs by popular lyricists from albums students bring to class. Examine how these songs follow patterns. Urge everyone to try writing his or her own lyrics—really poems. Then, later, if time permits, students who want to put forth the extra effort might work with the music department (or musically talented within the class) to put the words to music.

552-I *(Experiment/Essays) "Saying It Like It Is"*

Ask students to paraphrase a poem in their own words, in prose as in an essay. Selections are read orally and compared with the poem. Besides developing some poetic and rhetoric insight, students will also see poetry as the better way to express some thoughts.

553-C *(Experiment/Poems) "Graffoetry"*

To stimulate experimentation in poetry, have students create "found" poems consisting of words, sentences, or phrases found anywhere (billboards, newspaper articles, advertisements, recipes, even some walls). Arrange items in poetic form. Words may be left out or repeated, but no words are added. Share results.

554-I *(Interpret/Audiotapes) "For the Record"*

Let each student choose a favorite short poem to read into a tape recorder. Several practice readings before taping will improve results. Play back all the readings, making certain the words for some of the more difficult poems are available to read while listening. This approach is a good opening for discussion of oral interpretation of poetry.

555–C *(Interpret/Discussions) "Clash of Symbols"*

A relatively mature college prep class would benefit from the following idea illustrating there is no final interpretation of any poem, not even the author's. Write a poem yourself, then write out your own interpretation of it. Present your poem to the class as an anonymous poem and have them interpret it. They will be able to find and support meanings and symbols that you had never considered. When they are finished, reveal what you have done, show your interpretation, and explain how their versions are superior to yours.

556–I *(Interpret/Mixed Media) "Cut Out the Dissection"*

Awakening student sensitivity to poetry can sometimes be a problem. One way to sharpen interest is to avoid the usual explicative phase, at least initially. Assign a specific poem for each member to interpret in his or her own way. This interpretation may be in the form of an original painting, dance, music, a prose essay, or even another poem. This procedure encourages the student to explore poetry for its between-the-lines message.

557–T *(Interpret/Poems) "Going My Way"*

When studying poetry, a teacher can unwittingly antagonize students by foisting off a teacher interpretation when there really is no way to know. If a student tries but comes up with a different interpretation than the expected one, he or she should be encouraged to know that his or her opinion is as good as the next person's. Similarly important, use care when commenting on written papers that offer interpretations.

558–C *(Interpret/Recordings) "Auditory Imagery"*

To aid in understanding poetic imagery—symbol, simile, metaphor, and so on—bring in some record albums of image-rich songs. Any songs popular with youth are good. Play the song, perhaps several times. Hopefully, the students will be acquainted with the words. Then they can pick out the images, tell what they might stand for, and comment on effectiveness.

559-C   *(Interpret/Talk) "Greek to Me"*

To illustrate the role of sound in poetry, the teacher (or another bilinguist) reads several poems in any foreign language with which most students would not be familiar—even in "Jabberwocky" nonsense words. Through voice inflection, pause, rate, and other devices, the reader tries to project the general ideas and moods of the poem. See if the class can empathize on the basis of sound alone. Experiments in phonetic symbolism indicate that this can be done with a high level of accuracy.

560-G   *(Listen/Audiotapes) "Reading between the Lines"*

Poetry is often characterized by the saying: "What counts most is not what is said but what is not said—what the reader must discover." The student of poetry should be able to recognize how a message moves across the vacant space between images in a poem. To demonstrate, a small group can tape a word-association discussion outside of class. Members of this group speak spontaneously but use only one word at a time which has been suggested by the previous word. The tape is then played to aid discussion of the logic beind the flow of conversation: What single thought connected each image? Why did one word or image inspire the next? What were the cognitive aspects of the discussion?

561-C   *(Listen/Recordings) "Folk-Singing Young Folk"*

Analyze the poetry used by contemporary folk singers, noting the interrelationship of words, rhythm, and rhyme. Suggest putting some poems to music. Discuss the fit of both meaning and rhythm. Also try some original poem writing which could be sung by a student guitar-playing folk singer.

562-G   *(Read/Poems) "Togetherness"*

Let the class experience the fun of reading poetry through choral reading. Selections by Kipling, Poe, and Service are good starters. Encourage the class to work out some groupings to achieve special effects after they have learned how to read in unison effectively.

11 Evaluation

DRAMA

563–G *(Judge/Role Playing) "Try Tryouts"*

When studying any play, encourage students to act out key scenes. Have a contest between several groups (casts). This is a good way to analyze the characters' motives, emotions, and other traits, and to encourage creativity. The rest of the class decides which group (and individual) did the best interpretation.

HUMANITIES

564–C *(Compare/Games) "Humani-tease"*

To determine if students comprehend the correlatives of the arts, literature, philosophy, sociology, technology, and so forth, of an age, play a random drawing game. Call it "Humani-tease" or something better. Provide six small boxes that will hold 3×5 index cards. Label each box with one of the following: Traits and Ideas, Literature, Architecture, Sculpture, Painting, and Music. Place in the first box a number of cards each bearing a key trait of a period, say the Romantic, e.g., emotionalism, individualism, and nationalism. Then place the names of titles of various works of art (or artists) of the period in their respective boxes. Assume at least two teams of six players each. Each team player is caretaker of one box while his or her team has its turn. The first card drawn gives a trait or idea. Each of the other players must go through their boxes until they find a work that reflects that idea or trait. (Cards may be filed in alphabetical order to save time or may be in a jumbled state.) The chosen cards are then compared with a master list held by a monitor or the teacher. Allow one point for each correct card among four. The game progresses until a team reaches the preselected top score.

565–G *(Extrapolate/Demonstrations) "Renew the Review"*

A literature review can even become exciting if the class is divided into committees, each of which is responsible for producing a fifty-minute program characterizing the literary period the group selects to cover. The groups use art galleries, libraries, museums, and other sources to gather material. Their programs might incorporate filmstrips, slides, records, appropriate costumes, pictures of literary figures, puppets, or other props. After the shows have been presented, the best ideas could be worked into a program for other English classes or even the entire school. Of course, students can be evaluated on their contributions.

NONFICTION

566-C *(Identify/Biography) "Propped Up Book Reports"*

Everybody in the class independently chooses a biography to read. As part of a book report, they must illustrate, nonverbally with gestures and props, the famous person. The class must guess who the book is about. Some type of prize could be given to the person(s) with the most successful guesses. This activity requires good character analysis.

NOVELS

567-C *(Compare/Cartoons) "Charlie Caulfield vs. Holden Brown"*

Compare comic strip characters with people in books. Students can learn much about Holden Caulfield *(Catcher in the Rye)* by comparing him to Charlie Brown *(Peanuts)*. Let the class cut out specific comic strips or cartoons that illustrate a point they want to make about a book character. The similarities can be amazing.

568-G *(Compare/Games) "Miss or Match"*

The object of this game is to match a character with a well-defined personality trait or a situation with its significance in the story. Two sets of cards are prepared. The name of a character or description of a situation appears on each card in one set. The personality characteristic (or significance) is written on a card in the second set. The cards are distributed randomly throughout the class. Then one player with a character (or situation) card reads it and waits for a classmate to complete the matching trait (or significance). The student who thinks he or she can, reads his or her card when called. If there is a match, that student gets a point; if not, the point goes to the student who first reads a card. It is important to have unambiguous clues.

569–G   *(Compare/Skits) "Characters in Search of Plot"*

This exercise helps students understand interdependence of characters and plot. Two different groups present for the class an improvised scene based on a single idea supplied by the teacher, e.g., a crowded bus, a supermarket checkout counter, an ice cream parlor, and so on. They will work independently of each other and give their performances at different times (neither seeing the other's). Each group usually gives a different improvised interpretation of a single-idea plot, and the characters take on different personalities. A strong similarity between the two performances still provokes good comparison discussions on how the plot was altered through the characters' different personalities. If both presentations could be videotaped, the two groups could share each other's effort.

570–I   *(Extrapolate/Books) "Plot-It-Yourself Kit"*

The plot, almost always interesting and usually neglected because it is so obvious, should be used to develop an understanding of a novel's theme. One approach, when giving the next day's reading assignment, is to tell the class not to read beyond the assignment but rather to imagine the rest of the plot and jot down anticipatory notes. Since through plot direction the students must frequently change their idea of the theme, they gain a greater understanding of the term. Both teacher and student can then check on understanding.

571–I   *(Extrapolate/Cartoons) "Comic Pick"*

In just about any daily or Sunday comic strip, one can find the literary devices used in structuring a novel. Evaluate ability to pick out such elements as satire, irony, and allegory as students see them exemplified in various comic strips. Each example can be pasted at the top of a short explanation of how the strip illustrates the particular element.

572–C   *(Extrapolate/Games) "For the Game Room"*

This game is a technique for checking on understanding characters and plot details in drama, short story, the novel, or even poetry. The idea is to create nonsensical allusions, obvious puns, or outrageous similarities, or find song titles that will match and identify the predetermined list of titles and characters drawn up by the teacher. Examples include the following:

Giants in the Earth—"The Sounds of Silence"
The Iliad (referring to Helen)—"That face, that face, that
  marvelous face"
Moby Dick—"The Impossible Dream"
The Odyssey—"Bill Bailey, Won't You Please Come
  Home"
The Odyssey—(referring to the cannibal Laestrogonias)
  "People Who Need People"
The Old Man and the Sea—"One in the hand is worth two
  in the bush."

573-I   *(Extrapolate/Papers) "Extra, Extra!"*

A quick way to discover if students understand the basic plots
or themes in novels is to let them write headlines:

"Soldier Missing in Action Returns to Fight" (Plot)
  (The Red Badge of Courage)
"Youth Finds Self up a Tree" (Theme)
  (A Separate Peace)

This technique can be expanded to writing a news article about
the event, using facts from the novel. Or the teacher can make up
headlines for a matching section in a literature test.

574-I   *(Extrapolate/Papers) "Moving Bulletin Boards"*

When teaching long, thematic units using several sources,
keep track of the basic points by building a progressive bulletin board. As the unit moves along, list the elements of the
novel across the top: Plot, Characters, Setting, Style, Emotional Effect. As each element is studied, a few students at a
time write very short summaries (1) defining the element and
giving its function in the novel, and (2) telling how the element affected them. Their papers are then placed on the board
under the proper headings.

575-I   *(Extrapolate/Tests) "Self-Tests"*

Students can prove they understand the novel under consideration by preparing a test, with answer key, which checks on
familiarity with characters, basic theme, and plot. The teacher
then selects the most comprehensive test and administers it to
the class. If desired, the teacher may do a little editing to improve a question. The test writer then helps the teacher evaluate the results.

576-I   *(Identify/Discussion) "Conceptual-eyes"*

To elucidate an abstract concept in a literary work, ask each
class member to write his or her own definition of the concept in as

few words as possible. Faith, honor, courage, and patriotism are some of the concepts that might be examined. This statement could be the starting point for comparing and contrasting student ideas with an author's. Not only does this activity stimulate discussion, it also allows the shy student to share ideas in a relaxed atmosphere.

577-C   *(Identify/Discussion) "Drawing Blanks"*

Spice up a literature review and generate interest in new authors by distributing to each student short passages from famous authors. Obliterate the main characters' names. By analyzing the unknown author's style, structure, apparent opinions, and other clues, the class narrows the piece to a particular literary period and then to a particular author. For some classes it may be necessary to use works of authors already studied.

578-C   *(Identify/Discussion) "Slipping into Lit"*

As a review of the impact of a novel, ask each reader to write on a slip of paper some key questions or feelings about the novels. These slips of paper are collected and then used as a springboard for class discussion. Each student draws one slip and leads the class in discussing whatever it introduces. The procedure is repeated as long as interest is maintained. The best questions can be saved for final testing.

579-I   *(Identify/Displays) "Cool Coats"*

After a reading unit on *King Arthur: Tales of the Round Table,* allow students time to explore their interest in legendary emblems by designing their own coat-of-arms. A student's emblem will reveal many things about personal beliefs, self-concepts, interests, abilities, and needs, and will reflect historical knowledge about his or her family. These designs can then be placed on book jackets, lockers, sweaters, blazer jackets, and T-shirts.

580-C   *(Identify/Games) "English Inquisition"*

This game enables students to review literary facts and develop the skill of asking questions. One student thinks of a certain author or character and gives the rest of the class the first letter of the name. They then begin to ask questions to identify the mystery subject. Whoever guesses the word gets points and begins another game. The vital clue to solving the mystery name is in the questioning procedure, so some time should be spent prior to playing the game on how to ask questions that move from broad generalities to narrow categories very quickly. This approach gives everyone an opportunity to participate and gives the teacher a chance to hear how everyone thinks.

581-C   *(Identify/Games) "He's a Card"*

A valuable literature review game can be created by listing about a hundred facts pertaining to different fictional characters. Enter each fact on a card and shuffle cards. Each participant randomly chooses an equal number of the fact cards. The remaining cards are placed in one stack. In a round, a player puts down a card, reads the fact on it, and identifies the character. For each card handled successfully, the player is able to draw another from the stack, continuing until he or she misses. Then the next player continues. Scores are based on the number of cards each player has before him or her when an agreed-upon time limit is reached.

582-C   *(Identify/Games) "Panting for Pantomime"*

Relying on their own reading background for material, students play a game of charades with the following categories: authors, characters, titles, and quotations which the teacher or a student committee prepares on slips of paper. One team tries to guess whatever one of their teammates draws to pantomime. Before beginning the game it would be helpful to review the useful pantomime gestures such as ones to identify categories and certain insignificant words.

583-C   *(Identify/Games) "Slip Me the Answer"*

Limiting their activity to books familiar to the class, pupils draw up lists of questions about authors, titles, plots, themes, characters, and settings. They write on small slips of tagboard and place the questions in a box. Someone acting as questioner draws a slip from the box and reads it aloud. Each class member who answers correctly can keep the slip. At the end, the person with the most slips wins the game.

584-I   *(Identify/Notes) "Spicy Review"*

This literature review is a cooperative effort and particularly effective with slow learners. A number of volunteers choose characters from one or several novels and make up three clues about each choice. In turn, these are presented orally to the rest of the class who makes notes about the clues. Using their texts if they wish, the class brings in a list of the correct characters the next day.

585–C *(Identify/Paragraphs) "Author Bee"*

Discover if pupils have developed a concept of style through an "Author Bee." Divide the class into two teams. Read a paragraph written by one of the authors studied. The teams must guess who wrote it. Each member who answers correctly gets to sit down. (Why should the winners suffer on their feet?) The first team to seat all its members wins.

586–G *(Identify/Role Playing) "Role It"*

To see if students can identify characters, persuade them to act out key scenes or to interpret dialogue from selections under study. Encouraging them at times to give their own free interpretations promotes discussions about the controversial adaptations.

587–G *(Judge/Conferences) "Take Five"*

Gear literature study to include both rapid and slow readers even though the class is reading the same novel. The first five students to finish the novel have a group conference with the teacher. They are then assigned another novel based on the same theme or topic. The next five to finish have their conference and are assigned a shorter novel or even a group of poems that relate to the novel. Each five to finish confer with the teacher and receive additional assignments that can be completed in the remaining time. In this way the slow readers can read at their own pace and not be inundated by more work than they can handle. Everybody is challenged to the extent of individual ability. Then at the very end, the whole matter can be brought together through several days of panel discussion on the various materials covered by groups.

588–I *(Judge/Papers) "Texture Titillation"*

To capture a student's overall insights into a novel's plot, imagery, and symbolism, assign key chapters or sections to each student on which he or she writes a short critique. These papers are shared orally before the class and act as a catalyst for class discussion.

589–I *(Restructure/Notes) "Dear Diary"*

Students fabricate a diary that might have been kept by the most or least likeable character in a novel read by the class. The specific selection of notes will tell whether they have learned the technique of characterization. Instead of being written in one or two sittings, the best diaries develop over a period of several weeks during which time the student "lives" the character's life.

590-T *(Restructure/Journals) "New Heights for Wuthering Heights"*

When teaching the culturally disadvantaged, nonreaders, school haters, and so on, don't force upon them books like *The Scarlet Letter, Wuthering Heights,* or other works that may further alienate them. To begin, offer a choice of contemporary selections more in keeping with their particular social and cultural concerns: *A Hero Ain't Nothin' But a Sandwich* (Childress); *City Cool* (DeJongh and Cleveland); *I Never Promised You a Rose Garden* (Green); *The Outsiders* (Hinton); *Dinky Hocker Shoots Smack* (Kerr); *Cold Feet* (LeRoy); *Keeper of the Children* (Hallahan); *Go and Catch a Fish* (Stolz); *Nectar in a Sieve* (Taylor), or *Nothing Ever Happens Here* (York). Give them previews of each book on the suggested list, and let them choose ones they prefer to read. Have students keep journals in which they record their daily personal reactions to the reading. Stress that the journals are not to be graded and that the students are free to discuss their books in any manner they please, as long as they write a certain number of pages weekly. When a student completes a book, have an individual conference which might begin by discussing journal reactions—positively, of course.

591-I *(Restructure/Plots) "Summarily Speaking"*

Unfortunately, some teachers assume that they alone can handle the summarizing of major and minor events in works studied. In an exercise calling for plot summaries, students write down in chronological order the main events of a section they have just read. This gives the teacher an indication of how well pupils are keeping up with reading assignments. Let the summaries serve as springboards for discussions.

592-G *(Restructure/Skits) "Lit Skit"*

To evaluate student understanding of character development in an assigned novel, let two or more students present a skit dramatizing character-revealing scenes from the story. For example, in Salinger's *Catcher in the Rye,* Holden and Mr. Spencer consider Holden's exam. Holden does not want it read aloud; Mr. Spencer insists on it. Two students build on this impromptu scene, each trying to keep the character in role.

593-C *(Restructure/Skits) "Skit-Lit"*

The learning accomplished by accurately and successfully portraying character development in a skit (as in idea 592) can be transferred into an original, relevant situation reflecting modern-day crises. The entire class can then discuss how well each character was interpreted. The best situations grow from areas of student interest: relating to peers, getting along, socializing, examining the weird and grotesque, or finding an inner peace.

OVERVIEW

594–C   *(Compare/Games) "Concentration Creation"*

Especially helpful and entertaining for junior high classes is a literary game much like "Concentration." In this simplified form, the students match author cards or questions with the correct title. Each correct match uncovers a section of a rebus puzzle which, when fully revealed, depicts either a notable quotation from one of the works studied or from another famous title. To win the game the student must also guess the rebus. Of course, the game can also cover short stories and poetry—or any other forms. Use large sheets of tag board or newsprint mounted on the bulletin board for overcoming the logistics problem.

595–I   *(Compare/Papers) "Pardon My Melancholy, Baby"*

If teachers expect students to be creative in their written work, they would do well to phrase assignments imaginatively. The return on an assignment like "Write an 800-word paper on 'How Lavinia in O'Neill's *Mourning Becomes Electra* Can Be Compared with Her Legendary Greek Counterpart' " predictably is going to be dull and repetitious. But asking students to contrast their personal knowledge of or direct experience with one instance of Lavinia's behavior is assurance that there will be as many uniquely individual papers as there are students in the class.

596–C   *(Extrapolate/Games) "Abstraction Attraction"*

A lively way to approach understanding of metaphors so frequently used in literature is a game called "Abstractions." Everyone guesses which class member is the subject a player has in mind by asking questions such as "What magazine is he most like?" or "What would she like to do on a vacation?" Then the class can discuss what traits were conjured up by certain abstractions and why. The teacher observing this activity will be able to tell if the students are understanding the concept of metaphor.

597–C   *(Extrapolate/Games) "Team Up"*

In the manner of charades, divide the class into two or more teams. Give one member from each team the name of a character or describe a situation. The member whose team is up first chooses someone from his or her team who most resembles the character to be guessed (or the characters involved in a situation). The team member then gives stage directions to the character(s) for carrying out activities that will help other members of the team guess the right answer. The "actors," of course, do not know the answer either and must follow through in the same impromptu manner as the "director."

598-I *(Extrapolate/Illustrations) "Can You Picture that?"*

As an alternative to the usual written report on a piece of literature, each student draws or locates pictures for a collage to illustrate the main theme of one's selection. Pertinent quotations may accompany the illustrations. Display finished projects on the bulletin board. By this approach the student reveals if he or she has caught the essence of the literary work. Best of all, the typical and overused written book report can be omitted.

599-I *(Extrapolate/Journals) "Logging Literature"*

Journals can be very useful in teaching and evaluating literature as well as composition. Instead of asking students to write extensive papers, allow them to keep journals in which they record anything they want—opinions, emotions, anger, arguments—while they read their assigned or free readings. Several times each term set aside a class period to share these ideas. The instructor reads the journals, regularly writing comments to encourage additional exploration and development.

600-I *(Extrapolate/Papers) "Pick a Card"*

Instead of a constant "diet" of written book reports, allow students to use this writing time for more reading. Yet, some written "report" can be made. Students write short reports on 4 × 6 file cards (author, title, subject, brief commentary, and personal reaction). These cards are kept in the room for two reasons: to interest other students to read the book, and to enable the teacher to make up a question or two for an impromptu evaluation while monitoring reading assignments for individuals. Sometimes the teacher uses the cards to locate students who can share what they have read when it best fits into the class lesson.

601-I *(Extrapolate/Pictures) "Unfolding Personalities"*

To determine if students understand the role of characters in a play or novel, have each student prepare a file folder on one character. These personality folders include on one page a montage of pictures portraying the subject's personality—appearance, likes, dislikes, interests, occupation, and the like—

on one side, and on the other a detailed explanation of the illustrations. When completed, the picture portion of each card or folder is displayed for class discussion and identification. How well the pictures reflect the role of the character will reveal how well the student understood the character. (See related idea 34 for student personality folders.)

602-G   *(Extrapolate/Talks) "Need to Lead"*

One way to tell if students understand what they read is to let them share with the class. Try this for small groups. Assign each literature book section to a group. They must plan their own original way to handle a presentation. They need not do all the work, but they must take leader-roles. Just moving from lit book selection to selection (or section) in the same way— teacher leading always—can be deadly.

603-C   *(Identify/Games) "Enveloped in Lit"*

Test knowledge of novels or plays through subjective or objective questions in this game approach. Write a series of questions on slips of paper placed in sealed envelopes (sealed for heightened suspense), one for each student. Progressing in some sequence, each student takes turns opening his or her envelope and giving an impromptu answer. If the student cannot reply, the question is offered to the class. This becomes a good method for assessing preparedness before a test, for a review, or as a game. The students may even be graded on answers.

604-C   *(Identify/Games) "Pair of Aces"*

After reading the works of several authors, the class can play "Who Am I?" Before the class begins, each student writes several sentences about an author. Then, either in pairs or two or more teams, participants try to guess the author. The score is based on the number of statements needed to identify the author. The fewer the statements, the higher the score. This same procedure can be used for characters or any other aspect of literature study.

605-C   *(Identify/Games) "This Is Your Strife"*

Pupils need involvement and opportunities to express themselves in the classroom. A "This Is Your Life" review provides that opportunity and will also show who is informed about authors, poets, playwrights, and artists studied in class. A skillful group can lay the groundwork by preparing a number of biographies listing key events in the lives of those studied. Through the type of conversational dialogue used in the popular television show, the clues are given so two teams can compete for points in making the right guesses to identify the "mystery person."

606-I *(Judge/Book Reports) "Atypical Not a Typical Report"*

Measuring a student's knowledge of a book is most frequently through book reports (perhaps "book reviews" is a better name). Try this variation—"focused reports." Example openers might be:

" (Name of book) has everything I want to find in a book."

"Some incidents in _____ really stretched my imagination."

"If I could rewrite _____, I would change. . . ."

607-I *(Judge/Conferences) "Do-It-Yourself Reading"*

To enhance those free reading periods which allow students to pursue their own reading interests, some adjustment to environment is needed. If books or funds are available, provide a special reading room or arrange for converting a section of the library for this purpose. Contacts with publishers or distributors will often succeed in obtaining a supply of free, or very reasonably priced, appealing paperbacks. Changes in evaluation may also be in order. Students should be told they will be evaluated on the amount of reading, on the quality of choices, and on their understanding. Individual conferences are the most effective because they allow for differences both in ability and interest. Most of all, students learn best by doing what they enjoy most. Book reading is no exception.

608-T *(Judge/Questions) "Why How?"*

In directing literature discussions, ask "how" and "why" questions, not "who, what, when, or where." For example, "How do we know what will happen at the end of the story?" not "What happens at the end of the story?" Or ask "Why does Santiago want to catch the giant marlin?" and not, "Who is Santiago?"

609-C *(Judge/Talk) "Debate Is De Bait"*

Debate—the intelligent, constructive exchange of ideas and opinions—is one of the most valuable learning and sharing situations the classroom can help develop. Used in the right manner, it can be a most effective way to criticize literature. In this activity the teacher can act as Socratic guide, Devil's advocate, prompter, arbiter, and interpreter, offering alternative opinions rather than giving the "correct" one or "the truth."

610-G *(Restructure/Discussion) "Past in Review"*

Divide the class into small groups, each responsible for a particular author the class has studied during the term. On an appointed day, each group presents its panel, giving in-depth analysis of the author. They may wish to conclude with a brief quiz. In this way students do their own reviewing.

611-G *(Restructure/Games) "Exciting Citations"*

Covering literature in a classroom need not be routine. For instance, at appropriate times the class can be divided into two groups. The teacher (or student) gives clues (questions, statements) to elicit information about key episodes in the novel. The group that gives the best response and actually cites the desired portion of the story gets two points. The group reaching twenty points first is the winner.

612-C *(Restructure/Games) "Game for a Game?"*

Based on the TV game "Tic Tac Dough," this game serves as a good literature review. A Tic Tac Toe frame with the conventional nine sections is drawn on the chalkboard. Students have submitted questions on cards covering nine areas concerned with a literature review: authors, characters, plots, quotations, settings, themes, critical reviews, true or false statements, outstanding parallels—or any other pertinent areas as substitutes for the nine. These questions are placed in separate boxes marked with the category. The boxes are laid out in rows of three each way to emulate the game board. The first of two teams selects a category, as the question drawn at random from that box is read. If the person can answer, a circle or an X is placed in the graph area that matches that category. Added excitement comes with having to answer a question simply to block the other team. The boxes may be switched every other round so that a player could stick with a favorite category.

613-G, C *(Restructure/Games) "Lit Wits"*

Following several weeks or possibly an entire semester with students engaged in outside readings, the class divides into two equal teams for competition between those who prefer modern and those who prefer classical literature. All students working in groups within the two large teams prepare questions on all aspects of their preferred readings: comprehending form, plot, implied meanings, and themes; clarifying settings and characters; and judging craftsmanship. Each group preparing questions gets an identifying alphabetical letter to place on all its questions so they won't get called upon to answer their own. Then the questions written on cards with answers on the back are collected so that a quizmaster or mistress on whom everyone can agree can ask selected questions to the large teams, each participant taking turns in some planned way. Points are tallied, and the winning team is treated to a party by the losers.

614-C *(Restructure/Games) "Question My Answer"*

Here's a literature review game that all ability levels will enjoy. Make up five categories within the work of literature being studied, e.g., Characters/Settings, Story Line, Main Plot, Subplot, and Implied Meanings. Five teams frame four questions and answers in an assigned category. When called upon, one team member draws a question from each of the other four teams. His or her group must answer these within a time limit. For each question they answer correctly, they get one point; for each incorrectly answered question, the team submitting it gets two points. At the end of the playing time, the team with the most points wins.

615-C *(Restructure/Games) "Play Ball"*

Middle or junior high students enjoy this game in the spring when baseball is in the air. Divide the class into two teams standing on opposite sides of the room. The teacher "throws out" questions to the first team: questions on authors, their lives, and their works. Each question answered correctly is a base hit, if incorrectly, an out. Three outs for the first team give the other team members a turn "at bat." Use an overhead transparency of a baseball diamond to show progress.

616-C *(Restructure/Puzzles) "Sometimes a Crossword"*

Instead of the typical ways to review short stories, plays, novels, or poetry, involve the students in building games and puzzles. Since the crossword puzzle has proven to be a great brain teaser and a good way to approach study questions, teachers spend hours constructing them. Let students build these puzzles, singly, in groups, or in pairs. The best ones are chosen for the class to work.

617-C *(Restructure/Puzzles) "Switchword Puzzle"*

As a variation of the regular crossword puzzle approach to review titles, characters, authors, and the like, pull a switch.

Bring to class a puzzle already filled in. Ask the students to make up the clues to the answers. This provides variety when crosswords may be overused.

POETRY

618–I, C   *(Identify/Discussions) "A Quo-Test"*

Some students like to memorize entire poems. Others should be encouraged to attempt memorizing portions of popular, well-known poems. The satisfaction gained from being literate among peers and family will outweigh for some the necessary practice to improve ability to recall. The memorization can be shared effectively through class discussions in which one student recites a memorized portion and the others guess the source from a background of poetry studied in common during the year. Additional discussions can cover such matters as meanings, figurative language, sensory images, sounds, rhythm, and tone of the lines presented.

619–C   *(Judge/Audiotapes) "Orally Speaking"*

Before the class meets, volunteers who are some of the better readers tape record individual interpretations of the same poem. After hearing the tapes, the class selects the best interpretations, giving reasons for their choices. This exercise covers many hard-to-get-at items for poetry understanding.

620–G   *(Judge/Music) "Five by Five"*

Since musical lyrics are a form of poetry, go music. Five groups of students review the lyrics of the five most popular hits—one for each group. First, among themselves, each group criticizes verse quality based on what they know about poetic structure. They may even rewrite the lyrics to improve the verse, keeping in mind the music. Then the class is given the opportunity to react to each group presentation.

621–C   *(Judge/Recordings) "Can You Beat This?"*

In your next poetry unit, encourage students to build a room library of their favorite record albums. Over a period of time, by class vote and a process of elimination, select the four best songs. Rate them 1 to 4. Write the lyrics on the board and have the class assess the qualities that make these songs so

good: the rhythm, beat, lyrics, emotion, or whatever. Then find
poetry with these same qualities and follow the same procedure
as above. If one of the students plays the drums, let that student bring drumsticks and practice board to beat out the time
for some selections. To assess learning, let students write comparison papers showing how both mediums have many of the
same qualities but how poetry has greater artistry of language,
more depth, and deeper feeling.

622–C   *(Judge/Sentences) "Nice and Concise"*

When reading shorter poems, such as Emily Dickinson's works,
the students can write one-sentence summaries of what seems
to be the main theme. Pass these around for class reaction.
This is a good way to judge understanding and to start discussion.

623–C   *(Judge/Talk) "Inner Action"*

Poetry is the product of a mind sensitive to innermost feelings
and to both natural and supernatural worlds. Encourage students to become aware of this sensitivity. Also emphasize an
oral approach to poetry. Either assign a short poem or a passage in a longer poem to be memorized or read for a presentation to the class. Allow choices from the class anthology or
anyone's favorite. The class then evaluates each presentation,
noting the reader's manner of capturing and conveying the
intended feelings of the poet. This method calls for close examination of what lies behind each poem.

624–C   *(Restructure/Poems) "Scramble One"*

Type or write selected scrambled stanzas from popular poems
on separate pieces of paper. Pass out one complete set to each
class member. Ask the individuals to reorganize stanzas into
their original positions. Although this activity relates most to
"story line," it can also be used to check on structure.

SHORT STORY

625–I   *(Compare/Models) "Keep Plotting Along"*

After some study of the short story, use the following to see if
students can discriminate between good and trite plots. Begin
by describing a typical plot. Then provide three endings: one
improbable or even trite, another fairly predictable, and the
third original and very unusual. After rating them 1, 2, and 3,
students will hopefully show that they prefer the original
rather than the trite endings. Have about a dozen examples—
originals or from little-known short stories.

626-C *(Judge/Lists) "Plotting the Plot"*

To quickly check on the students' understanding of plot, hand out a list of incidents from a short story. The students are to check only those they feel are important to plot development. These checked items then form the basis for a discussion of plot development. Once the plot is well in mind, students can proceed to other aspects of the work.

627-C *(Restructure/Models) "Loose Interpretation"*

If a short story doesn't seem to have been well-liked and the class is dissatisfied with it for any number of reasons, try this. Let them see if they can do better by changing the characters and plot to the way they would have liked the story to happen.

628-C *(Analyze/Movies) "Seen and Heard"*

After reading a short story in class (for which a film is available), decide what the main points of the plot are, how they are sequenced, and why they are important to each other and to the entire story. In the next class meeting, review these points and show the film. Students compare the events of the film with those of the story, discovering similarities and differences. Considering "why" can be very interesting and informative.

629-C *(Experiment/Role Playing) "Playing Up the Ending"*

A useful device to give students practice in thinking "on their feet" is a modification of the old *commedia dell'arte*. After a short story involving a few characters has been briefly summarized, have the students act out spontaneously what they think is the climax.

VOCABULARY

630-C *(Identify/Lists) "Get the Word"*

While reading an assigned book or short story, individuals find words they cannot define (or even pronounce). Each such word and the sentence in which the word appears (underlined) is placed on a 3×5 index card. These cards are then exchanged in some appropriate way so that students can help each other figure out a suitable definition. It's noisy but instructional, and the knowledge gained usually remains. The teacher could collect some of these cards for later evaluations.

12 Application

631–C *(Construct/Mixed Media) "Scraps of Life"*

After a drama unit, find out what students have learned about life as reflected in the play(s) just covered. The class could prepare one large collection of current events that reflect incidents that are closely parallel to those in the plays. This collection could be placed in a large scrapbook. But each student could also construct his or her own booklet to include newspaper or magazine articles—even advertisements—which make the past come alive. If *The Crucible* were the play, clippings might include examples of contemporary "witch hunting" to show that history can repeat itself.

632–C *(Construct/Newspapers) "Roman Gazette"*

After studying certain Shakespearean plays, such as *Julius Caesar,* construct a newspaper with students contributing articles, crossword puzzles, cartoons, and advertising written in the vernacular of Shakespeare's time. Suggested articles might focus on Caesar's assassination or soothsaying, or there might be a feature on Portia's household hints. Choose a staff that includes an editor, typist, a few star reporters, and an artist to be responsible for the layout. The final product can be displayed in class or in a hall display case. It could also be printed and distributed throughout the school.

633–C *(Construct/Pictures) "Seen Scenes"*

As part of a drama unit, encourage the amateur photographers in the class to make a photo story of scenes from the play(s). Students pose in tableau fashion with minimum props and costumes. It is surprising how effective a bedsheet can look in a black and white picture. Make a hall bulletin board display using quoted lines from the play to identify each scene.

634–C *(Perform/Play) "Mirror, Mirror"*

Drama, it is often said, is a mirror of life and ourselves. After reading one or more plays, students assume roles of characters in the play but not in the context of the play. Instead, they must justify their conduct or actions in the play based on the demands of modern society.

635–C   *(Perform/Play) "Play Day"*

One way to create interest in any play is to update the script for a class presentation. After reading a good family play like *I Remember Mama* or a one-act play such as *Happy Journey to Camden and Trenton,* the class can re-create the key scenes or the entire play using any modern ethnic or regional approach. Keep the basic theme and characters' names but change their personalities and lines. This helps foster the slice-of-life about good drama.

636–I   *(Perform/Play) "Putting Them On"*

After studying plays, choose a good one-act play for the class to act out instead of reading it in the usual fashion. Members of the class do the tryouts, directing, acting, and producing. Some might design simple backgrounds painted on large sheets of wrapping paper. If the finished product is good, put it on for the entire school.

637–C   *(Perform/Recordings) "For the Record"*

Plays are often more meaningful to actors and an audience when read silently. Suggest several one-act plays, one to be chosen by the class for a tape-recorded radio performance or videotape. Students must plan narration, sound effects, background music, and so on. Tapes could be exchanged between two classes for sharing.

638–C   *(Perform/Videotapes) "Dry Run"*

If the school has a videotape recorder, student filmmakers will find it useful for running through scripts and trying out camera angles before committing the action to the permanency and expense of movie film.

639–G   *(Solve/Mixed Media) "Switcheroo"*

Divide the class into small groups and assign a particular scene from a play being studied to each of the groups, who will present the material in any way other than a dramatic script. Some may choose a short story format, others a photo essay, still others may write a radio script or a series of tableaus. Each group then presents the new version for the class. It is interesting to see the different interpretations of plot and character.

640-I *(Solve/Mixed Media) "The Play's Their Thing"*

When working with students of widely varying ability levels, allow for a variety of applications of learnings. The entire class can study the story line and characterizations. Abler students can go on to learn the basic theater conventions, enhancing the understanding and enjoyment of drama. The most advanced can study the technical aspects of play production. They might do a research paper on costuming or scene building. The many facets of drama accommodate individual differences.

641-I *(Speak/Discussions) "Review the Reviews"*

After seeing or reading a contemporary play, students search newspaper library archives to locate reviews of the play when it was first produced. Some reviews can be shared through discussions. This approach encourages students to work with back issues of periodicals or microfilm copies.

642-I *(Speak/Role Playing) "Behind the Scenes"*

Naturally, before a play can be performed on stage, it must be developed through a series of steps. Select a popular play as the hypothetical model. Assign each student a position: stockholder, theater manager, ticket manager, costumer, advertiser, producer, actor, and others. Each student must research how his or her role works in the real situation. Students then share this information with the rest of the class. Very often this aspect of drama is left out. It shouldn't be.

643-I *(Write/Papers) "Hand Them a Line"*

On cards the teacher presents famous lines from plays (identifiable by the quotations). Even though several students may have different quotes from the same play, each student gets a card and must write a short paper explaining such lines as Biff in *Death of a Salesman* saying, "I'm a dime a dozen," or Frankie in *Member of the Wedding* saying, "All people belong to 'we' except me." These can be shared by the entire class.

644-I *(Write/Plays) "Being Play-writes"*

Motivate aspiring actors and writers to try their wings by following these simple directions. On a half sheet of paper sketch an imaginary scene, complete with props and characters. Underneath, list the characters involved in the picture and write a brief description about what is happening. From this sketch, each one then writes his or her own one-act play or one scene using that setting and those characters. Several plays are selected for staging. The authors are their own directors. Finally, the plays may be judged by the class for qualities discussed earlier.

MEDIA

645–I   *(Construct/Book Reports, Mixed Media) "Talking Display"*

After reading a book, students take turns using available bulletin board space. They fill the board with pictures, quotes, and original art. Each item bears a number. These numbers help identify items mentioned on a taped narration from a tape player placed on a small table next to the display. Earphones permit individuals to tune in on the would-be written book report which now has taken a new and exciting form aided by the display material.

646–C   *(Perform/Role Playing) "An Inner View"*

Following the reading of a novel, play, short story, or poem, two members of the class pose as author and literary critic on a radio interview show. By projecting themselves into these roles, students will have a nearly first-hand experience of coming to grips with and articulating the intentions of the work. They will also apply past learnings to forming useful questions for examining a piece of literature. This process may be handled in small groups or with an entire class.

647–I   *(Perform/Book Reports, Mixed Media) "Bringing Out the Artist"*

WOOPS!

Surprise a class by suggesting that their book reports can take just about any format other than written or oral: collages, photographs, scrapbooks, poems, dioramas, models, even cartoons and original paintings or drawings. Another approach is to use one project such as listed here as part of an oral book report. This helps spice up the report and gives students an opportunity to express creativity and spare the audience from three days of "My book is _____. It was written by _____. It is about _____. And I like it because _____."

648–I   *(Speak/Television) "TV by the Week"*

As a regular Monday assignment ask one student to report on worthwhile TV movies or specials scheduled through the following Sunday. Very often these television specials and documentaries tie in with much of the literature studied in school. The reporter can strengthen the oral presentation by having available printed materials supplied by newspapers or network broadcasters. The focus might be on the purpose of the programs, originality of plot, effectiveness of settings and special effects, quality of the acting and dialogue, or the application to our own lives.

649–I *(Write/Book Reports) "Boost or Bust a Book"*

Since most students are very familiar with the format of television commercials, let them adapt this method for "pushing" or "panning" a book or any type of literature they either like or dislike. They should include some quotes from the work itself. This style of book reporting sparks new interest in an old subject.

650–I *(Write/Commercials) "Getting Personal"*

As a means of reemphasizing personification, draw students' attention to the many TV or media commercials that employ the device: "Let your fingers do the walking" (yellow pages). "Fly the friendly skies . . ." (air line). Students will be able to suggest many more. Following this activity each student creates a hypothetical product and commercial employing personification.

651–I *(Write/Critiques, Films) "Film Extras"*

For extra credit, students review films adapted from novels or plays. They write critiques which include how the film and the story differ, how certain elements were kept intact in the film version, how characters remained or didn't remain true to the originals, and so forth. Such an exercise serves to sharpen literary perception and to focus on the different techniques.

NONFICTION

652–I *(Speak/Book Reports, Discussion) "Friendly Persuasion"*

A study of persuasive literature and techniques can be a vital experience when students are given a stake in planning and carrying out the activities. A student chooses, reads, and shares a book with the class by defending or rejecting a certain point of view expressed in it. Lively debate ensues when the class's ideas clash. The fringe benefits of this assignment are discipline in logical thinking and the demand for exact verbal expression.

653-I *(Write/Biographies) "VIP Lit"*

Develop a "Great Persons" unit to give each student an opportunity to explore the life of an author he or she has read and admired. Culminating activities may run the gamut but should include some writing. As all the books and information are located, the student also learns more about using the library and its variety of resources.

NOVELS

654-C *(Construct/Books) "Novel Novels"*

Wouldn't it seem logical that a student could prove real literary knowledge of a novel's structure by writing one? Yes, students can write a novel—a novella, which is a very short novel. A novella does not take any more time to write than a typical research paper. Further, the novella might just evoke more student interest and possible continuance.

655-I *(Construct/Display) "Boxing Show"*

Students type out a brief description of one conflict or the climax from a chosen novel or short story. Then, in a small cardboard box, they re-create that scene in miniature, using toy figures, dolls, cutouts, drawings, or whatever seems to work. They finish the project by covering the box attractively and pasting their names, the book title, author, and the typed description on one side of the box where viewers can see it. These dioramas are then placed on exhibit.

656-T, G *(Construct/Mixed Media) "Meet You at the Service Station"*

Secondary teachers can use an idea from elementary teachers who use learning centers or the station approach to teaching. Set up around the classroom (or library) five to ten work areas where students can apply what they have learned after reading a novel. Groups of five to seven students rotate through the stations. Printed assignments at the stations direct individuals (or groups) through projects such as skimming the novel for specific reasons, constructing things that allow abstracting through symbols, drawing or completing any artwork, listening to tapes and taking notes for a purpose, viewing films and filmstrips, reading related short works of themes similar to the novel, engaging in group discussions, or researching one or several topics that relate to the novel. A culminating activity would finally bring the class together again.

657–I *(Construct/Mixed Media) "Scrap of an Idea"*

After studying a novel let the students prepare a Character Sketchbook, with each page containing an accurate, easily recognized character sketch. Students may cut out pictures from magazines or draw their own. Below each illustration they might place a caption, possibly a quote from the book or a brief explanation why the picture or drawing is appropriate for the character. Since this activity succeeds well with ninth and tenth graders, this cut-and-paste approach is not to be limited to grade school use.

658–I *(Construct/Discussion, Displays) "Alas, Poor Silas"*

One approach to the study of a nineteenth century Victorian novel, in which the development or destruction of one character occurs *(Silas Marner* or *The Mayor of Casterbridge),* would be to discuss how this character might act if faced with the varied problems of today's industrial society. In preparing for the discussion, students make montages or other simple displays illustrating the elements in today's world that would interest the character under study and would affect him or her in some way.

659–I *(Perform/Book Reports, Role Playing) "Characteristically Nine"*

Basically there are nine methods of revealing a character in a book. Students should know these by the end of the year. Let them apply what they learned by each selecting one famous character from literature read in or out of class. The presenter goes through the following steps illustrating what the character is like. (A partner may be used for role playing.)

1. Describing the person's clothing and environment
2. Telling the kind of person he or she is
3. Showing how the person acts
4. Demonstrating speech patterns
5. Relating character's thoughts
6. Revealing what other people say *about* the character
7. Demonstrating how other people talk *to* the character
8. Showing how others react because of the character
9. Demonstrating how the character reacts to others.

If done well, a "book report" has been completed.

660–I *(Perform/Role Playing) "Take on the Author"*

Encourage the students to apply their knowledge of characterization by letting several pretend they are characters in the novel and are having a conversation with or writing a letter to the author. They may question the author's motivation or rea-

soning, complain, compliment, suggest ways to make the character look better, offer another way to end the story, and so on.

661–G *(Perform/Skits) "Acting Out"*

In conjunction with reading and studying novels, discuss how
strongly authors are influenced by the times in which they
lived. Then let students put their knowledge to work. Divide
the class into groups, one group representing each literary
work studied. Let the groups produce skits depicting situations
typical to the era in which each writer wrote. Skits need not be
elaborate. (Four chairs with driver in front and two seated
behind can be a horse-drawn cab.)

662–G *(Speak/Discussion) "Four on the Floor"*

Divide the class into four symposia, each to characterize
through research and example
one of these four areas of
English literature: classical,
neoclassical, romantic, and
modern. Class time can be given
to group meetings, although
out-of-class work should be encouraged. The final two weeks
of the unit are devoted to presenting the symposia research
as imaginatively and differ-
ently as possible. One group may take a straight discussion
approach. Another might videotape a presentation. Others could
do a slide-tape program. The possibilities are limitless. Let the
students' imaginations reign.

663–G *(Speak/Discussion) "Let Your People Go"*

Allow students to form small groups, each group reading a different novel and presenting a panel discussion on the book to
the class. Consult a list of novels appropriate to the age and
interest level of the pupils to guide choices. By this method the
class is introduced to several novels instead of the customary
one or two. Invariably students are enticed to read novels on
which others report.

664–G *(Speak/Discussion) "Panel the Room"*

Give college-bound or advanced classes an opportunity to express themselves orally by arranging a unit in which they
work in groups to study additional books having the same
theme as a novel read by the entire class. Each group takes a

different book, and all the information is brought together in a class discussion.

665–C *(Speak/Role Playing) "Opportunity Mocks"*

Many classes have had successful mock trials. Students who desire to be lawyers or actors do very well in this activity. Opportunities to use debate skills will occur, for example, in determining the guilt or innocence of a character (before continuing the reading to discover how the author handled it.) Another approach would be to try the author for libel or for writing prurient literature for adolescents. Staff the trial with judge, jury, prosecuting and defense attorneys, and others.

666–I *(Speak, Write/Book Reports) "Real Characters"*

Students compare or contrast a character in their books to a person they know in real life or someone they have heard or read about. This activity helps students see that most novels are true to life, and it encourages them to become more critical of reading choices.

667–I *(Write/Papers) "Precise Précis"*

Following the reading of a novel, e.g, Hemingway's *A Farewell to Arms* or *For Whom the Bell Tolls,* assign a one-page précis of the novel. Ask students to try writing it in the style of Hemingway or as a book reviewer on the staff of an important periodical. The requirements of précis writing—concise exact expression—demand a thoughtful review of all the material studied.

668–I *(Write/Papers) "Families of Yesterday and Today"*

After reading a novel such as *Tom Sawyer,* students write papers comparing the relationship between Tom and Aunt Polly. Or, based on *Life with Father* as the related reading, they compare that family with their own. Or, for the really advanced student, compare family life three ways: Tom Sawyer's, Father's, *and* the student's.

669–I *(Write/Papers) "Take Four or Five"*

Throughout the semester individuals read at least four books by the same author. This array can be the basis of a critical paper comparing the several works, tracing trends, similarities, differences, stylistic matters, and so on. By studying one author in depth, students gain a better understanding of how he or she writes.

OVERVIEW

670–I   *(Construct/Anecdotes, Bulletin Boards) "All Aboard"*

In the study of a certain historical period of English literature, students are frequently exposed to major facts and happenings of that era. How these facts and happenings affect the personal lives of the authors makes the subject alive and arouses student interest. Encourage pupils to be on the lookout for literary anecdotes that they can share with their classmates. This could be a bulletin board project.

671–I   *(Construct/Book Reports, Artwork) "Tailor-Made Jackets"*

For a different kind of book report, students make book jackets for their selections. Along with the title, they create an illustration of an important incident in the book. They may use any medium (chalk, crayons, paints, magazine cut-outs, etc.) Inside the book cover, on the two flaps, they are to fasten a brief book report including a summary of the illustrated incident. The jackets can be fashioned directly on the books they depict or can be mounted on the bulletin board.

672–I   *(Construct/Book Reports, Displays) " 'Now' Book Reports"*

Add some art to the room decor. Using large poster board, students prepare magazine picture montages that depict an idea, the theme, or key scenes from a book. Pictures can share space with quotations and key words from the book. The purpose, of course, is to entice others to read the books "postered" around the room.

673–I   *(Construct/Book Reports) "So Many, Many Ways"*

Here, in the proverbial nut shell, are some fifty or more paired down ideas for either complementing or replacing book reports: depict scenes, make posters, produce a movie (film, rolls, or flip book), use a flannel board, dress character dolls, create sand table scenes, record musical backgrounds, paint a mural, do excerpt reading, dramatize, role play characters, retell incidents, write a letter to a friend, compile a scrapbook, review a book, engage in conversations, illustrate a lecture, ask questions after a report, and give a sales talk or report the news. Others are round-table discussions, puppet shows, chalk talks, pantomimes, critiques, time lines, maps, book jackets, movie scripts, interviews, spot advertisements, peep boxes, three-dimensional scenes, mobiles, costumed character(s), book previews, collages, book award ceremonies, and time capsules. Students might write a newspaper out of the book's era or even bring in the book's author—the sky is the limit.

674-I *(Perform/Book Reports, Role Playing) "Five Pluses"*

Let the class present oral book reports in which they impersonate the main character. This exercise has several desirable effects: (1) allows students to empathize with characters and obtain a greater sense of development and mood, (2) helps students relax since they are not themselves, (3) serves to interest rest of the class, (4) makes it possible for the teacher to verify student understanding, and (5) allows "characters" to be characters, which often spells f-u-n.

675-C *(Construct/Magazines) "Read All about Us"*

As a culminating activity to a literature unit, guide the class in publishing a literary magazine. It might contain reviews of books, plays, or essays that have been read by the class, or perhaps original student pieces. All art work, layout, writing, and printing is done by the students. The teacher serves only as a resource person.

676-I *(Construct/Pictures) "Visual Reporting"*

Some students don't speak well and some don't write well. Some do neither well. Let students (who request this) use a small bulletin board area toward which class desks can be faced. The students, having searched through "tons" of picture magazines each English room should have, presents a pictorial summary of the book—typical settings, how the characters might look, several characters speaking (captions attached), etc. With this incentive and security, the reticent reporter will get up and do a grand job narrating the display, and when finished—lo! . . . a book report!

677-G *(Speak, Write/Book Reports, Discussion) "Great Integrator"*

Integrate subject matter whenever possible. Work with the social studies teacher on a Civil War unit. English students read Civil War historical fiction while they study that era in social studies. Expand the "arena" by involving the drama coach in producing a related play or choral reading—maybe even a musical by adding the music teacher to the team.

678-T *(Speak, Write/Book Reports) "Free for All"*

Often teachers limit book reports to fiction classics (usually their own preferences) or books they think should be read. Stu-

dents should be permitted at times to use biographies, autobiographies, or works of literary critics. If students want to
read a nonfiction book, they should be encouraged, not discouraged. The book report form is more easily adjusted than
student interests.

679-I *(Write/Papers) "Quote Note"*

On the bulletin board post a fairly well-known quote from
prose or poetry. For extra credit or a continuing contest, students identify the author and the specific work from which it
came. Leave the quote on the board for several days so students have enough time to research and discuss it in a short
paper. Why is it an important quote?

POETRY

680-I *(Construct/Books) "Saying It Poetically"*

Let the entire class join in constructing a poetry scrapbook.
Students cut out interesting poems found in newspapers and
magazines and organize them into sections of the book. These
sections can be on meaning, form, societal struggle, or whatever. Such a project appeals to nearly everyone's interests and
motivates them to read poetry other than that assigned or discussed in class. The scrapbook clearly demonstrates the variety
of situations put into verse. The completed book can be displayed on a dictionary pedestal in the main hall or be donated
to some worthy organization or person.

681-I *(Construct/Pictures) "Poetry Cut-Up"*

Each student chooses a poem about which he or she has particularly strong feelings. The student draws or locates pictures
that interpret personal feelings about certain stanzas. These
selections usually initiate interesting discussions. This approach lends itself to a sound-slide presentation. If students
can be persuaded to donate their efforts, a teacher could have
a collection of visual presentations to be used for future study.

682-I *(Construct, Write/Pictures, Poems) "Steeped in Poetry"*

After having explored the world of contemporary poets (they're
more likely to grab student interest than those of 'yore), each
student selects a poet whose work really seems attractive. Next
comes in-depth reading of more of the poet's work as well as
biographies. Then comes stage two: presenting one of the
poet's works to the class. Background music and other audio-
visual aids are encouraged. Following the reading, the student

leads the class in a discussion: speaker, theme, tone, imagery, diction, rhythm, and meter. The final step is writing a paper on the poet and his or her contributions to the field.

683-I *(Construct, Write/Pictures, Poems) "Pick't Sures"*

Have students locate several related pictures that have strong emotional impact. Let this be the motivation to write a short poem attempting to catch the same mood.

684-I *(Perform/Dance) "Let's Dance"*

Poetry can be interpreted kinesthetically as well as literally. Let students select a line or stanza from an especially descriptive or musical poem and try to interpret the message, mood, and rhythm through modern dance. If students are too reticent, perhaps a dance class in the school or community would welcome such a creative project.

685-I *(Peform/Music) "Live, on Record"*

Music-minded students can choose a favorite poem and apply an appropriate melody to it, appropriate to tone, movement, and subject matter. They can then either sing it, accompanied by a musical instrument, or possibly record it on tape.

686-I *(Write/Books) "An Anthology and Annotations"*

To help create the feeling that poetry is an expression of an individual experience, encourage each class member to make a personal anthology of original poems or those written by others. Each selection should be followed by a brief comment on why it fits into the collection.

687-I *(Write/Poems) "Poetry Add-itions"*

After they have learned various poetic forms, such as the sonnet, ballad, blank and free verse, students write their own verse using words or lines cut from magazine display ads—not copied, *cut!* The difference in typography adds another dimension to the poem. Poems can also be written so that their words are shaped into the contour of the subject. Lines may be constructed tightly, loosely, or in vertical or horizontal shapes to depict certain moods, too. Sometimes these poems are called "concrete poems."

688–I *(Write/Essay) "Take the High Road"*

Students read "The Road Not Taken" (Robert Frost). Relating the poem to its general theme—blazing a trail vs. conformity—the class writes a short one-page paper on how the poem would have ended had the narrator taken the *other* road.

689–C *(Write/Magazines) "Booking Poets"*

A common classroom activity is a poetry magazine to which students may contribute original poetry. More unique are mini-mags. Each student decides on a particular interest and "publishes" a booklet of specialized poetry: humor, western, nature, inspirational, patriotic, and so on. These booklets can be developed over a long period of time (say, a half year). Students develop their own mini-magazines or can work with a partner to gain experience in several areas. The students' magazines can then be displayed later in the year when parents can visit or at a Creative Arts Festival.

690–I *(Write/Poems) "Good Trips"*

To motivate an aesthetic awareness of the beauty all around, arrange a "senses field trip." This could be merely imaginary, though students would undoubtedly prefer an actual trip to a lake, the business section downtown, or a nearby park. Students list impressions at random as they become aware of them. Then each could find or write poems relating to what he or she felt and experienced. Have students use the flow of consciousness technique activated by their being reminded of a past experience by the sight or sound of something. Perhaps a familiar odor calls forth an early childhood experience. The polishing can be done later.

691–I *(Write/Poems) "Life-Lifting Poetry"*

It's a common project for students to illustrate a poem with pictures from magazines, photographs, or drawings of their own. Although this helps make a poem more visual and meaningful, more could be done with this idea. For example, some classes have recycled old greeting cards. Using the illustrations, they replaced the messages with appropriate lines from famous poems or from their originals. The cards were then sent to the elderly, to shut-ins, or the hospitalized. The class artists might do the illustrations as well.

692–I *(Write/Poems) "Poetry Pot"*

Bring a bean pot to class. Paint on it the words *Poetry Pot*. During the year, invite students to drop into the pot their ideas for poems on cards or slips of paper. Just the first line or a title is enough of an idea to create a poem or two after having studied poetry. Ordinary things make the best poems—water dripping into a bucket or puddle, a butterfly on a flower, the thermos bottle that wouldn't open at lunch, waiting for an important grade—all just seeds that could sprout when taken out of that pot from time to time to be worked on in class. Individuals can dip into the bean pot, too, for ideas.

693–G *(Write/Poems) "Together We Conquer Poetry"*

Pupils need more evidence that poets are ordinary people just like themselves, sensitive to everyday events. Occasionally one of these events triggers a response, which compels the poet to express in verse. Thus, encourage the class to share similar experiences. At first, limit their audience to small informal groups. Each student-poet brings his or her poem to the group where it is read, interpreted, and changed if need be. This procedure is repeated until a half dozen or so poems emerge from the group. Then they vote to select the best one to be discussed with the entire class. Each group submits one poem and the entire class selects the best one.

SHORT STORY

694–G *(Construct/Mixed Media) "Picturing a Story"*

Assign groups of five or six pupils a different short story. Each group decides what the story line is and how best to present it to the class. There are several possibilities: a graphic presentation on a bulletin board, a chalk drawing (traced lightly in advance and filled in as someone tells the story), skit, poem, slide-sound presentation, or even a lecture by a dynamic student.

695–I *(Perform/Mixed Media) "A Moving Story"*

Two essential components of a well-written story—dialogue and description—are vividly highlighted by the following demonstration. First, have the class dramatize a short episode with much dialogue and no stage movement. The second time through, let students combine dialogue and movement. Here, the value of description and narration as related to dialogue is demonstrated. Finally, have the class rewrite the episode using description but no dialogue. A successful attempt proves mastery of many literary techniques.

696-G   *(Perform/Play) "Everybody into the Act"*

Using a short story with much dialogue, let the class adapt the story into a play. One group does the writing, another plans the costumes and makeup, other groups choose appropriate music and sound effects, and still another group gives the actual performance. After the presentation, a group that has studied the art of criticism presents their critiques of the play and how it was produced. This project exemplifies the type needed to give everyone a task suited to interest and ability.

697-G   *(Write/Books) "Inspired Stories"*

From preliminary work on the Bible as literature and having studied short stories, students write a short story that has a biblical symbol, motif, or theme. Stories in the Bible have often been given a modern setting. The Bible itself is literature with many literary techniques that can be studied. Teachers can look for an increasing number of resource books for teaching the Bible as literature.

698-I,C   *(Write/Essay, Discussions) "Seeing Ourselves in Others"*

After reading a story like "The Secret Life of Walter Mitty," students write a short, one- or two-page paper reacting to Mitty. This should help them better understand themselves through their reactions to a literary figure. The variety of student reactions will stimulate discussion on the reasons for such differences. This way they learn to examine literature closely to see what evokes a calculated response and how this occurs.

699-I   *(Write/Movies, Short Stories) "Short Subject"*

Following a study of the short story, show a short film dealing with a situation in which the students can become very emotionally involved (a chase, a fight, or a race, for instance.) Each student is to imagine himself or herself as having experienced first-hand what occurred in the movie. Then, as an author wanting to share these moments, the student writes a brief narrative based on the episode. For useful feedback, discuss the film and the student versions, considering how individual opinions of the facts vary. View the film again to discover the real facts. Discuss what can influence viewer or reader perception and a writer's viewpoint. This exercise helps illustrate the fact that the reader—and not just the author— brings meaning to the page.

700–G   *(Write/Papers) "Learn by Doing"*

Students cooperatively write an original short story after discussing and planning characterization, plot development, theme, and so on. Some write the beginning, others the middle and the end. The project is then read aloud and discussed to determine if the finished product met all of the requirements of a short story.

Part Four

READING

13 Introduction

Note to teacher about Part Four: Reading and writing skills should be developed together, each supplementing the other to double or triple the chances of learning in one operation. This section on reading includes hints for teaching both reading and writing, as well as listening and speaking, and is especially for students with learning problems. But ideas could be changed slightly for any ability level.

JOURNALISM

701-T   *(Read/Newspapers) "Paper Route"*

A unit on the newspaper helps develop the slow reader's ability to think critically about what he or she reads. It also arouses reading interest in readily available periodicals. A typical unit includes judging the logic of editorials, investigating language use in advertising, studying the appeal of human interest stories, and comparing different treatments of the same news item covered by several publishers.

MEDIA

702-T   *(Discover/Topics) "Treasure Chest"*

To stimulate the flow of ideas for writing exercises, the teacher can bring to class a Chinese wicker suitcase, a chest, or simply a decorated box loaded with interesting collections of pictures, magazines, flyers, booklets—anything worth looking at and reading. Students can freely add their own contributions so everyone will have a source of usable materials when they need pictures or ideas for writing assignments, covers for homemade books, montages or collages, and so on.

703-T   *(Read/Mixed Media) "Change in Command"*

Are you a victim of "great expectations"? Reading assignments need not be confined to the traditional classics such as *Great Expectations* (Dickens). Current newspaper and magazine articles along with contemporary paperback books and even comic books can be used more effectively in some classes to achieve the same reading skills as those offered in the classics. Contemporary novels, for example, may encourage more slow readers to read more books. *Huckleberry Finn* (Twain) may be a classic, but will it serve any better than *Pickpocket Run,* a story about a boy destined to follow in his dishonest father's footsteps? Consider some of these titles destined to be classics if they are not already: *Across Five Aprils; Alas, Babylon; All Creatures Great and Small; Bless the Beasts and Children; Catcher in the Rye; The Contender; Cry the Beloved Country; Farenheit 451; Lord of the Flies; Lord of the Rings; Ordinary People; The Outsiders; The Pilgrim; Roots; A Separate Peace; Shane; Sounder; That Was Then, This is Now; To Kill a Mockingbird; Watership Down; When the Legends Die;* and many more.

NONFICTION

704–T   *(Read/Circulars) "Souped-Up Reading"*

A good, economical source of high interest reading material for middle and junior high school boys can be found in advertising circulars, brochures, and booklets supplied by sporting goods, motorcycle, and automobile dealers. Have stacks of such materials available in the room. When possible, base simple assignments on this type of literature.

NOVELS

705–T   *(Discover/Definitions) "It's a Plot"*

To make the study of literature as meaningful as possible for the low ability students, try to present literary devices concretely rather than abstractly. When using such abstract terms as *plot, symbol,* and *theme,* express these ideas in terms they can understand. Students who don't know what "plot" means can easily tell what "happens" in the story.

706–G   *(Discover/Discussion) "At Any Rate"*

When teaching a novel to the entire class, a teacher can accommodate various reading speeds by allowing students to read as quickly as they like and then to form small discussion groups as they finish. The teacher can meet with one group while the others read. Those who finish early can be directed into other activities. (Also see ideas 471 and 497.)

707–C *(Discover/Discussion) "Pet Theory"*

Literary discussions can follow a specific format so that the slower students can participate even if they can't read well. Begin the discussion with questions on the literal level—the *plot*—so that everyone knows the story. This can be just a simple summary by a capable student. Next, cover relevancy of the material, considering the varying *experience* levels among the students. Everyone must feel the selection is worth reading and does in some way reflect the way things are in this world. Here, too, students consider the new material within the framework of past experience. Even the slowest students can enter discussions at this critical level. Finally, move to the inferential level—the *theme*—where the readers must consider what the writer has said "between the lines" and how the author said what he or she has through the structure. This is, then, the real message. Thus, compare initiating a literary discussion to the act of dropping a pebble into water. The rings radiating outward represent moving from the concrete to the abstract, from specific to general; thus, from *plot,* to *experience,* to *theme.* This should become the English teacher's P-E-T discussion approach.

OVERVIEW

708–T *(Discover/Artwork) "Curiosity Piquers"*

Before getting into the words of a book, pique student curiosity by displaying some artifact from the book, e.g., reproductions of the raft from *Kon-Tiki,* Hester Prynne's pillory and scaffold, a guillotine from *A Tale of Two Cities,* and so on. Bring in Tom Sawyer's straw hat, the dagger (wood or rubber) from *Macbeth.* Start the reading by discussing the incidents surrounding these items without giving away the plot, of course. How do you get these items? One source is projects made by former students motivated to display their various talents.

709–T *(Discover/Books) "Recycled Resources"*

Don't throw away those overruns on duplicator copies. Save those old workbooks. Provide file folders labeled by subject and skill. File duplicator copies and ripped-out workbook pages. Encourage students who need extra help or a challenge to go to this valuable resource file.

710–T *(Discover/Books) "Five for Three"*

If your school needs more books and budget is a problem, organize a paperback project. Appeal to students, parents, and book dealers. Have a book exchange. Participants bring in five books and receive three in return. The school gets the surplus to keep or to sell to raise funds for the library. For all these books, construct your own book cases of cinder blocks and boards.

711–T *(Discover/Books) "Reading Deeply"*

Provide opportunities to acquire and practice the following reading skills for understanding literature:

Follow sequence of events
Predict outcomes
Recognize reality from
   make-believe
Interpret figurative language
Identify with characters

Visualize characters and
   incidents
Create mental images
Recognize mood, tone
Infer from clues
Re-create settings

Since students do not acquire these skills by sheer exposure, they need competent guidance and practice, including a chance to exchange ideas with other classmates.

712–T *(Discover/Problems) "All about Reading"*

Reading problems occur within five basic areas: (1) word recognition (context, structure, phonics, usage), (2) comprehension, (3) sight word vocabulary (words known without recognition skills being employed), (4) rate and adjustment to reading difficulty, and (5) study skills (following directions, locating information, selecting and evaluating information, recalling and organizing information). Exercises in reading improvement involve all these areas. Concentrating on one area at a time will benefit both the student and teacher.

713–I *(Discover/Selves) "Fifth to Eleventh Eighth-Graders"*

Usually a wide range of reading abilities exists in any single class. Generally there is about a two-and-a-half-grade span both ways: a possible five-grade spread in a single class. Many teachers, failing to realize this range, force all students to work at the same reading level. This is both unrealistic and unfair. Remember individual differences when dealing with literature. Supply a variety of material from which the students can choose something appropriate to their own ability and interest level. The task of the teacher then is guiding individuals to conquer their own reading problems and to progress as their abilities allow. Discover what community or school help is available for the most seriously incapacitated readers.

714-C *(Discover/Selves) "Last but Not Least"*

This idea is a new twist on a frequently-used demonstration lesson on why we should follow directions carefully. The key, of course, is to read the *first* instruction and follow it. Individual copies of the test—or call it a problem—are available to each student but are returned after the activity, which, by the way, is less vocal and noisy than some versions of this bit of useful trickery.

A Simple Problem in Modern Math

Directions: First of all, read the full page of instructions carefully.

1. For this item and all the others, you will need a sheet of paper numbered from 1 to 11. For item number 1, look at your watch or the clock and write the exact time without the colon (i.e., 1:15 becomes 115) after number 1 on your paper.

2. Look at five students seated closest to you. How many of them are wearing brown or tan shoes? Write that figure (or 000) after number 2. (You will follow this procedure when answering remaining items. Keep all figures in straight columns.)

3. How many boys in the class are wearing blue shirts or sweaters?

4. How many blonde girls are in your class?

5. Count the number of pieces of gum under your desk or chair arm—not the chair seat—without getting out of your seat.

6. How many students are in your class today? Include yourself.

7. Count the number of individual light fixtures in the room.

8. Look at the student directly behind you (or to your left or right) and count the number of buttons exposed on shirt or blouse.

9. Find a book near you and open it to a center page. Write the left hand page number.

10. Using this same book, open it and stand it upright on your desk to show that you have finished all but one question. Then write the figure 30 after number 10 on your paper. Then re-read the directions and read item 11 below.

11. Now that you have finished reading all the instructions, don't do anything. Sit quietly and wait until those who can't follow directions complete the tenth step. For something to do, while you wait, see how long one person takes to get to number 11. Do not reveal the secret of this exercise.

715-I *(Discover/Selves) "Who Is Me?"*

Culturally deprived students often have trouble developing a self-concept. Until they have done so, they will have difficulty understanding the feelings and experiences of the characters they read about. The following three suggestions will help give such students mental, auditory, and visual pictures of themselves: (1) Assign a free-wheeling, unthreatening paper that tells what the student's shadow would see when following him or her around for a day. (The student looks at himself or herself more objectively than through the "I am" approach.) (2) Allow the student to talk into a tape recorder and then to listen to himself or herself speaking as an authority on a subject. (3) Photograph students working diligently and closely with classmates on room projects. Find a good reason to place such pictures on the bulletin board.

716-I   *(Discover/Topics) "Unfolding Personality"*

Each student receives a plain manila file folder and prints his or her name on the tab. In a few days each student brings back the folder bulging with memorabilia: photographs, favorite magazines, souvenir menus, playbills, concert programs, clippings, box tops—things that reflect each one's life style, hobbies, and interests. The result will be an idea collection to help the teacher suggest student composition topics to write, books to read, and ideas to share in discussion.

717-T   *(Discover/Tutors) "Learning by Doing"*

Be alert for students who can readily explain a word or describe (demonstrate) a concept to their peers when the teacher may flounder. Use them as tutors or aides for younger children (fourth through eighth grades) who need practice in reading. This tutoring program gives high school students a chance to review reading skills at a lower level and increases their confidence about their own role as readers. The younger students benefit from the individual attention.

718-C   *(Listen/Audiotapes) "Air that Lit"*

To help slow readers, ask several good readers to tape crucial portions of the selection being studied. Play back this tape while the class follows along in the text. Lacking this possibility, cover key portions orally in class. Since students understand more words by sound than by reading or writing, their chances of grasping and being able to discuss a selection are multiplied. Being forced to rely only on reading outside of class is terribly frustrating and defeating for the slow reader.

719–C *(Listen/Discussion) "Little Sir Echo"*

The Echo Game is an enjoyable way for students to learn that listening for content is an active, not a passive, task. Start a discussion on a subject of special class interest (current events, dating, spectator sports, new fads). After the discussion is under way, interrupt it and tell the class that from then on, before anyone adds a comment, he or she must first paraphrase what the previous speaker has said to that person's satisfaction. The resume the discussion. After the game, discuss how the echoing rule affected individuals.

720–T *(Listen/Talk) "On the Alert"*

Suggestions for projects often arise from overhearing student conversations or monitoring discussions. A teacher must be an alert observer, a good listener, and a skilled practitioner to zero in on student interests in this manner. But being a bit of a "snoop" will reap benefits through improved student attitudes toward school.

721–T *(Observe/Mixed Media) "Reading en Masse Media"*

Teachers often overlook the mass media as an incentive for reading. Books on which movies and television shows are based can be used with great success. Discussions of current events such as items on conservation, public transit, or crime statistics may encourage voluntary reading. Comic books have been used with some success though they are limited in enrichment opportunities and, because they tend to be overused, they inhibit progress for cultivating new tastes.

722–T *(Read/Books) "Reading Tree"*

Choose a corner of the room offering a cozy place for students to relax with a book. Decorate it with a "reading tree," an actual trunk with branches, reaching from the floor to ceiling. Its bare limbs can leaf out again with book synopses written and illustrated by the students after they complete a story. To add interest, let students hang other favorite items from the branches: small pictures of movie or television stars, clever buttons with slogans, and many other things. Cut outs can be in shapes of common tree fruits.

723–T *(Read/Books) "Teacher Reading Readiness"*

The task of improving reading through the subject field is always easier if needs are anticipated and prepared for in advance. These simple guidelines may be helpful:

1. Provide material at suitable vocabulary levels.
2. Select material to include all interests.

3. Offer materials from simple to increasingly complex.
4. Avoid situations that embarrass or frustrate.
5. Plan for a variety of activities.
6. Individualize as much as possible.
7. Use fresh, imaginative methods.
8. Provide for successful experiences.
9. Praise and encourage.
10. Record progress regularly and clearly.

SHORT STORY

724-G   *(Listen/Audiotapes) "Reel Short Story"*

Assign a small group of volunteers to tape a short story, a play, or skit for other classes to hear. Let one student be the narrator. The others will read the dialogue using as much expression as possible. Ray Bradbury's story "The Playroom" is a good beginning. This is one way to cover a number of stories quickly and effectively if tapes of different stories are shared among classes.

725-C   *(Listen/Books) "Hey, Teach! Your Turn"*

Try reading to the students, no matter what their ages. Through embarrassment teen-agers may show reluctance at first to be read to, but in a surprisingly short time they will request the reading of exciting, suspenseful stories. Fill the hour with animated reading. This activity improves reading interest and auditory skills. Try to select only those stories that can be completed within the hour.

STUDY SKILLS

726-T   *(Read/Books) "Skim This"*

Skimming and scanning are valuable skills in improving reading ability. They form the bases of many related reading skills. Skimming is reading rapidly for meaning—just hitting the main ideas. Scanning, on the other hand, involves looking for specific information—rather like looking for a particular name in a phone directory. Easy to confuse, the two words are often differentiated by equating the two m's in skimming with "main meaning." Take every opportunity to get students to practice scanning or skimming. For example, try a Scanning Relay. Divide the class into three equal teams. Ask a question about a story then tell everyone to hunt for a sentence or sentences that will give the right answer. As soon as the sentence is located, the participant raises his or her hand and reads it aloud. If the student is correct, his or her team gets five points. The first team to earn twenty-five points wins.

727-C *(Observe/Skits) "Playing Library"*

Introduce younger students to the use of the library for locating information by creating a "play" centered on the use of the card catalog. For the drawer fronts, print segments of the alphabet on cards attached to chairs. One simple skit approach is to give each student a card (lettered large enough to read across the room) naming a familiar book and its author. Then tell the students to stand behind the correct "drawers" (chairs) in the proper order of a title card section, then for an author card, and finally for a subject card. For the latter they may have to do a little guessing. More elaborate sequences can be planned for other library resources such as the *Readers' Guide to Periodical Literature.*

728-C *(Research/Libraries) "Relaying Information"*

This idea requires cooperation from the school librarian who provides a box with book catalogue cards. In the library, arrange students in relay teams of five to ten pupils. Children draw a card from the box, race to find the book, bring it to their team table, and tap the next person who continues the relay. The team that gathers the most books in the set time wins. Arranged beforehand with the librarian, books obtained could become the room library. This helps instill skills for locating information.

729-I *(Research/Mixed Media) "Armchair Travels"*

Distribute picture postcards from various geographical locations. Ask each student to imagine that he or she has been to the place and to write an expository paper about it. Encourage the use of encyclopedias, road maps, and travel booklets. In this writing, students learn to use and cite resources and increase their knowledge of English and geography simultaneously.

VOCABULARY

730-I *(Discover/Lists) "Using the Right Type"*

Those who are unmotivated by simply copying lists of spelling words or vocabulary, or sentences containing these words, often find the typewriter an interesting way to put these lists on paper, especially if they are unhappy about their handwriting. Typing will also force the student to analyze words carefully.

731–T *(Discover/Problems) "Text Looks"*

Examine class texts for reading problems that may overtake average and below average readers. Anticipate specific problems in word recognition skills (context clues, structure, phonics, dictionary), sight vocabulary, comprehension (literal, critical, inferential), rate and adjustment, and study skills. For the teacher relatively uninformed about reading, a visit to the school's or system's reading specialist will be most helpful. A good textbook on teaching reading is invaluable. We tend to take reading skills for granted until we find some students who don't even know the purposes and locations of the table of contents, glossary, and index. Many don't know where to find the copyright date nor what it represents.

732–C *(Discover/Tutors) "Expert Ease"*

Assign one or two words from the vocabulary lesson to each student who is then to become an expert on the words. He or she then teaches them to the rest of the class in some interesting way (riddle, pictures, games).

733–C *(Read/Cards) "Flashy Cards"*

Help students enlarge their vocabularies by defining new words in reading assignments. Each day three different students bring to class four unfamiliar words from the assignment. The words are placed on 3×5 cards with the word printed in large letters on one side (upper and lower case so that capitalization will be recognized) and the appropriate definition on the other side. These cards can be used for class or individual practice.

734–I *(Observe/Pictures) "Snap into It"*

To increase sight vocabulary, take snapshots of familiar objects and people. Attach the appropriate words to the photos. If placed on small cards, these word-builders become flashcards with some visual impact. Lacking photographs, use good illustrations from picture magazines.

735–T *(Read/Lists) "Minimatch Flashcards"*

As new vocabulary is encountered, have students print words (standard manuscript) on small cards that will fit into small match or pill boxes. Some teachers use snap rings and punch a hole in the cards so they can be fanned out around the ring. Have the students make the words a little larger than the average handwriting. The teacher uses these flashcards for individual drill in root words, syllabication, or classification, for instance, and the student then also has his or her own list of troublesome words to carry around in purse or pocket for use when there are moments to spare.

736–C *(Research/Dictionaries) "Box Scores"*

Construct an attractively decorated box with a slot in the top. Encourage children to deposit words they do not know how to pronounce or define. Every few days draw a slip from the box. Place the word on the bulletin board. Then have several students find the pronunciation and write a sentence using the word in each of its various definitions (uses). Have them write these sentences below the word. The results are then discussed in class. The newfound words should then be used as frequently as possible in the regular classroom activities.

737–I *(Research/Lists) "The Big Ten"*

To make vocabulary study practical, each student takes from a newspaper ten words he or she does not understand. From the individual lists, compile a master list of the most common difficult words. Have students look up the definitions in their dictionaries or make up their own. Chances are very good that such a list will be more useful to the students than a literature-based list.

WORDS

738–T *(Discover/Definitions) "Fear of Fonix"*

Phonics in reading instruction often throws fear into teachers just beginning to learn some of the fundamentals. Terms like "blends," "digraphs," and "diphthongs" tend—needlessly—to give the most trouble. Once understood, this aspect of word recognition problems can be dealt with. Here are some remembering devices:

   Digraphs, as *di* denotes, are of two types: consonant and vowel. The *ph* also illustrates consonant digraphs, two consonants sounded as one. (A vowel digraph is *au* in *caught.*)

   The word *blends* has two sets of letters illustrating this definition: *bl* and *nd* or two letters having two separate sounds —usually the original sounds of each letter. Blends are associated only with consonants.

   The vowel counterpart of a blend is the *diphthong* (*di* meaning two and *phthongos,* voice). Examples of diphthongs are *oi* in *oil* and *oy* in *toy.* These two-letter combinations often give beginning readers a problem and deserve to be emphasized in vocabulary and spelling exercises.

14 Deliberation

LETTER WRITING

739-T *(Practice/Letters) "Drop a Line"*

Letter writing is not easy for many students. They need much practice. Bring to class local (and some national) names and addresses on 3×5 index cards. Let each student pick one at random. This will be the addressee who will receive an actual letter asking for a catalog, obtaining free information, ordering some merchandise, asking for an autograph, or making a comment. A little booklet called *1001 Valuable Things You Can Get Free* (N.Y.: Bantam Books) could be a source. Also check with your local Chamber of Commerce.

MEDIA

740-G *(Organize/Mixed Media) "Wanted: An Ad"*

Advertisements are often overlooked as a source of reading matter. Ask students to bring to class a newspaper or magazine advertisement for a particular product (autos, fashions, or furniture, for instance). The students form small groups and arrange their ads into categories according to type of appeal (economy, prestige, adventure, or quality, for example) and find an appropriate name for each category. The last and most important step is to analyze the effectiveness of the advertisement by answering several questions about each ad: Why is (product) important? How does this product give (category)?

NARRATION

741-C *(Consolidate/Talk) "Chain Reaction"*

Study narration by letting the class compose its own story to read aloud. Either the teacher or a student begins by offering an introductory narrative paragraph, preferably involving the classroom or the school and, of course, class members. Going around the room, each student adds a section. A tape recorder is needed unless each student writes his or her contribution.

When the story is complete, it should be one within the students' experiences, interests, and vocabulary.

742-I *(Experiment/Myths) "Fabricated Fables"*

Most children like fables and myths. After reading some published versions, the teacher writes and reads a simple one. This is usually a good beginning because published myths can be too involved. Students then write their own using the teacher's myth as a model. This assignment helps the teacher detect the more creative children, who can then help the teacher create model materials that will interest even the slowest reader.

743-I *(Interpret/Cartoons) "Filling Balloons"*

Select some of the students' favorite comic strips or cartoons. After removing the balloon captions, duplicate them. Students then write their versions of what they think the characters are saying. Keen observation of the action (pictures) will reveal the key ideas which the students will phrase succinctly. For the more advanced writers, use the same approach for comic books, which will require more complete dialogue.

NOVELS

744-T *(Analyzing/Books) "Being Critical"*

Some practical exercises to improve critical reading involve recognizing certain aspects of plot, characterization, setting, and style. A look at critical questions involving plot will suggest some for other areas:

1. Did the action interest me?
2. Was the action convincing?
3. Did it relate to me?
4. Did suspense build logically and adequately?
5. Was action lively or did it move slowly and unevenly?
6. Was the ending reasonable and inevitable, yet surprising?
7. For what possible reason did the author write this story?

745-C *(Analyze/Cartoons) "Comical Plotting"*

Students take Sunday comic strips (self-contained serials) such as "Blondie" or "Dick Tracy," and analyze them for characterization and plot (rising action, climax, falling action). This is a different way to practice using the elements of fiction. Also, most students enjoy comics even if they don't like to read, yet the basic structural differences aren't that great.

746–G *(Experiment/Games) "Monopolizing Adventure"*

In teaching a book like *Tom Sawyer,* emphasize plot sequence by letting the class work in groups to make up a simple game-board game depicting Tom's escapades. The markers, fashioned out of paper, can be key objects from the story, e.g., a tombstone. The goal can be built in as game hazards. As a follow-up writing exercise, each student submits a short paper giving directions for playing the game. The best of these can become the game rules.

747–T *(Interpret/Plots) "Causing an Effect"*

Inferences in reading are drawn from cause and effect relationships. Students need much practice to sharpen their ability to move from making simple inferences to more complex levels as illustrated here:

1. Find meaning in more complex generalizations than employed at the critical level.
2. Identify the purpose or main idea from what the author has included.
3. Equate certain statements or passages with that purpose.
4. Recognize literary devices such as symbolism, imagery, and allusion, as well as historical references.
5. Relate these literary techniques to the meaning of the work.

OVERVIEW

748–C *(Experiment/Chalkboards) "Chalk One Up"*

Reserve a section of chalkboard or supply a banner of wrapping paper for a "graffiti wall." A bulletin board for tacking up displays of words and appropriate pictures also serves the same purpose. Students are encouraged to write clever, nonembarrassing expressions and slogans. This activity provides an opportunity for informal writing and reading practice.

749–C,I *(Experiment/Mixed Media) "Fix It"*

To speed up reading rates and to increase the amount of printed matter gathered through a single-eye fixation, the following suggestions are offered:

1. Match pictures with captions in timed contests.
2. Beat the clock in choosing from the table of contents in a popular youth magazine an article (1) to read first, (2) to read

last, (3) for boys only, (4) for girls only, or other categories.
3. Race to pick out in three minutes a previously designated car from a page of classified auto ads.
4. Pick out preannounced key items from classified or display ads.
5. Bracket words that belong together in sentences of varying difficulty; read them as "single words," no pauses between them.

750–T   *(Interpret/Books) "Three-Tiered Trials"*

Reading comprehension occurs on three levels: literal, critical, and inferential. The literal level covers the act of translating the words themselves. Critical skills require an interplay between what is read and the reader's past experiences, while inferential reading involves reading between the lines—determining the deepest meanings in a work. Although all three levels are important for full literary appreciation, plots and story lines must be made clear to slow readers so they can enjoy the discussions at critical and inferential levels. Thus, reading is plot-oriented, experience-oriented, and theme-oriented. (See related idea 707.)

751–T   *(Interpret/Talk) "No Put-Down"*

Do not underrate the intelligence of slow readers. They may be slow academically but not mentally or emotionally. Respect and emphasize the qualities and abilities these students have rather than dwell on what they lack. Slow readers, for example, often compensate for their lack of reading and writing skills by becoming highly articulate in speaking. Thus, if they know the plot or the gist of a selection, they often outdo better readers in critical and interpretive discussion. (See related idea 707.)

752–T   *(Organize/Books, Papers) "Up Organization"*

The following list contains just some of the elements of organization skills that can be turned into practice exercises.

1. Central ideas through lists of questions
2. Central ideas into headlines
3. Events placed in proper order: chronological, space, importance, deductive-inductive
4. Chapter titles and topic headings
5. Main ideas found in groups of words and phrases
6. Outlines of main and supporting ideas
7. Signal words, e.g., first, then, next
8. Summaries and precise writing
9. Short synopses of paragraphs, pages
10. Titles for paragraphs or entire selection
11. Topic sentences
12. Words and ideas grouped and classified.

POETRY

753-C *(Experiment/Word Lists) "Qua-training"*

Develop an interest in writing simple original poems by practicing the suggestions below. Write on the chalkboard three
lists of rhyming words such as these:

Group 1	Group 2	Group 3
girl	stop	slow
pearl	shop	mow
say	Ann	walk
pay	pan	talk

Students then write a four-line poem for each group. When the
poems are complete, they should be shared and placed on the
bulletin board with some appropriate pictures. Here is an
example:

girl	What do you say,
pearl	When a favorite girl
say	Who despite your pay
pay	Would like things pearl?

Notice that the words do not need to be in the order they are
listed.

STUDY SKILLS

754-C *(Consolidate/Games) "Library Full of Treasures"*

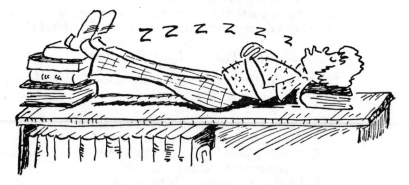

Allow students to practice locating information in the library,
particularly reference materials. Start a treasure hunt game.
At each step along the way, students must find a specific bit of
information. After finding one answer in the atlas, searchers
could be directed to the encyclopedia, from there to the *Readers'
Guide,* and so on. Of course, this must be carefully preplanned

with simple, easily followed directions printed on small slips of paper.

755–I   *(Experiment/Dictionaries) "Things Are Looking Up"*

To acquaint the student with the wide range of information that a dictionary offers, look through an unabridged dictionary and make up questions. For example: (1) In what century was Robin Hood supposed to have lived? (2) Why is a weasel like a skunk? (3) Why is "rodeo" a good name for that event? (4) Why is a "doubting Thomas" a Thomas and not a David, Donald, or a Douglas? Have students look up the answers in the dictionary after they determine the key word or phrase in the question.

756–C   *(Experiment/Games) "Follow the Flash"*

Practice following directions. Divide the class in half. Write a command on the board or use flashcards. Quickly remove the command. Call on a pupil. If the direction is carried out accurately, then that team gets a point. A typical instruction might be: "Open any book to page 33, then hold up the book."

757–I   *(Interpret/Authorities) "Going to the Source"*

Give students an opportunity to develop the skills of locating and selecting information by acquainting them with the *Guiness Book of World Records* and the *World Almanac*. Elementary, junior, and senior high students enjoy looking up the biggest, most, least, of anything. This activity is interesting, educational, and fun, and it broadens the students' informational horizons.

758–G   *(Interpret/Talk) "Telling It Again"*

This exercise provides practice in recalling information accurately. Although there are many ways to proceed, one approach is to have one student tell his or her neighbor something—an event or just an idea. The listener then tries to paraphrase exactly what was said. Whether this is done in pairs, teams, or class halves, it becomes an awakening event to discover the task is not as easy as thought.

759–C,I   *(Organize/Mixed Media) "No Penalty for Clipping"*

Clip short articles from the financial, society, sports, and general news section of a newspaper and paste them on cards. Shuffle the cards and pass them out to the class with these instructions: "These articles were taken from the newspaper. Arrange them under the proper column headings listed on the chalkboard (financial, society, sports, news) as quickly as you can determine the type of article." For variation, students can discriminate between articles that might be of interest to an athlete, for example, or a banker, housewife, seventh-grade girl, or business executive. Summaries of stories written by pupils can also be arranged in the same manner using categories such as travel, humor, adventure, fact, fantasy, or history. This activity allows practice in skimming and scanning. (See idea 726.)

760–I   *(Organize/Models) "Classy Game"*

To develop organizing and classifying skills, students practice putting together related things. For example, cut out common clothing, household, lawn, or auto pictures from catalogs. Place these illustrations on 3 × 5 index cards. Match words, also on cards, with these pictures. Place in file folders for storage and use them later as needed.

761–I   *(Organize/Selves) "T-Square for Building Study Habits"*

Students need to organize themselves as they study and deliberate about subjects being learned. Let them use T-Square—a formula for reading a textbook assignment. Train students to use these steps:

T: Take any textbook.
S: Survey quickly the assigned material to get a general idea and direction from introductory paragraphs, headings, charts, illustrations, as well as guide questions at the end.
Q: Frame questions in the mind or on paper, questions that can be answered by the material.
U: Understand where certain questions can be answered: underline if it is your book.
A: Answer questions from general knowledge or look up the answers.
R: Review more thoroughly the parts of the assignment that contain answers for the questions you could not answer.
E: Expand your knowledge of this assignment by seeing how it fits into the related material you already have learned or studied.

VOCABULARY

762–C   *(Analyze/Games) "Say and Tell"*

Help students develop an awareness of antonyms and synonyms with this exercise. Divide the class into two or more groups. The teacher pronounces a word and uses it in a sentence. Each pupil on a team has a chance to go to the chalkboard to write a word that has an opposite (antonym) or similar (synonym) meaning. The teams build points by their correct word choices.

763–I   *(Analyze/Pictures) "Words that Unfold"*

Use file folders for this vocabulary-building exercise. For example, inside place a picture of a West Coast Indian carving a totem pole. This provides a clue to a new word—"gouge." From a list of possible definitions printed on the opposite page, the student chooses the definition "to carve out, usually with a metal tool." Students can participate in developing these exercises by contributing interesting pictures that may suggest new words and ideas. The teacher can hand out blank folders for this purpose.

764–C   *(Consolidate/Lists) "Two Matches"*

Vocabulary words may be learned by matching two lists of words, a list of nouns representing occupations (e.g., minister, surgeon, author) and a list of verbs indicating what these professionals do (e.g., preach, operate, write). Adding adverbs would be a natural follow-up.

765–I   *(Experiment/Games) "Scrabbled Egos"*

"Scrabble" can be used effectively for a word-building game, but adaptations of the regular rules and procedures can also be made. For example, players can have two minutes to see how many words they can make from half a dozen letter tiles (without use of the gameboard). Or various prefixes and suffixes can be printed on short strips of wood or cardboard proportioned to match the tiles. Each player is given an affix and must see how many words he or she can make with a set number of letter tiles.

766–C   *(Experiment/Games) "Teach-Tac-Toe"*

The familiar game of Tic-Tac-Toe may be adapted for building vocabulary, by first drawing two game frames on the chalkboard. In one, print assigned vocabulary words in each box. The class is split into two teams. Individuals from each team are alternately called to pronounce and use in a sentence one of the boxed words not already used. For a correct response, a circle or an "X" is placed in a box in the other game frame. Instead of circles and Xs, use the words themselves that can be placed directly on the Tic-Tac-Toe frame by using an adhesive such as double-faced masking tape. To win, a team must earn marks in any three consecutive boxes, forming a straight line in any direction.

767–C, I *(Experiment/Mixed Media) "Perfect Practice"*

New words should enter the child's vocabulary through necessity. Even an abstract term such as *democracy* can be thoroughly learned in a series of steps: (1) write the word in syllables, (2) list word derivations and related words, (3) give the definition and write the new word in several sentences, (4) paste pictures from newspapers and magazines under the heading "Democracy is . . . ," and (5) take field trips to city or state government offices to see democracy in action.

768–I *(Interpret/Cards) "Cardology"*

Capitalize on a student's desire to substitute words when reading by encouraging a study of synonyms and antonyms. Prepare flashcards on which are printed the word, a synonym, an antonym, a definition, and an illustrative sentence. Students read all of this as it is flashed and, with practice, they will be able to give synonyms and antonyms by seeing only the original word stimulus. Another way to proceed is to devise exercises in which more effective and picturesque words are substituted for those in the original sentence, e.g., in the sentence, "The boy ran quickly from the car," "dashed" would communicate more feeling.

769–G *(Interpret/Games) "Check Mates"*

This checker game is designed for students who need sight-word drill. On the squares of a regular checkerboard paste the words to be learned (the Dolch sight-word list or any other suitable list). The two-color scheme of the checkerboard must, of course, be retained. Students play as in a regular checker game but must name the word on the square to which they are moving or over which they are jumping.

770–T *(Observe/Cards) "Build a Tach"*

A useful, do-it-yourself tachistoscope can be made by cutting one or several slots in a file folder. Trim off the tab to form a straight edge and tape this edge to form a sleeve. Cut another folder to form a single sheet or card which can be slid up or down inside the sleeve exposing words or phrases in the windows as slowly or rapidly as desired. To estimate timed exposure of words, count off by thousands to approximate seconds: "One thousand, two thousand, three thousand" is three seconds. Any speeds of less than a second should be confined to commercial equipment.

771-I *(Organize/Lists) "Measure Hunt"*

An effective way to teach spelling is to mark off three or four columns on a sheet of paper. Label each column with a desired category (depending on the subject under study). In lieu of any special categories, suggest "animal," "vegetable," and "mineral." Using dictionaries, students see who can place the most correctly spelled words in each of the categories in a specified time limit. This activity also teaches the process of classifying.

772-I *(Organize/Lists) "Words on File"*

Encourage students to write new words on the inside of file folders, which are stored for review and used by other classes to build vocabulary. Suggest creative ways to arrange lists such as finding meaningful definitions and sample sentences. Occasional pictures from magazines or drawn by the student will add interest and help clarify the words in these personalized classroom dictionaries.

WORDS

773-C *(Analyze/Cards) "Got a Pair?"*

This activity helps students who are having difficulty with any aspect of reading that requires word analysis. On the chalkboard or on a large poster, print word endings: *-an, -ould, -ead, -oop, -each,* and others. Prepare another list with initial consonants, digraphs, or blends (see idea 738) which when matched with the correct endings will complete the words. Students are asked to see how many words they can make by matching the endings. Set a time limit. The student with the most words at the end of, perhaps, six minutes reads his or her list to the class. Other students offer additional words. Then all can apply meanings to unknown words. (Idea 793 will help in a related area of affixes.)

774-C *(Analyze/Magazines) "Be a Cut-Up"*

Pictorial magazines can provide the stimulus for many aspects of teaching reading skills. For example, to aid in the practice of forming the consonant vowel combinations (see idea 738), have students cut out words employing whatever sounds are being studied. Sometimes parts of various words can be cut up to form syllables of specific words. The change in type design or size helps accentuate syllabication. Such a collection can be pasted in a scrapbook or notebook. This approach gives an air of practicality which sometimes doesn't come across in the average workbook exercise.

775–C,I *(Experiment/Chalkboards) "Long and Short of It"*

For practice in decoding polysyllabic words, prepare a list of phonetically spelled words to use in board drills. Write a word on the board, dividing it into syllables. Some of the syllables will be short words the students can read immediately. Others will have simple sound patterns that they can sound out by relating them to rhyming words. For example, *er* usually has the same sound as the letters *er* in the word *her.* In the word *plan* they can find the word *an.* Soon they also will become familiar with certain common sound patterns, such as *ing, ank, con, pre, tion,* and *tious,* and they will decode these combinations automatically. Here are some examples of phonetically spelled words that can be sounded by breaking them into syllables (each word has at least one hidden word in it which could help the student pronounce the word by splitting it into pronounceable parts):

apartment	continental	maximum
apparatus	illustration	operate
buffalo	imitated	peppermint
commanding	importantly	perforate
comfort	insist	pulsating
conductor	internal	satisfactory
confident	ligament	transcontinental
consistent	management	understandable
constricted	manipulate	workmanship

After some practice, have volunteers sound out the words to see if the other students can write them correctly.

776–C, G *(Experiment/Games) "Picture Clear"*

Show students a typical rebus puzzle then have them make up their own. Working in groups later, students pass around their papers so each has someone else's. Then each attempts to solve the rebus, carefully pronouncing the word. This exercise for learning syllabication can also be expanded to include entire sentences.

777–I *(Experiment/Pictures) "Sound Pictures"*

Show four or five magazine pictures (without captions) or place pictures in sets of file folders. Illustrations should suggest adjectives or adverbs. By questions try to elicit the best words. Responses can be oral or written.

778–C *(Experiment/Senses) "Snakes Alive"*

Give your class an interesting noun (sometimes with a picture) such as *snake.* Ask them to think of a sensory word describing a snake. The first replies may be *green* or *long,* but soon the class will use more descriptive words such as *scaly, slithery,* and *wiggly.* This can be either an oral or written activity.

779–C,I *(Experiment/Sentences) "Have a Pair"*

Write pairs of words that are easily reversed or confused because of similar configuration and sound, for example: *bear-bare, bridge-bribe, flight-fight, hoped-hopped, plum-plume, saw-was, shave-shove, their-there, they're-their, weather-whether.* Encourage close scrutiny of each word pair to note differences in form and meaning. Have students listen to these words in sentences read orally and then write the correct choice on paper.

780–C,I *(Interpret/Audiotapes) "Tap a Tape"*

To allow students to practice word recognition and spelling skills, tape some oral instructions (different for each student) that emphasize specific words you want them to learn; for example: *"Proceed* to the door, open it and *engage* in a brief *conversation* with the first person you see. Then *write* a note *explaining* what you have just done." Of course, you can modify the instructions to grade level. This exercise, which could be presented as a game, also gives students a chance for practice in following directions—an important study skill.

**781–C,
G** *(Interpret/Games) "Under the O"*

Play "Word-o" to develop word recognition. Prepare 8½ × 11 cardboard sheets blocked off like a bingo card with twenty-five squares, five rows of five. Or have each student fold a paper into twenty-five equal-sized squares. The center square is marked "free." Print twenty-five troublesome words or sight vocabulary words in the blocks. Students may do so from lists the teacher provides. Each card will have some of the same words but all will be quite different. The teacher has all the words on a master sheet or on small cards drawn from a box. As the teacher pronounces the word, the players try to locate the same word on their cards and cover it with a marker. The player who first covers five words in a straight line—vertically, horizontally or diagonally—calls out "Word-o" and wins the game. To make the game more challenging, require the winner to use the words correctly in two sentences before he or she can officially be declared winner.

782–I,C *(Organize/Lists)* *"Three Ways Better"*

Here are three reading exercises to help word recognition when reading a story: (1) List all the words in this story that are made up of a prefix or a suffix and a root word. Underline that affix (prefix or suffix). (2) List words in this story that begin with two-letter or three-letter consonant blends. Underline the initial blend in each word and so on. (3) List words in this story that have long vowel sounds.

15 Evaluation

EXPOSITION

783–I *(Judge/Papers) "Author Authority"*

This idea is a variation of one in which the student dictates a
story while the teacher writes it for the student to read later.
This time, however, the student tells the teacher about an activity, sport, or procedure which the student knows much about
and the teacher knows very little. The teacher then writes an
explanation based on information the student gives. The student reads the completed draft, usually quite eagerly. Then
both discuss how well the information was incorporated into
the composition and who is at fault if the explanation emerges
poorly.

JOURNALISM

784–C *(Identify/Newspapers, Questions) "Page One Start"*

Below-average ability classes are often motivated to read by
competing, especially competing with the teacher. Short daily
quizzes based on the local newspaper's front page are a start.
Give a grade of A to anyone who can ask a front-page question that the teacher is unable to answer.

NARRATION

785–C *(Extrapolate/Games) "A and B Stories"*

Assess ability to retell a story aloud by using the classic spell-
down. As usual, divide the class into two teams standing in
lines opposite each other. Begin with the first student on side
A who tells what happened first in the story. The lead student
on side B takes the story one step further. Students who cannot reply go to the end of the line and await another turn. A
second miss disqualifies them, and they must sit. At the end of
the allotted time, the team with the most students standing
wins. A slight switch can be made in this procedure by asking
each student to contribute five questions (with answers) on a
subject under study. Answers to these questions determine who
stands or sits.

NOVELS

786-C *(Extrapolate/Plots) "Predicting the Future"*

Assess ability to listen with understanding. After reading
some passages aloud, ask: Can you find the turning point in
the story? Do the characters act and talk like real people?
Illustrate. What is the moral or main idea of the story? Have
you read any other stories with similar ideas? Which ones? To
do this, the student must organize and recall information and
use inference. These skills need constant practice.

787-C *(Restructure/Games) "Expertease"*

To help develop good reading habits, plan a Stump the Panel
game either before discussing a novel (for testing knowledge of
plot) or after (for reviewing emphasized points). A chairperson
and panel of four reader-experts are selected; the remaining
students are challengers. They write questions about the plot—
who said certain important things, what some words mean,
which are the key passages, and so on. Questions can be on
file cards and should be checked for appropriateness. The following day, a moderator is chosen to call for questions, and a
recorder is picked to total points for either the panel or the
challengers.

OVERVIEW

788-I *(Compare/Audiotapes) "A Record Event"*

To encourage oral reading practice and to evaluate improvement, tape record a student reading an unfamiliar selection.
Then allow the piece to be taken home for oral practice. In a
few days record the reading again and compare the difference.
There is usually a great improvement.

789-I,G *(Compare/Charts) "Competitive Rating"*

Pair all class members. Have them choose some fairly easy
reading such as short stories or novels. Each student reads for
three minutes while a partner provides a word count and time
check. Both teammates compute a words-per-minute rate, and
the teacher (or students) charts the scores. Repeat this with
similar materials at least three times each semester. Students
like to see how their own progress compares with their peers.
After learning this charting procedure, students can show
progress in spelling, reading comprehension, vocabulary, and
even overcoming composition weaknesses. Such charts also
help the teacher tell at a glance an individual's progress.

790–I *(Compare/Charts)* *"Take Ten"*

Break word-for-word reading habits. Let the student compete with himself or herself and chart that progress. The reader establishes a baseline figure for a normal ten-minute reading. For each ten-minute reading exercise to follow, the reader must increase the pages read by one. This continues until the reader can no longer comprehend. Through various assessments such as comprehension tests (with 95 percent accuracy), the reader should be able to locate the most comfortable and successful rate for that type of reading material. Once this plateau is found, the reader can gradually increase rate as long as comprehension does not drop.

791–I *(Extrapolate/Questions)* *"Going to Press"*

Allow each child to write—or dictate for you to write—an important comprehension question for a story being studied. Duplicate these questions for the class. Possibly attach names to each entry. Students are thrilled seeing their names in print along with the question, and the review is invaluable.

792–I *(Extrapolate/Books Reports)* *"Audio Books"*

Allow slow readers to submit reports on books they have *heard*. Prepare an audiotape library of class-chosen selections that slower students can use as they follow in books kept in a special room library. This involves some work for the teacher of a group of student readers. By reducing the usual frustration, this method encourages slow readers to enter literary discussion. This way, they too can evaluate the work's quality, the author's objectivity, and other matters appropriate to critical and inferential reading.

793–C *(Identify/Lists)* *"Reading in the Round"*

Not all work with words and phrases needs be relegated to lists on the chalkboard or paper. For example, some teachers have had success with practice wheels, which can be made of anything from paper plates to plywood. After teaching such useful structural aids as meanings of prefixes and suffixes, provide additional practice through self-study use of the wheels. The following common prefixes and suffixes are among some which can be combined with root words to produce various words with different meanings, illustrating the importance of

knowing affixes. This same approach can be used for thought
units as well as for sentence parts.

Prefixes	Suffixes
ab—from, off	ation—state of
auto—self	ancy, ency—act of
bi—two	ful—full of
con, com—with	ing—act of
dis—apart	ish—resembling
mis—in the way	less—without
ob—toward	ment—state of, act of
pre—earlier	ness—state of
trans—across	ory—pertaining to
un, in—not	tion—state of

794-T   *(Identify/Problems) "Dunce Hat Still On"*

There is such a person as the much maligned "dumb kid" who
is unable to read or learn at or close to the achievement level
of the other class members. Some teachers do not understand
this soon enough. Some never do. Expectation levels need constant adjustment based on results of frequent evaluation. (See
idea 713.)

795-C   *(Judge/Books) "Once upon a Time"*

Motivate middle school or junior high students who read on
picture-book level. Encourage them to read aloud to younger
brothers and sisters or other children in the neighborhood or
school. In addition to the reading, they can also rate the picture books according to the reactions of their youthful audience. Ratings could determine whether these titles should be
included in a bibliography of recommended children's gift
books. They could also be rated for such elements as horror
(whether it is suitable for children), fantasy (whether it is the
right kind), or endings (whether they are believable). The final
ratings along with brief annotations are published for parents
to aid in book buying. How does this help the slow readers?
Prereading and other preparations help them improve their
own reading abilities. Stories must be read accurately and
with feeling to obtain accurate listener reactions. Then, too,
students are not embarrassed carrying juvenile literature for
important research such as this.

796-I   *(Restructure/Book Reports) "Hate Them Reports"*

As an alternative to lengthy written book reports, students
write brief descriptions and personal opinions on 3 × 5 index
cards headed by title and author. These cards are then filed in

a box according to title. Now students can read what others have to say about books they plan to read. If the descriptions are vivid and precise, curiosity may outweigh any negative comments about a book. The file box of book report cards can also be used by the teacher to monitor individual reading. Instead of a file box, cards could be placed in pockets inside file folders which, for the more popular books, have been decorated to resemble a book jacket. (See also ideas 600 and 671.)

797-G *(Restructure/Discussions) "No Danger of Copying"*

Teachers who are not too concerned with individual scores can administer a group effort review test. Divide the class into small groups of about five students each. Group members work together discussing each question before answering. In this way, learning becomes cooperative and not competitive. Students become less anxious and perform better. Since students do work together, the questions can be more complex than might be used for individual testing.

798-C *(Restructure/Book Reports) "New Roles for Book Reports"*

Reporting on biographies and autobiographies presents an exciting challenge to students when they can role play the main characters in the book. Let students who have read the same book form a panel of important visitors from the past who will present the main ideas in the book. This type of group activity often breaks through the psychological barrier slow readers have for the written book report.

SENTENCES

799-C *(Identify/Games) "Caught on Tape"*

The class reviews voice inflection rules governing periods, commas, and other marks of punctuation with this game. Play a tape recording of a study reading. The rest of the class follows along by reading the copy. Ask the students to call out "stop" when they detect a vocalized mistake. Such an error might be not dropping the voice at the end of a sentence or not pausing at a comma. Students must explain the violation they spotted. Points can be assigned for each correct find.

800–C *(Restructure/Games) "Neat Card Trick"*

A pack of fifty-two unlined, 3 × 5 index cards (colored preferred) is made up to contain ten each of nouns (some pronouns), verbs, adjectives, and adverbs. Fill out the remaining twelve using prepositions, conjunctions, and articles. The object of this game, "Sentence Rummy," is to create one or two complete sentences using ten words based on kernel sentence patterns (see idea 263) such as *subject* plus *verb* or *subject* plus *verb* plus *complement* (completer). Modifiers, of course, stretch out the patterns of key words. Emulating Rummy terms, if desired, call each sentence a "trick" worth one point for each word correctly used. To play, ten cards are dealt to each of four players (eight players if partners are used). Unless a player is dealt all the cards needed, at each turn a player draws two cards, either from the face-down pack or the face-up discard pile. The player keeps one card (one that can probably be used) and deposits the other in the discard stack face up. When a sentence or two can be assembled—after a draw and before the last discard—a player goes out. Going out counts two points. Thus, winning one hand scores twelve points: a maximum of ten for one or two sentences, and two points for going out. Players decide before the game what top score will constitute winning the game.

SPELLING

801–C *(Restructure/Chalkboards) "Moving Spelldown"*

Two students go to opposite chalkboards. Choose a judge for each student. The teacher stands in the middle of the room and says a spelling word. The two students write the word quickly on the chalkboard. Each judge checks for accuracy. The first student to write the word correctly on the board wins this round. The other student sits down and a challenger comes up. All students get a chance to participate.

STUDY SKILLS

802–I *(Compare/Charts) "Two Rs"*

Periodic reading rate improvement exercises will help students see the importance of reading rapidly while recalling the main ideas. In one such approach, have the class read short stories of 250 to 300 words. Using complete sentences, each writes the main idea of the entire selection. They may then write each paragraph's main idea and finally answer some comprehension questions. To keep it all in perspective, pupils keep individual progress charts indicating speed and accuracy. Pairs can check each other's rate and recall record.

803-G *(Identify/Games) "Auction Quiz"*

To check ability to recall information, divide the class into about five groups with half a dozen on a team. Each team is given twenty points at the start. The object is for a team to retain as many of these points as possible. Each team bids on an unknown question (possibly in an envelope). The team bidding the highest number of their twenty points gets the question. The more points bid, the harder the question. If a team fails to answer a question, they lose the number of points they bid. All members can collaborate on the answer, but only one answer is acceptable.

804-C *(Identify/Problems) "Accidentally on Purpose"*

This activity is designed to assess comprehending or recalling information and reading critically. After reading a story or article, each child writes a paragraph telling something about it, deliberately including at least one mistake (wrong word choice, incorrect fact, wrong name, or inaccurate time, for instance). These paragraphs are read aloud so the class can find and correct the mistakes. Paragraphs may also be duplicated and distributed to the class. Of course, some mistakes will be natural. These should be found and corrected also.

805-C, G *(Restructure/Games) "Square Game"*

"Categories" is a good game to build vocabulary and to practice recalling information. The words and categories can be tailored to suit many aspects of English (literature review, grammar drill, vocabulary building). Each student prepares a grid with an agreed-upon five-lettered word written horizontally over the top squares. Five or six categories are listed vertically on the left side of the paper. For each category, each player must fill in a word that begins with the letter at the top of the column as in the following grid. Enough time should be allowed for players to feel they have completed as much as they can. Then the sheets are scored. For each correct word any player who has it gets as many points as there are other players who did not have it. For example, if only one out of ten players wrote *Euripides* as a playwright beginning with E, it is worth 9 points. If nine out of ten players wrote Eliot they get one point each. The reward is for new and unusual names and, since the answers are read orally, all players profit. First names and titles (without the articles) can be used as first words.

(Possible Fill-ins)

	G	A	M	E	S
Authors	Gunnar Nordhoff	Andersen (Hans Christian)	Milton	Ernest Hemingway	Stevenson
Books	*Gone with the Wind*	*Arrowsmith*	*Mayor of Casterbridge (The)*	*Ethan Frome*	*Silas Marner*
Char-acters	Gulliver	Dr. Aziz *(A Passage to India)*	Madame Defarge *(A Tale of Two Cities)*	Catherine Earnshaw *(Wuthering Heights)*	Simon *(Lord of the Flies)*
Play-wrights	George B. Shaw	Auden	Moliere	Eliot	Shakespeare
Poems	"Go Catch a Falling Star" (Donne)	"Among School Children" (Yeats)	"Miles Standish" (Longfellow)	"Essay on Man (An)" (Pope)	"Snowbound" (Whittier)

806–C *(Restructure/Instructions) "Junior Cartographers"*

Organization skills are best evaluated when students can apply them to new and interesting situations. Provide each student with one of possibly three sets of instruction for what is a simple process except for the fact that the instructions are out of sequence. Exercises can include such projects as brushing or feeding a dog, cutting the grass with a power mower, planting a terrarium, or antiquing some furniture. Those with the same set of instructions may share and compare order, or the teacher can provide each with a key.

807–I *(Restructure/Paragraphs) "Orderly Sentences"*

On separate strips of paper, type or print sentences from short paragraphs. Place scrambled sentences into an envelope or file folder to keep them together. By arranging slips on their desks, students unscramble the sentences, making smooth-reading paragraphs. With available keys they can check their own organization. The same process can be used for scrambled paragraphs. Selections may come from the school newspaper, magazines, book passages, directions for assembling things, recipes, and many other sources.

808–C *(Restructure/Paragraphs) "Thoughts to Order"*

After studying such paragraphs, have students write (or re-structure prewritten sentences) paragraphs in which the thought progresses from:

1. The least important or interesting to the most
2. The familiar to the unfamiliar
3. The general to the particular (deductive)
4. The particular to the general (inductive)
5. One place to another (space order)
6. Earlier time to a later time (chronological or time order).

VOCABULARY

809–C *(Restructure/Games) "On Playing Vowel"*

Play the decoding game. Write simple sentences or short paragraphs for the students, omitting vowels. Have the student complete the sentences. For example:

Th—y d—n—t l—v— th—t d—n—t sh—w th—r l—v—.

810–I,C *(Compare/Games) "Matches Needed"*

In the center of a bulletin board, place a fairly large picture of a familiar object (car, airplane, house, garden, boat, etc.). Students must locate and cut out words from magazines and newspapers that help describe the bulletin board pictured item. With the class divided into two teams, find out which team can bring in the most words to put on their side of the bulletin board. You can vary this idea according to the word study activities of your class.

811–T *(Identify/Games) "Flash Recall"*

Make flashcards for basic sight vocabulary. Form two piles, with the words the student knows in one pile and those he or she has trouble recognizing in another. Have the student study the troublesome word list. Decide on a reward when all the cards can be placed into the pile of words he or she knows. See how quickly the student learns the words with this little extra motivation. Periodically review the words the student already knows.

812–I *(Identify/Games) "Look Alikes"*

Slow readers often have difficulty recognizing sight vocabulary words that look alike except for one or two letters. Perhaps this simple card game will provide needed but exciting practice. Using plain white 3 × 5 index cards, print two identical sets of cards containing troublesome vocabulary (because of similar configurations). One set is for the student and the other for a partner or the teacher. The partner begins by laying down one card at a time very quickly, word-side up. The student is to pick up a card only when it exactly matches the one on top of his or her stack. If the student picks the wrong word, the card is forfeited. If the student is right, he or she takes both. The object at the end of any number of games is to collect all the cards. For slow readers who overuse configuration clues, words like these may give problems: *want, went,* and *won't; these* and *those; them, theme,* and *then; house, hose, horse,* and *hours;* and sometimes even *was* and *saw.*

813–G *(Identify/Games) "Making Points with the Dictionary"*

Divide the class into five or six groups. Using the dictionary, one group picks out an unfamiliar word such as *buckram,* writes the word and its simplest definition on a piece of paper, and gives it to the teacher. The other groups, without a dictionary but using the same size paper, create their own definiticns for the word and hand them to the teacher to be combined with the correct definition. Then each group, except the one that chose the word, listens to the definitions being read and tries to choose the correct one. If right, the group gets five points; wrong, two points. When a group's definition is chosen, even though it is incorrect, that group gets three points for being able to write a logical-sounding definition. If the right definition eluded everyone, the group that chose the word gets ten points. Then the dictionary is passed to the next group and the procedure is repeated until each group has had two turns. The group with the most points wins.

814–I,G *(Identify/Games) "Pass or Fumble"*

The popular game of football can be brought into the classroom, modified, and used as a means of mental exercise in vocabulary enrichment. Draw a football field with proper yardline markings on a large sheet of green construction paper. Add some matchstick goal posts. The game begins on the fifty-yard line where a cardboard football is placed. The only other equipment needed is a stack of cards on which new vocabulary words are printed. In order to move the football a player must read the word on the card. If the word is pronounced correctly, the player moves the ball ten yards toward the opponent's goal. If the word is read incorrectly, it is considered a fumble and the ball is moved backward ten yards. When a player crosses the goal line, he or she earns six points. If the player reads the next word correctly, he or she gets the extra point. Then the ball is replaced on the fifty-yard line. This can also be a team game with the gameboard placed on an overhead transparency.

815–T *(Judge/Oral Reading) "Out with Doubt"*

Listen to individuals read. Be alert to words they ask to be
defined or those they clearly puzzle over. Select some of these
for vocabulary-building activities. These words are related to
immediate needs and interests.

816–I *(Restructure/Transparencies) "Word Pictures"*

Choose small pictures of objects that are familiar to a student
with a reading problem. Place them under a sheet of plastic.
The student or the teacher prints the name of each object either
on or near it. Each word should be pronounced aloud. Review
each word with the plastic still in place. Then remove the plastic and place it on an overhead projector or just hold it up. See
how many words can be recalled without the aid of the pictures. If the original pictures are clear line drawings in black
and white as in coloring books, make a transparency of them
before proceeding as above. The latter is especially useful
when working with a class.

WORDS

817–C *(Compare/Sentences) "Blankety Blank Story"*

The teacher chooses any illustration depicting a great deal of
activity and writes a short lively story to go with the illustration but leaves out several key words. From the context, students decide what the appropriate words should be. Compare
the students' choices with the original.

818–C,
G *(Restructure/Games) "Tic-Tac-Toe Know"*

Play Tic-Tac-Toe using three-lettered words. To score, count
each horizontal, diagonal, and vertical word (forward or backward) as one point. Two players take turns and each has a
grid. During each turn, a player places a letter in a square.
Whenever a word is built, a point is scored. This continues
until neither player can build any more words. Teams can also
be used. For example:

m	u	m
u	u	u
g	a	s

mum (2)
mug (2)
gum (2)
gas (1)
sag (1)
sum (2)

10 points

The same approach can be used for evaluating the ability to make up short words that employ letter diagraphs, blends, and diphthongs and are built syllable by syllable rather than letter by letter. (See Glossary for reading terms.) One player begins by putting the first syllable (or letter combination) of a known word in one box; then the other player takes a turn. The first player to complete a three-part word wins the game. (Tic-Tac-Toe need not be limited to nine squares. Sixteen would be more useful at times.)

819–C, G,I   *(Restructure/Games) "Ai, Ai, Sir"*

Here is a game that will reveal how well students understand vowel combinations in words. Begin by writing one or two vowel combinations like *ai* and *ea* on the board. Then five-student teams produce as many words as they can with each vowel combination. At the end of ten minutes, each team reads its list of words and receives one point for every real word correctly spelled. Vary the rules by scoring only for words no other team has.

820–C, G   *(Restructure/Lists) "Compound It"*

Word building becomes a competitive game when the entire class uses the following or similar lists of words to form compound words:

back	cook	milk	road
boat	drop	note	sail
book	mail	play	sand
box	man	rail	top
coat	mate	rain	wood

After writing these words on the chalkboard, give each student a sheet of lined paper. Tell the class they have five minutes to write as many compound words as they can, using only the words on the board. Students with the greatest number of words read their lists, and the one with the most correctly spelled is the winner of the game.

821–C   *(Restructure/Sentences) "Nice Idea"*

This exercise checks on improvement in written expression. Students substitute weak words in model sentences with more interesting words. On the chalkboard write sentences that need improvement, e.g., "Joe got a good used car buy and fixed it up to look real good." The class offers substitute words for *got, good, fixed it up, real,* and *good.*

16 Application

EXPOSITION

822-I,
G,C   *(Write/Role Playing) "Explore This"*

Reading and writing skills are best developed simultaneously.
To motivate students, have them write stories about imaginary
experiences in particularly appealing avocations or vocations,
e.g., airline stewards and hostesses, television camera opera-
tors, archeologists, or police officers. Have them find basic
information on the training and tools of the trade. Then ask
them to make up a log of a typical day or to write a more formal piece. These papers can be shared with the entire class or
read aloud in small groups.

JOURNALISM

823-C   *(Construct/Newspaper) "Small-Time Publishers"*

Empty writing assignments fail to interest many students,
particularly the slow readers. The following idea works as well
for them as for the bright students. If your school has a newspaper, students could submit jokes, crossword puzzles, games
and riddles, and even some news articles. All these efforts
involve writing and possibly some reading for research. This
idea gives everyone a chance to be responsible writers and
readers with a purpose. It also proves to reluctant learners
that speaking is not the only important form of communication. Some future jobs may very well depend on the ability to
read and write.

LETTER WRITING

824-I   *(Write/Forms) "Recall the Past"*

For the noncollege-bound students, useful, relevant instruction
on how to complete job-oriented forms will result in better attitudes toward reading/writing assignments than the usual abstract composition assignments. Begin with simple forms—
bank checks, W-2 forms, or applications for credit—and proceed

to personal letters requesting job interviews or seeking information about a trade school.

825-I   *(Write/Letters) "Count-to-Ten Words"*

Help children release inner tensions by frequently allowing them time to write a letter to someone, including the teacher, about something that angered them. This helps teachers keep in touch with children's attitudes and helps prevent explosions by offering them a safety valve. One teacher used this approach as a substitute for assigned compositions. He found that student attitudes toward composition improved 100 percent.

826-I   *(Write/Papers) "Take a Letter; Take Two"*

Have students make up a letter to the editor expressing a definite opinion toward a subject in which they are particularly interested. Each student writes a second make-believe letter to the editor expressing an opposite opinion on the same subject. The assignment can be carried a bit further if the student writes a short paper or gives an oral report examining both arguments point by point.

MEDIA

827-I   *(Perform/Book Reports) "Book a Show"*

Combine a creative puppet play with an oral book report. A taped narration, some stick or hand puppets, and a cardboard box can do much to improve the conventional book report.

828-I   *(Perform/Audiotapes) "Box or Tube"*

To encourage motivated writing as well as encourage reading with understanding, place students in teams of four. A team prepares a ten-minute radio program to be tape recorded. Give them rehearsal and planning time. Suggest linking the various group projects together for variety: soap opera, sportscast, newscast, commercials, etc. With equipment available, the skits could also be recorded on videotape.

829-I   *(Write/Papers) "Classified Research"*

Students read classified ads for autos. They cut out the ad for the car they like best. Then they attach the ad to a sheet of paper on which they write a brief statement on why they chose this particular car. (A car is a good subject since both girls and boys seem interested.)

830-C   *(Write/Papers) "Spare that Cartoon"*

To encourage recreational reading and a little writing, collect cartoons from newspapers or magazines. Group the cartoons by theme or subject. Paste them on poster board or in booklets. Students read these in their spare time or use them for projects. For example, find a cartoon series that conveys the idea that this is the "machine age." Prepare a short paper to tell how the cartoons show this.

831-I   *(Write/Papers) "This Idea Is Classified"*

Students find a particularly interesting classified ad (lost and found, personal, miscellaneous for sale, help wanted) and write the story behind the ad—how the item came to be for sale or why someone is looking for a ride to Connecticut. A variation is to have students tie together—juxtapose—two ads to form a comic situation. A third possibility is to let students respond to a classified ad specially prepared by the teacher. Comparing results makes learning to write almost fun.

832-I   *(Write/Sentences) "Watch Them Unfold"*

One or several pictures are pasted on one half of the inside of a manila file folder. The other half contains words that might be used with the picture(s). The two sources should help even the least creative writers to write a series of sentences telling whatever the picture suggests.

NARRATION

833-C *(Write/Papers) "From Print to Practice"*

After a story (or book) has been read, ask if anyone can identify in some way with the main characters (e.g., How many of you have owned a dog like the one in the story?). After a discussion that awakens many recollections among the class, students are urged to write a short narrative telling about their dog (or whatever) in some happening.

834-I *(Write/Papers) "Live and in Full Color"*

Character analysis becomes clearer for slower students when they consider a live model. After discussing character description, ask students to observe a television actor in a character role and to take notes while watching the program. Then have them write a description, including all the features and habits they noticed, and a summary of the character's personality. As an added attraction, let the rest of the class try to guess who is being described.

OVERVIEW

835-I *(Construct/Book Reports) "Grateful Integration"*

Here is a chance for a student to bring together many talents (their own and other's). Instead of the conventional book report, start with a skit centering upon a key scene in the story (several characters in costume before a simply constructed backdrop). The student giving the report can play the main character or be the narrator. Probably one or two of these a week can be handled, but the effort will be welcome and valuable.

836-I,G *(Construct/Demonstrations) "Research and Development"*

This idea is for individuals or pairs. They must use at least three books and a few articles to research a free-choice topic. Each presents his or her research to the class in any fashion. Make sure all audio-visual aids are available to the students. Topics may run the gamut from ESP to famous clowns.

837-I *(Construct/Displays) "Collage Graduates"*

"A picture is worth a thousand words" and may be effectively used to "tell" the plot or theme of a story. Depending upon the length and complexity of the plot, several pictures may be used to assemble a montage portraying action, theme, and characters more vividly. Conrad Richter's *Light in the Forest* is excellent for starters since pictures of Indians, forests, and pioneers are relatively easy to find or draw. Even so, the teacher should have a vast collection of magazines and catalogs. (See idea 702.)

838–C   *(Construct/Models) "Swinging Bookmobile"*

For an unusual approach to book reports have students make swinging book mobiles. Each student will need a clothes hanger and plenty of imagination. The first step is to cover the triangular base of the hanger with paper—plain, fancy, decorative, or textured. Next, make cutouts of characters in the book. Suspend these cutouts from the bottom rung of the hanger with thread, at different levels. Then write a synopsis of the book, mount it on colored paper, and fasten it on the back of the hanger. Hang these mobiles around the room and watch how they inspire other students to "look into" the books.

839–G   *(Speak/Books) "Being Party to Reading"*

Consider "reading parties" at crucial times during the year. Able readers from the class choose several favorite stories or poems. They practice until they can achieve a smooth, dynamic, oral presentation. Another class and parents may be invited to the event. Writing invitations can be an important facet of this activity. Students are motivated to do their very best reading and writing when the audience extends beyond the teacher or the class.

840–C   *(Write/Book) "Junior Book Makers"*

Does this teacher's case sound familiar? "A few years ago I was assigned to teach an English class. The required anthology contained selections which were either irrelevant or outdated and too difficult for my students to read. In response to my class's complaints, I challenged them to write their own book. Working in groups, they designed the cover and illustrated the stories, poems, and plays they wrote.

"Student-made materials like these could be collected over the years and kept in the classroom library as models and motivators. Perhaps such a book could be donated to a children's hospital or exchanged with other schools. Materials like these meet both the interest and reading levels of the creators. Even further, the pride of accomplishment is immeasurable."

POETRY

841–I   *(Write/Poems) "Poetic Grammar"*

Students can use parts of speech to write "near-poems" of five lines each. Ask them to follow these simple directions: (1) On the first line of your paper write a noun naming a person, place, or thing (or use your favorite definition). (2) On the next line write two adjectives that give some additional information about the noun. Separate each adjective with a comma. (3) On the third line write three verbs, also separated with commas, that tell what the noun does. (4) On the fourth line write a short phrase about the noun—anything that seems to follow the verbs or relate to the noun. (5) For the last line repeat the word you wrote on the first line or write a related word. Result? "Near-poems" such as these:

leaves	snow
red, golden	white, soft
flutter, glisten, float	falls, floats, covers
nature's decorations	winter sports
autumn	skiing

This activity makes students more aware that each word in a poem must carry much meaning and emotion and, thus, must be chosen with great care. For the slower student, such attention helps build vocabulary.

SHORT STORIES

842-I   *(Write/Forms) "Solve a Blank Problem"*

Students who have difficulty reading and writing can become very discouraged by a blank piece of paper and a stiff composition assignment. Help them by providing a short story, complete with key words, punctuation, and paragraphs. Leave blanks to be filled in with their own words and ideas. Completed stories can also be used later as springboards for grammar lessons.

843-I   *(Write/Papers) "Short Subjects"*

The structure of a major writing assignment on a short story or novel is not a stumbling block to students if they remember to answer the following questions in their papers:

1. Who is the main character?
2. Where does the story take place?
3. What does the main character set out to do?
4. What or who helps the main character?
5. What problems occur?
6. Does the main character succeed or fail?
7. How does everything turn out?
8. How does the reader feel about the book?

844-C,I *(Write/Papers) "What Happened Next?"*

The first half of a story is mimeographed and distributed to members of the class. Students are asked to finish it any way they want. Minimysteries are good for this purpose. Completed stories will be imaginative, uninhibited, and surprisingly revealing.

STUDY SKILLS

845-C *(Construct/Models) "Model Lesson"*

Accuracy in following directions is greatly increased when students are interested. The unusual motivates. Have each student bring to class a small cardboard box about shoe box size which can be cut with scissors. Then duplicate some written instructions (about three different forms) to be distributed on three colors of paper to assure better distribution of three projects. The students must then build what they read, e.g., a bird house or feeder with peculiar design, a psychedelic truck van, or an interesting store front. Scissors, felt pens, crayons, and construction paper are provided. No glue is needed if the directions instruct for making slots to hold roofs, wheels, awnings, and the like. The models need not consume much class time—about half an hour. The rest of the time can be used to compare each other's constructions and to view the three models the teacher built to help write the instruction sheets.

846-I *(Speak/Anecdotes) "Shares that Mature"*

Once a week each student "discovers" something in the library and, during a Friday, "know and tell" period, talks about it with at least one classmate. They could share information from a book, an article, or any reference. Each would try to explain his or her find in a well-organized, interesting way. Different partners could be chosen each week. This activity combines two desirable learnings in reading: locating and organizing information.

847-I *(Write/Instructions) "On Bows and Rugs and Things"*

Students write instructions on how to perform some sort of activity connected with a hobby or a craft. How to shoot a bow and arrow or how to hook a rug are just two examples for an assignment that puts into practice skills on organizing information.

848–I   *(Write/Papers) "New Designs on Composition"*

Draw a simple design on the chalkboard such as a wavy or crenelated line. Encourage students to complete the lines to make an object or a larger design. They then write a story or short essay which their sketch or design serves to illustrate. From this simple interesting approach, the students apply knowledge of organizing information around one central idea. To cite an example, one student imagined gear-like crenel to be the tops of two castle towers. In one, a young man was incarcerated and in the other, naturally, a young girl. How the two communicate and finally meet became an interesting story.

VOCABULARY

849–T   *(Solve/Puzzles) "Not So Crosswords"*

Collect crossword puzzles from every possible source, and make them available to your class during free time. If you can create some crossword puzzle addicts, you give these students a relaxing yet challenging recreation and also a lifetime source of vocabulary enrichment.

850–I   *(Write/Paragraphs) "A Wordy Story"*

Place four new words on a piece of paper. Select a willing student from the class who will take the list and write a very short paragraph or story using the same words in different contexts. That way the meanings are clarified in use rather than through unrelated dictionary definitions.

Part Five

ROOM MANAGEMENT

17 Introduction

18 Deliberation

19 Evaluation

20 Application

17 Introduction

In this revised edition of the Handbook, each of the original items in this chapter has been compressed as much as possible, some into several key sentences to make room for a frequently suggested addition. This new section is called "101 Test-Writing Ideas" and features many different ways to phrase English essay and objective test questions to make this section of Room Management an even more valuable resource. To conserve space also, the original format has been altered to retain only the main I-D-E-A headings and the content words used for grouping.

ATTITUDES

851   *"A Low Profile"*

Sometimes the best way to teach is to become inconspicuous, allowing the students to bear much of the burden of research and preparation. Frequently be a facilitator rather than a presenter. Keep a low profile when student interest is high and when they are self-motivated.

852   *"Bogus Checks"*

Students soon begin to ignore teachers who call for class attention then continue their "housekeeping details" at the desk. "Quiet!" means "something is going to take place now, so please listen." If it doesn't mean that, soon "Quiet!" will mean nothing to the class.

853   *"Creative Encounters"*

For some reason, educators and authors seem to restrict truly creative lessons to elementary school children. Older students are destined to days of dull discussions and test reviews unless the instructor improvises. For ideas about class projects, motivational techniques, and culminating activities, middle and high school teachers can search the volumes written about elementary school approaches. Displays, puppet shows, games, skits, and other activities can be as stimulating in high school as they were in those early years.

854   *"Feeling Ah-h-h!"*

Comfort is an important aid to learning. If the teacher is relaxed and allows students to relax, the general attitude and
learning process is heightened. Tend also to lighting, seating,
temperature, extraneous noise, and other essentials that affect
learning.

855   *"Great Leveler"*

A teacher must be honest and sincere with students. An open
mind to their ideas and opinions is imperative to command
their respect, stimulate their minds, and encourage their
participation.

856   *"Look to Yourself"*

Discipline problems often stem from the teacher rather than from
the class. Since no lesson plan will be successful in a class in
which the teacher cannot be heard over the noise, here are
some thoughts to keep in mind. Discipline breaks down when:

1. Demands, standards, and expectations of the teacher are
   too high
2. Students have too little work and not enough challenge
3. Extreme authoritarianism or its opposite become the teacher's pattern.
4. The teacher is inconsistent
5. Students can't keep up with the instruction
6. The teacher overestimates the attention span of the class
7. Timing of class activities is poor.

857   *"Look Toward the 80s"*

A successful junior high school teacher suggests this: "When
English is taught at the middle and junior high levels, subject
matter accounts for only 20 percent of the students' needs.
Ideally, the other 80 percent concerns care, attention, and
deepest empathy."

858   *"Moderate Joiner"*

Teachers' attitudes toward their jobs and their desire to keep
abreast in their field are often reflected through active membership in professional groups. English teachers are fortunate
to have one of the largest subject matter organizations in the
world—The National Council of Teachers of English. Beside
benefitting from its wide offerings of teacher resources and
journals (elementary, secondary, college, and English
education), teachers can participate in conferences and hold
office. Many states have English councils affiliated with
NCTE. Membership in both state and national English groups
should be a must for each English teacher.

859 *"Sensitivity Activity"*

After several days (up to a week) of school, use this to help you
and the classes know each other better. Students prepare montages (collages) made up of pictures (very small items) that
characterize them: likes, dislikes, hobbies, interests, ambitions,
homelife, and so on. For added interest, the class guesses
whose ID card they are examining via the opaque projector.

860 *"The SAP on Which Every Student Thrives"*

Successful classroom teachers need more than a good subject
matter background. They need to know how to bring the "SAP
of life" into the classroom, i.e., those three areas tied so closely
with basic human needs. Students need to feel the *security* of a
class where an unthreatening learning climate prevails. They
need to feel and share *affection* (or appreciation)—the knowledge that they are liked and needed class members. Finally, they
need a chance to have successful learning experiences, to
achieve full potential, and to apply particular talents—in
short, they need to gain *prestige* among peers and with the
teacher. Naturally, these three basic needs have many related
aspects, but following the magic "three" will help solve many
problems before they occur.

861 *"Write 1,000 Times: I Will Never . . ."*

In establishing and maintaining order within a classroom,
subject matter is never used as a threat. For example, to eliminate a disruptive element by requiring extra compositions or
memorizing poems actually defeats the purpose of the English
class.

AUTHORITIES

862 *"Para Pros"*

Take time in the beginning of the year to survey parents (perhaps a brief questionnaire sent home). Find out who can come
to talk to your classes: actors, poets, novelists, mimists, reporters, plumbers, architects, computer programmers, etc.

BOOKS

863 *"Buying Library Stocks"*

Students broaden their own reading backgrounds more readily
if good books are available. Start a classroom paperback library. At the beginning of the year collect about fifty cents
from each student in all your classes and order a wide selection of paperbacks (probably 100 to 150) to be attractively

stored and displayed. Students use the room library during free reading time or after school. They may also sign out books overnight. Then at the end of the school year and after the last class session, each gets a chance for the "grab-book"—reaching into a box for a book that he or she can keep, trade, or sell.

864   *"Do-It-Yourself Book"*

Not satisfied with a book or several you must use? Make up your own. Write and assemble (even with student help) the type of book you want. A publishing house will print small quantities using economical paper and offset plates. Copyrights should be no problem for class sets used in a single school if you credit sources.

865   *"Spice Is Right"*

Use a multi-text for variety. One source is short story collections. Some worth checking are *Black Voices: An Anthology of Afro-American Literature* by Abraham Chapman, editor, and *Women and Fiction* by Susan Cahill, both from Mentor. Others are *The American Short Story,* Calvin Shaggs, editor (Dell) and *The Comic Spirit in America,* John D. Massey, editor (Charles Scribner's). Of course, many other alternatives to a single textbook are available for improved motivation and wider understanding.

BULLETIN BOARDS

866   *"Dig that Display"*

Copy good bulletin board ideas on 3 × 5 cards which are classified and filed in a recipe box. Both teacher and students will then have many ideas on which to base new installations. Solve the lettering problem by keeping envelopes containing several sizes and styles of cardboard letters. Whenever a new bulletin board title is needed, these templates can be traced on colored construction paper. Incidently, placing letters on banners is easier than trying to pin them up singly.

867   *"Eye of the Beholder"*

When designing a bulletin board, try to fit your themes, ideas, and illustrations into a pattern that will carry the eye across the board. Use connecting lines, diagonal lines, semicircles, wavy lines, and other devices.

868 *"Leave It to Them"*

Select a student bulletin board committee to help you collect and file, as well as occasionally install, a display. (Also see idea 874.)

869 *"Living Color"*

The bulletin board is often the only source of classroom decor. Too often it is not used to good advantage. Take every opportunity to install bulletin boards coinciding with what is being discussed and investigated. Studying *Moby Dick,* for instance, provides the chance to display several vivid photographs of whaling and life at sea. Sources are weekly periodicals, travel magazines, and especially *National Geographic.* An empty or cluttered bulletin board speaks poorly of teacher planning.

870 *"No Board 'Em"*

Good bulletin boards reflect student backgrounds and interests. Consider, then, more than just displays of colorful magazine illustrations and posters. Use small picture hooks for fastening many kinds of items to the bulletin board: record albums, framed or unframed art prints, or miniature models from dolls to ducks. Anything in hardware should not be overlooked to enhance learning.

871 *"Try Trivia"*

Reserve a small corner of a bulletin board for a "Trivia Corner." Each week post a question the students can answer by going to a dictionary or other reference book. Questions resemble this: What two presidents in the twentieth century did not seek re-election? At the end of the week post the answers along with a new question. This serves many purposes, such as introducing students to subjects other than English and getting students to use reference materials.

CHALKBOARDS

872 *"Chalk Talk"*

Writing on the chalkboard doesn't seem to be a subject worthy of much attention. But many good lessons have gone down the drain because the teacher forgot some simple details:

1. Erase a dirty board with uniform up-and-down motions.
2. Write where windows do not cause a glare for some students. Use draperies or shades if available.
3. Learn to write so that you are not in front of material as it is being written. Stand to the side.
4. Keep the writing high enough so students don't need to stand to see.
5. Allow students to help write on the board at times— especially if you write poorly.

873   *"Phrase-y Idea"*

One way to spark interest in an otherwise unreceptive class is to use "asides." Each day write a one- or two-line phrase to the side of the chalkboard. If the sayings are clever enough, student discussions on meaning and application often occur.

DEMONSTRATIONS

874   *"Filling the File"*

Teacher demonstrations need resource materials. Provide a file folder for each chapter or unit. Fill it with relevant magazine and newspaper clippings, government bulletins, travel folders, etc. Get contributions, too, from parents through their students.

DISCUSSIONS

875   *"Roll with the Punches"*

Don't drag a sluggish lesson plan to its conclusion. Start a discussion on archaeology, ghost stories, smoke signals, or any subject about which you are informed. The class will appreciate the switch. So will you.

876   *"Warm Up"*

Tune in to the moods of your class. Hear what they are chattering about as they come into the room—last night's football game, a new record, a popular movie, a TV show, or a tragic accident. Start some days just "rapping" about their interests.

DISPLAYS

877   *"Go Psychedelic"*

A dull room environment can actually detract from good teaching and learning. For students to feel excited about English, science, or any subject, they should see exciting things in their classrooms. Placing modern, psychedelic posters or art prints around may inspire a story or a poem. Aquariums promote relaxing and thinking. Mobiles, purchased or homemade, can swing intriguingly from the ceiling, making even the dullest room more interesting. Terrariums are easy to make and keep, but perhaps the simplest and most effective decorations are flowers and plants. Students really appreciate a teacher with a green thumb.

878   *"Hobby Lobby"*

Reserve a table in one isolated corner of the room. Hang a sign over it: "Hobby of the Week." Students take turns bringing in and displaying a hobby, even if it is just a collection of books. All displays need not be subject-matter connected.

GAMES

879   *"T.G.I.F."*

Try to make Friday a better day for students and teacher. After four days of school, the class sometimes finds it difficult to settle down to serious work. Arrange an activity that does not bind them to their seats in silence. Group work, games, or free reading periods are some of the ways to go.

HANDOUTS

880   *"Complete Returns"*

If you have a habit of loaning pens to students and then forgetting to get them back, try one of these ideas: Remove the cap of the borrowed pen and set it upright on the desk in front of you as a reminder. No one wants a capless pen in a pocket or purse. Or write the name of the borrower on the corner of the board. This puts pressure on the student to return the pen or whatever was borrowed.

881   *"Pretty, Good Handouts"*

Do your class handouts begin to look dull—always the same? Try duplicating on colored paper or using art in the margins. Sometimes place copy in boxes instead of the traditional paragraphs.

INSTRUCTIONS

882   *"No More Excuses"*

When it comes to class assignments, prevent the usual "but I didn't know what I was supposed to read." Duplicate the assignments; include the dates they are due. One danger, of course, is that the frequent use of dull white sheets of paper will decrease the desire to read this outline. Avoid this by varying the color of the paper and the format.

LECTURES

883   *"Coming Attractions"*

Don't underestimate outline handouts. Use them to help students follow along the teacher's lectures, to describe a unit of work (topics, activities, culminating projects, and all), or to simply present a day-to-day guide for each week's classwork. This gives students a secure feeling.

884   *"Common-sensical"*

Unless the teacher is an exceptionally good lecturer, an oral presentation lasting more than fifteen minutes at a time can be "deadly." Shift activities at least twice during each class period.

885   *"Delayed Action"*

One way to handle class questions and replies that come out of sequence (but ones you want to come back to later) is to have a class secretary jot them down. Give credit for service jobs like that.

886   *"Maybe It's Not What You Say"*

Where you stand and how you move when presenting material to a class can enhance listening. Don't stand in front of a brighly lit window. Let students see your facial expressions. Move dramatically to emphasize a point or to change pace.

887   *"Punctuated Lectures"*

When preparing a lecture try to anticipate unspoken questions the students might have, especially in the difficult areas. At these points make a comment such as "take notice" or "listen closely." A few simplified illustrations and a probing question or two will also assure getting the point across.

888   *"Speaking Wisely"*

In the classroom use a normal, literate vocabulary. Do not talk down to the students. Get into the habit of using appositives, synonyms, or explanatory phrases without breaking sentence flow. For instance, "When Siddhartha joined the ascetics—the self-sacrificing group—he learned things he couldn't have learned in his rich home." When using a word like *asceticism*— the philosophy of denying the body to improve the spirit— write it on the chalkboard while talking. Students will learn to improve their vocabularies if you pay close attention to your own.

LIBRARIES

889   *"Research Me"*

Get your class into library research gently. For a while have them answer questions on a sheet by digging into various sources: What is a sissy bar? Name three songs by (popular music group). Which state capitols (if any) have the same name? and so on.

MIXED MEDIA

890   *"All Work and No Fun"*

Make full use of audio-visual aids to entertain as well as to teach. A child who has been having fun is more likely to accept a learning situation than one who is hopelessly bored.

891   *"Machine Overdose"*

The days that projectors, films, recordings, and the like can be used are limited. Gimmicks and electronic equipment do not always make live and interesting classes. Build plans around what can be spoken, written, read, or duplicated on paper, using the hardware as supplementary aids. Strive to create variety, enthusiasm, and novelty with traditional materials.

892 *"Pandora's Box"*

Provide a box in which students may deposit anything that has even the remotest bearing on what the class is discussing and what is happening in the world. Suggest articles, cartoons, books, photos, slides, films, tapes, records, magazines, toys, games, flowering plants, original stories, and poems. There is one stipulation. A note explaining how the item can be used in the class must be attached to the object. Select a student committee to empty the box periodically and to share with the teacher the ideas they think can be worked in.

893 *"Unconventional Thinking"*

One teacher uses the "top ten" songs of the week to teach spelling and reading. Students appreciate the unconventional, interesting teacher who is not always bound by tradition.

NEWSPAPERS

894 *"Extra! Read All about It"*

An economical textbook is the local newspaper. Get a class supply for at least several weeks (economical if the school gets a rate). Study what makes good reading. Are there parallels, say, in literature?

NOTES

895 *"A Big Stick"*

Communicate with each student at least once a week. Have mail boxes in the room or just a stick into which numbered slots have been cut.

896 *"Smile"*

Write happy notes to everybody. Get a few note pads printed up "From the desk of . . . ." Correspond widely with the staff and students. Tell a joke, quip, or draw a picture. It'll brighten their day as well as yours.

PERIODICALS

897 *"Recycled Resources"*

Read magazines and journals with a pencil handy. Write page numbers on covers. Then when you are ready to go to the paper bin rescue these pages for your files.

PICTURES

898 *"One for the Files"*

Manila file folders need not be relegated to dusty file drawers. In folders (some are available in colors) fasten interesting, individualized assignments created around colorful magazine illustrations. The main advantage is that folders can be labeled and filed in some order for reuse. These assignments can serve as strengthening exercises or extra challenge work. Once shown how, students can create their own sets of instructional materials or learning packets, an excellent resource for student tutoring.

PLANS

899 *"Bridging the Gap"*

Gimmicks may be employed as motivation for learning, but true motivation exists only when the students experience a gap—a curiosity gap, knowledge gap, generation gap, credibility gap, or whatever. This gap must be recognized directly at the start of the hour and with such force that everyone will want to "hang in there" until the gap has been bridged. The clever teacher doesn't lay the final plank until just before the hour is up.

900 *"Good IDEA"*

Lesson plans need not be elaborate. If overly detailed, they only discourage planning. Paradoxically some teacher education methods courses have forced a lengthy type of planning which will never be used even though all teachers need to plan. Use the acronym *IDEA* to sketch out the essentials of any daily plan with built-in variety (even useful when considering unit plans).

I means instruction (what should be taught), stated in several brief, student-oriented learning objectives.

D is demonstration (from simple models to feature films) to clarify instruction.

E is for evaluation (feedback to find out if the instruction got through), usually oral questioning but sometimes a written quiz.

A refers to application (putting the skills or concepts to use, outside the classroom as well as in, because unapplied ideas are soon forgotten).

A lesson plan, then, is a simple set of objectives and procedures—reminders—implementing the four phases of any lesson. Sound familiar? It should. This *idea*book is built around a similar format. (For related idea see Appendix.)

901   *"Just You and I"*

Plans should allow some time for the teacher to meet with each student for ten or fifteen minutes (alone if possible) once every report period.

902   *"Listen and Learn"*

Use students' ideas freely. Plan a unit now and then that is made up entirely of students' objectives and the procedures they suggest to achieve those objectives.

903   *"Look, Listen, Stop"*

Stop if you are getting clues that your class is becoming bored or that you are not getting across the information. Plan each lesson, but plan flexibly so that if you are in trouble you can change technique or even the entire plan. Lesson plans are guides, not masters.

904   *"On Being Weaned"*

Junior high, middle school planning must gradually move from teacher-directed activities to self-direction. Students who never get to progress on their own fall apart when this freedom comes more naturally in senior high school.

905   *"Peer Group Disapproval"*

Opening up a classroom for student-centered activities and assignments does not mean that the teacher becomes a teenage peer to students, nor that respect for the teacher gives way to anarchy. The open classroom is a way to achieve more comprehensive communication but without negating individual responsibility or plain hard work.

906 *"Positively Controlled"*

Good planning shows a teacher who cares: one who sets achievable goals, believes all students can learn, seeks ways to reach everyone, accepts differences, adapts teaching methods to a wide range of individual needs, utilizes student strengths and natural interests, builds in praise, and rewards frequently.

907 *"Roll Role"*

One way to avoid wasting teaching time with housekeeping duties and procedures is to assign room responsibilities to students. For example, one can take the daily roll call. Several can be responsible for the distribution and collection of materials. When tasks are performed consistently, students will soon feel responsibility for both discipline and learning.

908 *"The NCTE's of Written Comp"*

By using the abbreviation for the National Council of Teacher's of English (NCTE), a teacher can easily recall the four main aspects introducing any composition assignment.

> *N* is for *needs*. This area can be divided two ways: between an individual's composition needs (from one paper to the next) and the need to write with a realistic purpose—not an empty exercise for a grade.
> *C* is for *climate*. The atmosphere of the room must be conducive to relaxed, good writing. Providing unsurmountable hurdles is not the way to make eager writers.
> *T* is for *topic* (or content). Each composition assignment must be broad enough to reach all interests and flexible enough to meet the ability levels of everyone.
> *E* is for *evaluation*. No assignment should be overcorrected. Using a fair but challenging grading system that considers individual differences is a must. Eliminating fear of grades will help encourage more fluent writing.

909 *"2 W's + 2 H's"*

A well-written learning objective is meaningful as well as specific. A test for a good objective is to ask four journalistic-type questions: Who? What? How? and How well? A meaningful objective tells or implies *who* it is for, *what* the learner is expected to be able to do if the objective is achieved, *how* this learning is to be facilitated (sources of helps, conditions), and *how well* the learner must perform to achieve the objective. Certainly not all objectives can or should contain each of the criteria, but the more information stated, the more specific and measurable the objective will be. (See also the Appendix.) Here is an example of such a four-level objective:

Who? (Easily determined from wording—preferably student oriented)
What? To spell twenty words
How? To spell twenty words from the list of twenty-five in chapter one
How well? To spell twenty words from the list of twenty-five in chapter one and do so with 90 percent accuracy.

PROJECTORS

910   *"Up the Wall"*

It the movie screen is missing, use a wall, back of a map, even the ceiling with kids lying on the floor. Project a theme on a chalkboard so that corrections can be written in.

SLIDES

911   *"Spice Is Nice"*

Add a little spice to your slide shows by including a few of your own. The class erupts when a slide of you at the beach gets "mysteriously" mixed in with "The Life of Dickens."

TALK

912   *"Is Anybody Listening?"*

Teachers too often do not develop students' listening skills. Create a unit in which listening is the key skill. This is an addition to frequent oral tests and notetaking.

913   *"Shy Guy"*

A shy student should speak to a small group in class several times before presenting to the entire class.

914   *"Why Me English No Good?"*

Students need to know that standard English is a goal but that speaking a dialect has a place in our society. Learning English is a process of "addition," not "subtraction."

TELEVISION

915 *"Channeling Interests"*

Take advantage of the educational resources available via television. Watch for announcements of stimulating programs and dramas. Assign classes to watch those that tie in with current units or are of special interest. This activity is useful for slower students who cannot read well. Networks and other agencies provide special program guides for schools. Try to get on their mailing lists.

TRANSPARENCIES

916 *"Not Live but in Full Color"*

To make your own transparency or "translift": (1) locate a picture or map on clay-coated paper (the kind that sticks to wet fingers); (2) heat laminate the inked side; (3) soak the paper and the plastic in detergent water; (4) peel off the paper so that the ink remains; and (5) when the ink has dried on the plastic, laminate the other side so that the ink is sandwiched between. A slightly inferior translift can be made using clear adhesive contact film and eliminating the heat lamination. The process and results are basically the same.

TUTORS

917 *"Do-It-Yourself Kid"*

Find out strengths of your students. Each one can tutor another student in some area of school work.

918 *"Peer Teachers"*

Occasionally allow a student to present the lesson on a relevant topic, but give the student at least a week to prepare. The history behind a novel, play, or poem would be good for such an assignment.

18 Deliberation

BULLETIN BOARDS

919 *"Board of Education"*

A participation bulletin board is a way to "discuss" content through relevant drawings, photographs, and items in print. Each student plays a part.

CHARTS

920 *"For the Record"*

Design a recording system by which students can keep their own progress charts—one that is easy to read but informative and motivational.

DISCUSSIONS

921 *"No More Disgusting Discussing"*

Some teachers fail as discussion leaders. The technique is simple but takes practice: an interesting, worthwhile topic; common-sense ground rules (no interruptions, etc.); clear goals; open-ended questions when needed; and a good wrap-up.

922 *"Somethin' Brewin' "*

Little is known about what creativity really is, but research has indicated that it can be fostered and developed. One way is to separate idea production from evaluation. During class discussions individuals should feel free to express any thought that comes to mind without fearing ridicule or the consequences of a lowered mark or adverse teacher opinion. Many good, creative ideas are sure to develop in a permissive atmosphere.

923 *"Something Old, Something New"*

Lead into a class discussion of new material with a few well-chosen questions prepared in advance. Questions should deal with something with which all the students are familiar: some relating past studies to a new material, others relating to world problems or student experiences. Questions should deal with comprehension of facts, vocabulary, and inference. Whatever the lead-in, it should pique student curiosity for the new material.

924 *"Talking in Circles"*

The "circular response" discussion is effective for involving every class member. Too often discussions are monopolized by a few but not necessarily by those who have the most to contribute. In this plan the class is seated in a circle. A question or topic is introduced and someone begins the discussion. The person sitting to the left of that speaker is next to speak (or can pass), and the discussion moves clockwise around the entire circle. No one person is allowed to speak out of turn. When a question has been thoroughly discussed, even though all students in the circle have not spoken, the next question is introduced where the other left off. While some students learn better by listening and others by talking, there is no reason for not involving the quiet ones.

FIELD TRIPS

925 *"Questionable Field Trip"*

Before a field trip ask each student to write out and hand in one question about the trip (the subject to be explored) that he or she would like answered. After the field trip use these questions for test reviewing the results of the experience. If desired, students can be graded not only on the questions answered but also on those asked.

GAMES

926 *"Altogether"*

Whether you are teaching in a middle school, junior, or senior high, competition can be used to build strong motivation. For a unit project divide the class into teams to compete for the best-project award in any one of several categories (best designed, presented, or written; most humorous; etc.). Or have one class compete with another.

927 *"Are You Game?"*

With a few changes in rules, such classic games as Monopoly and Easy Money can be used to practice recent learnings. Game boards can be drawn on plastic and, with an overhead projector, can be projected for all to see. Players' markers can be small circles, stars, squares, or triangles which are silhouetted on the screen to show moves. For further suggestions consult the Index of this book under "Games."

928   *"Going on Record"*

For review games use some hardware, in this case, a tape recorder. Have all questions on tape along with electronic beeps to time answers. The process could go something like this: "Team One, the correct answer to the following question is good for a six-space move (on the board) and may be discussed by your group. You have one minute to answer this question: 'Judging from the action in the story, when would you say it took place, last half of the nineteenth century, early twentieth century, or the present?' " Then sixty beeps are followed by a "ding." If the team gets the answer before the bell, it moves its marker, and the tape then "cues up" the next team. This can get very exciting because there is no way to vary the speed of the action. Besides checking on knowledge, this approach tests ability to listen carefully.

INVENTORIES

929   *"A Couple 'a Words"*

Word relationships can be fun and are good practice for students who plan to apply to universities. Make up a series of multiple choice analogies that give the reader practice in analyzing a situation. For the educational value, include some words that are not familiar. For example:

Gas : (is to) car : : (as) _____ : _____ .
(a) scepter : king
(b) food : man
(c) oil : engine
(d) scale : music

LECTURES

930   *"Sensible Consensus"*

Sometimes students will dispute the teacher's ideas or statements. Although such disagreements can be resolved by comparing evidence for both points of view, inevitably some teachers finally use their authority to settle the matter. To avoid this, write the objection(s) on the chalkboard. This gives time to think, and it indicates the students' point of view is worth considering. Matters reflecting differing cultural values or beliefs may be unresolvable but are worth discussing. Other, more factual, statements can be deliberated to attempt consensus.

LIBRARIES

931   *"Cutting Class"*

To help the class become more familiar with the school library and what it has to offer, send students to the library in small prearranged groups of five or six. This can be done on a daily basis after necessary instruction and information has been presented. This keeps the class size more manageable and tends to cut down the disturbance of sending an entire class.

MIXED MEDIA

932   *"What Next?"*

Discuss the various ways of communicating: oral or written methods, photography, painting, sculpture, music, body movement, and so on. Then class members think up one idea they want to share with others. They must find at least one way to present this idea other than formal conversation or writing.

PLANS

933   *"On Being Unpredictable"*

Be unpredictable during the deliberation phase of the teaching-learning sequence. Every once in a while forget teaching English for a day; instead, introduce a wide-open discussion on current issues that affect students—changing life roles, educational innovation, new ways to handle world problems, to name a few.

QUESTIONS

934   *"Ask Me Anything"*

After students have become familiar with whatever is being studied, divide them into two groups. For fifteen minutes, have each group make up questions to ask the other. They use their books for this phase. Then have each side question the other (without books), giving one point for each correct answer. There are many different ways to design the questioning procedure, e.g., switch each time or go on until a side misses. This is an excellent review procedure.

935   *"Mutual Aid"*

A switch on students writing review questions is to have them write questions they cannot answer. Collect the questions and involve the entire class in answering. Chances are good all questions will be answered. A few might appear on the next test.

SEATING

936   *"Classy Arrangement"*

Don't resist a preset seating arrangement. It helps in learning names, the first step toward rapport. If students can move around for group work, team work, and round-table discussion, they won't resent sitting in assigned seats for formal classroom activities.

937   *"Seat of the Problem"*

The basic horseshoe or circle seating arrangement is still a good idea to promote discussion and involvement since students feel more like participating. Just as the teacher wants to be able to see all the faces, each student wants to watch classmates react to what he or she says. In this seating arrangement, the teacher becomes more *a part* of the group, rather than *apart*.

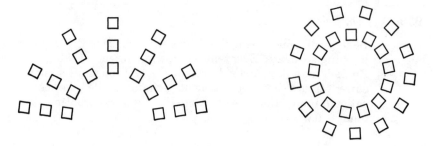

Other Arrangements

TALK

938   *"Breaking Up the Class"*

To give each student a greater opportunity to speak and be heard, reorganize formal class sessions into group workshops. Try to place at least one energetic, cooperative leader in each group. Workshop projects are unlimited; anything from covering the textbook to assessing the human condition.

939   *"Meeting of Minds"*

Students need to practice democratic living. Classroom meetings run by a class president and secretary provide opportunities to practice *Robert's Rules of Order*—a baseline program for better human relations.

940   *"Party Line"*

Demonstrate the need to communicate clearly. Give one child a short sentence. He or she whispers the message to the next student who, in turn, whispers what was heard to the next. This process continues until all have participated. The last person then announces what he or she heard. In an attempt to trace the message breakdown, each student—beginning with the last—repeats what he or she heard. Generally the original message is changed unintentionally at least once.

941   *"Shoring Up the Shy One"*

Offer alternatives to the students who find it difficult to speak in front of the class. One approach is to conduct an interview. The person interviewed may be another student, teacher, or visiting dignitary. The fact that two subjects are sharing the limelight may be just the thing to "crack the ice." Panel discussions serve a similar purpose.

TUTORS

942   *"T-Day* the *Day"*

Plan for student involvement when one student a week plans a fifteen- to twenty-minute teaching presentation or demonstration—anything from teaching a golf swing or skateboard stunt to a discussion of occupations that are disappearing. Let them use audio-visual aids, too.

19 Evaluation

ATTITUDES

943 *"Bang in the Eye"*

Students are *looking* at the teacher as well as listening. Instead of sitting motionless behind the desk while presenting information, the teacher should move and use meaningful gestures to maintain interest. Annoying habits such as rocking back and forth and playing with the hair (women and some men need to keep their bangs out of their eyes) only detract from the oral demonstration. Most important of all, the voice should be effective. If the presentation is weak or distracting, the class won't listen long enough to find the message.

944 *"Best Four-Lettered Word"*

Be K-I-N-D to students. Use positive reinforcement.

945 *"Boxed Ears"*

Too often teachers wait for their own evaluations until the end of a term or year when it is too late to change anything for the current students. Even if you read some comments you don't like, the trends in student remarks should be helpful.

946 *"Change of Angle"*

Advising a school club or chaperoning a school activity is a learning experience for you, the teacher! It helps to know your students from different vantage points. Sometimes it will completely change the way you regard them in class.

947 *"Duds for Duds"*

The teacher sets the pace in the classroom. A teacher who looks dowdy and dull in face and figure turns off a class. Having a sparkling smile and tasteful and interesting clothes (even to cover up a sad mood) goes a long way to improve student evaluations of their teacher and to enhance learning.

948   *"Fifty-Fifty Split"*

If two students are caught cheating on a written test, there is an alternative to taking away both papers and giving zeroes. Suppose the two wrote papers worth ninety points each. Divide the score equally so that each gets forty-five points, obviously a failing grade, yet, no points or papers have been taken away, and both copier and copyee receive equal credit—probably F.

949   *"How'm I Doin'?"*

Periodically allow the students to grade themselves and comment on their progress. The teacher need not rely on this grade as one to be recorded, but often it works out that way. From this type of evaluation, teachers can assess their own accomplishments.

950   *"Let's Get Personal"*

Show students that teachers are human, too, through personal anecdotes. Pick up on subjects that bother students. Relate, if true, that as a youth you were self-conscious about a "deformity": skinny legs, small bust, boney shoulders, ribs that could be counted, facial pimples, protruding ears, large nose, or even the "wrong color hair."

951   *"Shake, Pal"*

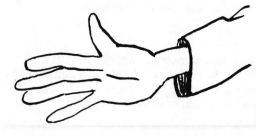

Becoming friends with the school custodian will pay dividends when you need those extra services—a new bulletin board, some clay pots for flowers, a change in the seating arrangement, or a quicker response when someone parts with a too-hasty lunch.

952   *"Switch Roles"*

Each time you give a letter grade to a student, check the objectivity of your judgments. The following experiment may help you discover the value of this approach. When you grade a problem case, write down the reasons for giving that grade. Then imagine you are that student and ask yourself if you can accept the reasons the teacher gave to explain your grade. This self-test allows you to discover whether your basis for assigning grades is subjective or objective.

953   *"Three Reasons for Promptness"*

Barring an emergency, the teacher should see that homework
and tests are returned to the students promptly for several
reasons: (1) The more immediate the feedback from the teacher,
the more valuable the assignment to the student. (2) It shows
that the teacher recognizes the importance of the work in time
and effort. (3) The teacher builds student rapport by showing
consideration for their anxieties. When the teacher returns
papers promptly, the class learns to expect it as a regular
practice.

954   *"Why You're You"*

You and your students can evaluate attitudes with different
assignments such as these: (1) completion statements like "The
thing I like best about myself is _____." (See also idea 972.); (2)
one thing that would make you most happy; (3) three things
that make you feel good; (4) four things that make you angry;
(5) ten things you are good at; or (6) three beliefs (views) you
support very strongly.

CHARTS

955   *"Spot Check"*

The unusual and accurate evaluation technique is to check off
on a seating chart the students who participate in class discussion each day. At the end of the week, by looking at the "scat-
ter pattern," the teacher has concise knowledge of which students are and are not participating. The latter can then be
brought into the discussions.

CONFERENCES

956   *"Grading Goes Live"*

Avoid too much emphasis on letter grades. Use personal conferences and extensive written comments. This gives students
a more accurate evaluation of themselves. What does the rest
of the class do during conferences? Hundreds of ideas in this
book can help.

957   *"Information Please"*

Conferences with students can be more effective with some
advance planning. First, the student should have information
on progress. The best for this is a collection of important assignments saved in a file folder or envelope. Next, the student
needs to know his or her standing for the inevitable grade. A

point chart or some kind of profile will suffice. (See idea 157.) Finally, the teacher should have specific objectives set for each conference.

FIELD TRIPS

958   *"Be a Sport"*

Attend the school's athletic and social events. Students are quick to notice who is really interested in what they do and who is not. Students like to know that someone enjoys the same things they do.

959   *"Getting to Know All about You"*

If you are new to a school system, get acquainted with the school and the community before the school year begins. Two things are gained by this evaluation. First, you become aware of the teaching resources available in the school and community. Second, you learn how this community differs from others you know. This may affect your entire teaching approach and will certainly reveal many unique opportunities for special assignments.

FORMS

960   *"Color Me 'A' "*

Prevent the grade book from becoming a mass of illegible letters, numbers, checks, and symbols. Arrange it so that it is clear at a glance what grade applies to what type of assignment (for both instructor and student). Use colors in the vertical columns, keying each color to different areas of work. (See idea 961.) Each color color could have a different weight in relation to the final grade. Another way to avoid confusion is to place cumulative points in the boxes, with the last entry always representing the total at a given time. This final figure can be easily translated into a letter grade without adding.

961   *"Color-Vision"*

Need a quick way to distinguish marks or scores for various assignments? To differentiate easily between small, medium-sized, and major projects and tests, record the marks in pencil, blue ink, and red ink respectively. When it is time to average marks, count the pencil marks once; the blue, twice; the red, three times, in a system of weighting by thirds. In fairness to them, tell students whether an assignment is to be level one, two, or three. As a double check, always identify each column of marks by a name, page, or exercise number.

INSTRUCTIONS

962   *"Cannot Tell a Lie"*

After the procedural tasks are dealt with the first day of school, relax and get to know your students. One activity that will appeal to most of them is "To Tell a Lie." Students are to describe themselves accurately but to include one "white lie." The class tries to guess from the talk or the paper being read what portion is not true. Some students will telegraph clues when they reach the exaggeration. Others will handle it well. Start off with your own offering as an example.

963   *"Rules, Rules, Rules"*

The first day of class is the time to introduce at least a few rules for the students to follow. You will be tested anyway as to your expectations, so speed the process by telling what you expect. Pages and pages of "do's" and don't's" may look impressive but will probably introduce more problems than they solve.

INVENTORIES

964   *"Belief Relief"*

Teachers often have two problems when teaching: relating the past to the present or vice versa and helping students express themselves well orally and on paper. One way to accomplish both is to use a questionnaire to obtain student beliefs about man, religion, government, and so on. Discussing these in class will provide writing topics.

965   *"If I Were the Teacher"*

Students generally appreciate the opportunity to write one-page papers describing what they would like to have you teach in the English class. Tell them that from these papers you will get ideas on which to base class assignments and longer units of work.

966   *"Drawing Out a Class"*

If you are concerned about your effectiveness as a teacher, try this different way to get feedback. Ask each student to draw a picture or design conceptualizing the class. Indicate you are more interested in an emotional rather than simply a physical response. Show a few samples from previous classes to awaken imaginations. Since the drawings need not be signed, some truthful responses should occur. Watch to see how large you appear in the drawings, perhaps an indication of you as an authority figure. Other traits to check are whether or not colors or shapes are dark and foreboding or light and cheery. A drawing cluttered with many objects might reflect on your neatness or on how your instruction is coming across. Generally, the more normal and beautiful the picture, the better the student views your class. By studying these impressions and selecting trends, you should be able to obtain a fairly good overall picture of yourself.

967   *"No More Complaints"*

A common student complaint is too much homework. On the second day of class the teacher can assess student feeling regarding homework and the pattern of their study habits. Tell them which units are to be covered, and how much they will be writing and reading. Explain the school and class requirements. Students and teacher can then work out a general outline that will suit both parties.

968   *"Psych 'em Out"*

To create a sense of group identity in the first few days of class, ask students to rearrange the seats to permit good eye contact among themselves. Do not give any directions. Do not appoint any leaders. The results will help answer these questions: Are the students auditory learners? Can they take oral directions? Who are the class leaders, the followers? Do the class members work well with each other? Who becomes involved and who does not? This information can be used to plan instruction.

969   *"Self Check"*

To discover the students' interests and to keep a check on yourself, devote an entire class session to such questions as "What is English class to you?" "What would you like to see happen in English class?" Answers to these questions are needed for successful teaching.

970   *"Teacher, Take Note"*

The task of writing out final grade reports becomes easier and more accurate if you select two or three students each day, observe them carefully, and take brief notes. In four weeks you can have an observation file on a class as large as forty. This will help prevent blanks in your memory when you have to write comments, when you must decide between a C+ or a B–, or when a parent comes in to talk about his or her child's performance in class.

971   *"Triple Treats"*

Early in the school year use this method to help your students get to know each other. Divide the class into groups of three students each. Have the group members tell each other about their happiest day. Then continue by sharing their saddest day, telling of a world leader they admire, discussing their favorite magazine, or revealing what they were like as a fifth grader. Do this for a half hour daily for the first week, switching groups so that every student has talked with everyone in the class.

972   *"Who I Am and How I Change"*

Make up a form containing twenty to thirty projective statements that the students can complete quickly. Ask them to fill out this form at the start of the year and twice later. Consider their opinions to statements such as: (1) My mother (father) is _____ . (2) School is _____ . (3) I would like _____ .

LECTURES

973   *"It's a Vocal Thing"*

Teachers who are not particularly ardent scholars can still be effective if they will master the art of communication—cultivating a good speaking voice and using natural, meaningful gestures and facial expressions. Yes, the voice can be improved. Practice with a tape recorder.

974   *"Get to the Point"*

Students are often reticent when it comes to reciting in class. Encourage participation and less lecture by rewarding acceptable recitation with points that will help raise grades earned mainly through written means. Let a student aide keep track by using a copy of the class list.

NOTES

975   *"Open Card Test"*

If you have prepared a comprehensive objective-essay test highlighting a unit, tell the class that they may bring with them one 3×5 card of notes containing as much information as they wish. This will help relax many who block when being tested. It is surprising how much can be written in such a small space.

PAPERS

976   *"First Aide for Paper Evaluation"*

Your school cannot afford lay readers? Well, you're not alone. Get some volunteers—retired teachers, English majors in college, particularly adept parents, and capable students (as in a future teachers' club). Students need to write a lot, but they won't if you are the only evaluator.

PROBLEMS

977   *"Just Shy of a Project"*

A small effort that pays dividends is taking the time to discover the special interests of a shy student. A word after class about a stamp collection, for example, can create a bond and draw the student out of the proverbial shell—or at least crack it a bit.

QUESTIONS

978   *"Checking the Traps"*

Some teachers use tests to trap students—just to show them why they should have listened to the teacher more carefully. Testing is as much an evaluation of teacher effectiveness as it is of student learnings. Good tests are prepared with the course objectives as guides. Tests of this type are not likely to trap.

979   *"Discriminating Tests"*

The best indication of a good test is how each test item succeeds in discriminating, for example, between the top third and the bottom third in the final scores. Any question that is answered correctly or incorrectly by the same number of students in both the upper and lower thirds must be examined for its value. A simple tally of right and wrong answers for the two student groups will give the needed information on whether a question is "pulling its load."

980 *"Everybody's Test"*

When preparing tests, remember that the less academically inclined students need some incentive to at least try. If the test is too difficult, they may panic or, even worse, give up. Include some simple questions they can answer. Naturally, enough of the difficult questions will be used so better students will also be challenged. Nothing is more defeating to student ego that not being able to answer a single question.

981 *"Nothing but the Facts"*

In an essay test, plan to include several "outline only" questions for which composition skills are not a major factor in answering. Thus, the student who must rush through essay questions to finish or the student whose poor grammatical skills are obstacles in presenting ideas is not penalized. In addition, you avoid much of the padding common to essay replies.

982 *"One of Our Own"*

Students could review for a test by preparing their own test in advance. All can contribute questions and prepare study guides. Also don't forget that students can prepare short quizzes, for example, for a literature lesson.

983 *"Students Turned On"*

For reasons most of us can supply from our own experiences, a student is frequently alienated by some of the questions on an essay exam. In such an event, what are the alternatives? One way is allowing the student to frame a question of equivalent worth and then write an essay answer to it. This alternate approach allows students to take the initiative in deciding what information is important, gives an opportunity for self-motivation, and serves as a better learning experience by testing the students on what they know instead of what they do not know.

984   *"Testing the Test"*

Step one in quality test construction is to write each question on a 3 × 5 file card. The advantages are: being able to prepare a test or exam again with slight content changes to fit different emphases; keeping track of incorrect responses on back of the card to be used later to improve the question or gather even better multiple choice alternatives; keeping track of correct/incorrect responses to make sure the question is differentiating between the top third and the bottom third of the class. (See also idea 979.)

985   *"Test Plus One"*

Teachers should add the following question to every test they write: "Has this been a fair test of the material we covered?" If the student can explain why a test has or has not been fair, he or she should receive extra credit. Students who hedge on that question are doing so because they fear retaliation. This should cause the teacher to reexamine his or her own attitudes and teaching methods. Solid trends among answers to the question provide more accurate feedback than most other approaches.

986   *"Testworthy Tests"*

Guidelines for writing test questions could fill a complete book. Here are a few examples mainly for improving objective tests.

1. Keep questions and directions clear and explicit.
2. Prepare only plausible incorrect alternatives for multiple choice tests.
3. Avoid overlapping responses.
4. Make alternatives grammatically consistent with the stem sentence.
5. Take care that correct alternatives are no longer or shorter than the distractors.
6. Do not use qualifying modifiers like "always" or "never" in the alternatives.
7. Vary the positions of correct answers.
8. Place in the stem all words that must be repeated.
9. Do not use double negatives.
10. Provide at least three, preferably four, response alternatives for each multiple choice question.
11. Confine matching elements to no more than ten per side.
12. Keep to only one basis for matching, e.g., all names, all events, etc.
13. Do not keep the same number of elements in each column when matching.
14. Avoid trick (deliberately misleading) questions.
15. Provide an accurate key made after you take the test.

101 Test-Writing Ideas

We break format here, appropriately at Questions, to present this very comprehensive list of 101 model test items which can be used to give variety to teacher-made tests and to provide suggestions for evaluating specific English content. Occasionally, items are merely suggested by using a few words, symbols, or dashes.

Definitions of Types

Alternate Choice	Student chooses between two items.
Completion	Complete a sentence or a stem to the end punctuation (not just missing words in a sentence).
Essay	Student writes at least several sentences, possibly a paragraph or a full page.
Fill-in	Words are placed in blanks created within an otherwise complete sentence.
Interlinear	Student line edits, underlines, or marks out incorrect items in sentences.
Matching	One column of items is matched with items in another column.
Multiple Choice	Select the correct response from three, four, or more alternatives.
Sequencing	Student places items in order or rearranges.
Short Answer	Write several words, not necessarily complete sentences, as in an Essay test.
True or False	Student writes True or False, T or F, + or 0 or other ways to tell if a statement is correct or incorrect.

Alternate Choice

1. Decide whether or not the word over the number in each sentence is right or wrong. If it is right, place the letter "C" in the numbered blank; if it is wrong, write the correct word in the blank.

   ```
                  1
   Tim and Rob was close friends.      1. _____
         2          3
   They did'nt argue or dissagree.      2. _____

              etc.                      3. _____
   ```

2. Read each item and decide whether or not it is a sentence. If it is a sentence, place an X in the S box. If it is not a sentence, place an X in the NS box.

   S   *NS*

   ☐   ☐   1. An article of bad news

☐ ☐   2. They decided to go

☐ ☐   3. Since he is my brother

☐ ☐   4. It is here

3. Some of the following sentences are simple (s), some are compound (CD), some are complex (CX), and some are not sentences at all (N). Circle the type you see.

1. The man, when he arrived, slept. S   CD   CX   N
2. A few ate, but most ignored.   S   CD   CX   N

4. In the numbered blank, write the word in parentheses that makes the sentence correct.

_____ 1. Every student must do (his, their) homework.
_____ 2. If anybody disagrees, let (him, them) suggest a better idea.

5. Fill in the blank with the sentence letter that is described by each numbered phrase.

A. Tom saw his idol on television. He was saving people in trouble.
B. On television Tom saw his idol save people in trouble.
1. _____ begins with a phrase.
2. _____ begins with a subject and verb.

6. Is a comma required at the slash mark? Write "Yes" or "No" on the line after each statement.

1. A tired/thirsty runner flopped down under the tree. _____

7. On the line before each number, write A or B depending on which sentence is correct.

_____ 1. A. She paid three dollars for a hat, and five for shoes.
           B. She paid three dollars for a hat and five for shoes.

8. Write "clear" in the blank if the reference is clear; write "not" if it is unclear.

_____ 1. Dan told Diane that the horse had kicked him.
_____ 2. Pauline is an accomplished pianist, which she began at five.

9. Place a check mark on the line in front of the choice that you think is better and place a second check mark on the line in front of the reason that explains your choice. (Sentences, paragraphs, or items marked A and B precede.)

_____ A is better than B.
_____ B is better than A.
Because:
_____ 1. The setting was too unrealistic.
_____ 2. The characterization was flawed by the. . . .
etc.

10. Below you will find selections of poetry (or whatever) in pairs. Examine each pair carefully and decide which selection you regard as the better. If the selection you choose is the left of the pair, mark an X in the left circle; if the selection is at the right, mark an X in the right circle.

1. .... 1. O O
....
.. ..

11. In making decisions about important issues it is important to be able to distinguish between arguments that are *strong* and those that are *weak*. Strong arguments must be both important and directly related to the question. Weak arguments may not be directly related even though they may be important; or they may be of minor importance or related to trivial aspects of the question. Below is a series of questions. Each question is followed by three or four arguments. For the purpose of this test, you are to regard each argument as true. The problem is to decide whether it is a *strong* or *weak* argument. Mark the appropriate line with an X.

1. Does the author show the same ability to portray characters as in her earlier book?

	Arguments	
	Strong	Weak
No, she fails to establish them clearly.	_____	_____
Yes, since the main character is so clear.	_____	_____
etc.		

12. Each of the following numbered items is the main topic for one of the paragraphs in a theme. Five details are listed after each topic. Four of these details apply to the topic and should be used to develop the paragraph. On your answer sheet list the letter of the *one* detail that should not be used.

_____ 1. Topic: Pests in the neighborhood
a. Where pests are located
b. Types of pests
c. Size of the neighborhood
d. Dangers from pests
e. People in the neighborhood

Completion

13. In the space provided, write the word or words that correctly complete the statement.

1. A story about a person's life and is written by himself is called an _____ .
2. Letters added to the beginning of a word to change or modify the meaning of the word are called _____ .
3. The selection that best typifies the title of the literature unit is _____ .

14. In each of the sentences below, one or more words are needed in the numbered blanks to make the sentences complete and true. Place the answer in the correspondingly numbered blanks to the right.

1. Main characters are (1), (2), and (3).   _____ 1.   _____ 4.
2. Support characters are (4), (5), and (6).   _____ 2.   _____ 5.
                                               _____ 3.   _____ 6.

15. Add three lines to complete this verse:
    I saw old winter in its muffled robe
    _____
    _____
    _____

16. Complete any three of these five quotations. Do not fill in more than three. One word or several may be used.

1. "M ... .
   ... .
   ... ... and _____ ,"
2. "Do ....
   ... . _____ ?"
                etc.

17. Complete each statement by writing in each blank the word of words that will make the statement true.

1. _____ are the first ... ...
2. _____ became the ones ....

18. The ways to complete the following statements have been listed underneath. Using the number of the completer you want, place that number in the blank before each statement.

_____ 1. There are ....   _____(1)_____ .
_____ 2. Some of the ... ...   _____(2)_____ .
_____ 3. A few .. . .   _____(3)_____ .
                etc.

    a. many selections without rhyme.
    b. two or three.
    c. the Andersons.
                etc.

19. After each statement find three nearly correct ways to complete the statement. Ahead of each numbered blank write the letter of the best of the completing choices.

_____ 1. In the story the plot reverses itself when _____(1)_____ .
      a. Tom asks .. . .
      b. Tom questions . .. .
      c. Tom ... ...

Essay

20. Name three characteristics of the story just read which differentiate it from the previous story.

21. In a few sentences explain why the answer you have chosen best illustrates the characteristics listed in your answer to question one.

22. Name four stories that deal with the problem of growing up. For each story tell:

    1. what the problem was
    2. how the problem was solved
    3. your opinion of the solution.

23. From the following list of characters in .... 's _____(Title)_____ *choose two to compare and contrast.*

           (List of characters follows.)

24. The end of ...... 's _____(Title)_____ has two endings. From the list of descriptive terms below, choose two or three that you feel best describe the author's work. Then, in a short paragraph, explain your choices.

           (List of terms follows.)

25. Listen to the recording and draw some conclusions about the author's work.

26. Turn to page 95 of _____ . Here .... makes a brilliant statement about .... Find the section and tell why or why not you think it is a good statement.

27. Each of .... 's friends represents a type of person. Write a well developed paragraph on any of these friends and show how the author develops that character.

28. Based on what we have discussed about character development, describe one of the main characters from _____Title_____ in terms of:

    1. the way the author views this character
    2. the way others view this character
    3. the way the character sees himself.

Your answer should be well-written and be in acceptable essay form not exceeding 500 words.

29. Compare and contrast the characters of ..... and ......, giving examples to back-up your statements. This may be done by:

    1. recalling their actions in specific incidents
    2. telling how they interact with other characters
    3. knowing what others have said about them
    4. remembering what they said about themselves.

30. In front of the room is a Van Gogh print called "..... ..... ." What do you think the artist is trying to convey? Does this picture recall any of your own experiences? What is the mood of this picture, and what contributes most to this mood?

31. In one or two brief paragraphs explain why you selected one of the lists below to describe ___(character)___ in the book we just read.

a	b	c
stuffy	indignant	childlike
matronly	flighty	impulsive
sensitive	obstinate	frantic
thoughtful	powerful	sensitive
moody	haughty	idealistic

Fill-in

32. In the space provided at the left, write the word or words that best fit the blank in the statement.

    _____ 1. ___(1)___ is the author of ....
    _____ 2. In (Title), ___(2)___ has the role of narrator.

33. Fill in each numbered blank on your paper some form of the word indicated. Choose the form that patterns best in the sentence.

    1. He is a handsome man, but his brother is even (handsome).
    2. Yesterday was the (happy) day of my life.

34. Insert the correct form of the verb for each sentence.

    1. She _____ the package on the table ten minutes ago. lay
    2. Each of the officers _____ congratulated by the captain. be
    3. He had just _____ down when the doorbell rang. lie

35. For each of the following sentences, choose the connecting word (among those in parentheses) that will tie together the ideas effectively.

    1. Three or four times he looked in my direction, _____ I lay so still that he could not see me. (but, and, for)

36. Here is a recipe for a cheese omelet with certain connecting words omitted. Fill in the blanks so that the recipe can be followed accurately. Use the words listed below the paragraph.

__(1)__ , break eggs into a small bowl. __(2)__ beat slightly to mix until batter can be taken up on a spoon. __(3)__ add the seasoning.... etc.

finally	then
next	first
and	or
before	at once

37. In the blank space of each sentence, insert the correct subordinating conjunction that deals with the quality in parentheses.

 1. I had finished two years of college ___(time)___ I went into business.   (Answer: before)
 2. __(Reason)__ he knew he would be called upon, he did not come to class.   (Answer: When)

38. With your book open to page 223, place the important transition words on the bridge between the paragraph diagrams below:

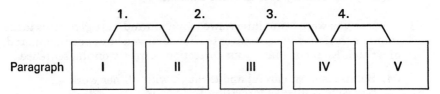

39. From the groups of words following the passage, choose the one word you think best conveys the sound or feeling needed. Each blank in the passage is numbered to correspond with the group of words bearing your selection.

 As the strong wind blew the sails and rigging ___(1)___ as if in agony. The deck ___(2)___ mightily with each ocean swell until the passengers wished they were dead. The terrible ___(3)___ that floated from below deck almost decked myself.

 1. moved   swayed   groaned   sounded
 2. raised   moved   went up   heaved
 3. odor   smell   stench   scent

40. (A passage appears first with sentences numbered.)

 1. The passage above includes an introductory sentence called a topic sentence. That sentence is number ____ .
 2. The first sentence to include a coordinate conjunction is sentence number ____ .

Interlinear

41. Read the following passage and decide which punctuation marks should be used at each numbered point. Then mark the punctuation in

the space provided after each number. If no punctuation mark is needed, write "N" in the blank.

He asked$_1$ why the bus had stopped$_2$ Before I could answer$_3$ he had left$_4$ "Is the book$_5$ that I borrowed here?$_6$ he asked$_7$ As you know$_8$ he was a man of unusual abilities$_9$ and he taught us many$_{10}$ many things.

1. ____   6. ____
2. ____   7. ____
3. ____   8. ____
4. ____   9. ____
5. ____   10. ____

42. Each of the following sentences lacks punctuation marks. Place the proper punctuation *where needed*. (Type with much space.)

    1. Ive seen many beautiful buildings recently and I think the style is both useful and decorative
    2. Should I tell Mr Landers that Marthas cat is in the tree
    3. Boy did Tommy ever hit that baseball

43. Suppose you were being interviewed for a job and were given this task: Improve the following sentences to show that you have good command of written English. Make your corrections directly on the sentence.

    1. Bonnie is most careful and through with all her work.
    2. Someone is always forgetting their book.
    3. Me and Lou were not late.
    4. The number of people that have gone to Washington is astonishing.

44. Underline in the following sentences whatever is asked for after each sentence.

    1. His first act was to buy several expensive items at the supermarket. (the noun modifiers: adjectives)
    2. All employees must replace all breakages; noncompliance will be grounds for dismissal.   (the noun markers that are derivational suffixes.)

45. Read the following sentences and decide which are correct and which ones are run-ons (run-together sentences). Correct all the run-on sentences by rewriting them on your paper and using the proper connecting devices or by using two sentences if they are not closely related.

46. For sentence variety shift the italicized words to another position in each of the following sentences. (Place a caret mark (∧) where you place them. In some you may have to make additional minor changes to avoid sounding awkward.

    1. Janet had left the office *before her boss could say another word.*

47. Make all the necessary changes to comply with the directions found after each number. All sentences must be complete.

   1. Add a period after the word *novelist.*
      Ernest Hemingway was a great novelist whose best known works
      are ___(Title)___ , ___(Title)___ , and ___(Title)___ .
   2. Add a period after the word *noises.*
      The silence was interrupted by many noises especially the faint
      tapping of a typewriter in the next room.

48. The following paragraph with all punctuation and capitalization left
    out consists of fifteen sentences. After each number on your answer
    sheet, write the first and last words of each sentence as they occur.
    Capitalize each first word. Put the appropriate end mark (period, ques-
    tion mark, or exclamation mark) after each word you place last.

49. Read each sentence. Decide which word or word groups should be set off
    by commas. After the number on your answer sheet, put the needed
    comma and the word just preceding it.

50. Where in each sentence can the phrase or clause in parentheses be
    placed? Answer by placing the position number or numbers in the space
    to the left of the number on your answer sheet.

    _____ 1. (1) The slave (2) kneeled at the desk (3) and asked for
              mercy (3). (when the captain arrived)

51. Make all the changes in the sentence as indicated and include any other
    necessary changes.

    1. Change *lives* to *life.*
       More important than material things are the lives which are lost
       in war.

Matching

52. Match each word in column A with its correct definition in column B by
    placing the proper letter in the space provided. (Note: Include more
    items in column B than in A.)

	A	*B*
_____	1. hesitation	a. scoff
_____	2. reserve	b. causes suffering
_____	3. scorn	c. pause
_____	4. herald	d. express sorrow
_____	5. grievous	e. set aside
_____	6. bewail	f. announce
_____	7. recapitulate	g. move back
		h. summarize

53. Match the lines of poetry with the list of poetic terms in the right column.
    Explain briefly why you selected the term. (Note that some letters may
    be used more than once.)

	Poetry	*Terms*

_____ 1. "···· ······ ·······
······· ···· ···· ···· ,
······ ·······"

a. blank verse
b. hyperbole
c. free verse

_____ 2. "···· ···· ···· · ,
·········· ··· ·· · ;"
···· ···· ····· ···· ·"

d. onomatopoeia
e. sonnet
   etc.

etc.

54. Select two descriptive phrases (words) from column B which best fit each character in column A. Briefly tell why you chose the adjectives to describe each person. (The same phrases (words) may not be used for more than one person.)

	A	B
_____ & _____	1. N ····· H ····	a. frugal
_____ & _____	2. Mrs. G ·····	b. brave
_____ & _____	3. M ···· T ····	c. easily deceived
_____ & _____	4. Aunt J ·····	d. quick to anger
	etc.	e. puritanical
		etc.

55. For items 10 to 15, select from the five principles at the right the most closely related to the statement at the left. Mark your answer in the space provided.

Statements	*Principles*
_____ 10. ··· ······· ······· ····· .	a. ···· ···· ·····
_____ 11. ····· ····· ···· ··· ·· .	b. ···· ··· ·····
_____ 12. ···· ····· ······· ···· ··· .	c. ··· ···· ·· ···
etc.	etc.

56. In each group of words below, match the numbered word or phrase with the lettered word that most closely corresponds in meaning to the numbered word.

_____ 1. antelope
   a. fruit   b. springing gait   c. animal   d. introduction

57. In the parentheses at the right of each phrase in the right column place the letter of the word or phrase in the left column which, together, will complete the statement accurately.

1. A small business may obtain the aid of:

a. the Dept. of Agriculture	in protecting its invest-ment.	( )
b. the Interstate Loan Agency	in eliminating the dan-ger of overspending.	( )
	etc.	
	etc.	

58. Read each question carefully and decide which one of the answers (matches) is best.

_____ 1. Which pair of .... in _____(Title)_____ is not correctly matched?

    a. B ·· D ··· & U ····· M ····
    b. T ·· N ···· S ··· & P ·······
    c. etc.

59. Read each sentence and consider how each numbered word in the sentence is used. Match that number with the sentence part.

We walked into the library and found the book that we wanted.
  1   2   3   4   5

_____ preposition
_____ subordinate conjunction
_____ direct object
_____ subject
_____ coordinate conjunction

60. After each numbered statement below put the letter a, b, c, or d. (A separate answer sheet can also be used.)

    a. if it ··· ·· ·· ··· ··
    b. if it is ··· ··· ·· ·· ··· .
    c. if it can ·· ····· ··· · ·
    d. if it ·· ····· · ·· ··· · .
      1. The first of the ···· ···· ·· ··· ··· ·· ···· ·· ··( )
      2. The story of···· ··· ··· ··· ··· ··· ··· ···· ··( )

61. Each of these quotations (passages) expresses some idea found in the poem. Insert in the blank before each quotation the letter of the idea the quote expresses.

Ideas Often Expressed

    a. Immorality   d. Imperishable beauty
    b. Futility   e. Strength in a supreme being
    c. Modesty   f. The destiny of man

_____ 1. "····· ····· ······· ······· ······· · · ·
        ···· ········ ···· ····· ········ ···· ,"
        ··· ········ ····· ········ ····· ···· ."

_____ 2. "··· ··· ········ ······ ··· ,
        ···· ······· ···· ··· ·· ·· ;
        ····· ··········· ······· ."

62. Below is a series of items in numbered pairs. The first set list five *things*. Only four things are related. The second set lists five *categories*, to which the four related things might belong. For each list of *things*, mark the answer space that corresponds to the one thing that does *not* belong to the same category as the other four. For each list of categories, mark

the answer space that corresponds to the letter of the one category that *best* explains the relationship of the four remaining things in the first list.

Things	*Categories*
a. antibiotics	a. factors for diagnosis
b. microorganisms	b. ways to acquire immunity
c. intravenous tap	c. forces to control hypertension
d. diet	d. hemotological controls
e. chemotherapy	e. none of these

Multiple Choice

63. In the space provided at the left, place the capital letter of the item that correctly answers each question.

    _____ 1. Who ... ... ?
         a. ....   c. ....
         b. ....   d. ....

64. In the space provided at the left, place the letter of the combined items that correctly answer each question.

    _____ 1. Which of the following are plays by Shakespeare:
         a. "Macbeth"   c. "Death of a Salesman"
         b. "The Tempest"   d. "Major Barbara"

    The correct combination is:
    A. b, c, d   C. a, c, d
    B. a, c   D. all of these

65. Which of the following settings are found in ___(Title)___ ?
    Place a small "x" to the right of each correct answer.

    ocean island   cave
    boat marina   cabin
    forest   school house

66. Number your paper from 1 through 10. Find the ten misspelled words in the following list. Write each misspelled word correctly next to the numbers on your paper. (Use at least fifteen words.)

67. Select the proper form of the words in parentheses. Write your answers on a sheet of paper with numbers corresponding to the sentences.

    1. (Lady's, Ladie's, Ladies' Ladies) jewelry is on the main floor and (men's, mens, mens') is on the second.

68. Of the three choices below, which combination or single item best describes R ----- M --- and S ------ ?

    a. decisive and self-serving
    b. hopeful and vindictive
    c. competitive

Circle the correct answer:
b   b and c   a and c   all of them (a, b, and c)

69. Choose the letter of the correct word among the four suggested to improve the underlined word in the sentence.

1. Don't Tom live in Lexington any more?
   a. no change   b. Doesn't   c. Do   d. Doesnt

70. The cartoon (photo, drawing, etc.) shown best illustrates:

a. - - - - - - - - -   c. - - - - - - - - - - - -
b. - - - - - - - - - - - -   d. - - - - - - - - -

71. Pick out one of three sentences that gives the reader the best mental picture of the factory in ____(Title)____ .

(Three sentences follow; each with a letter.)

72. Circle the best choice of the three in each sentence.

                    I
1. My mother and myself will be happy to attend.
                    me

73. (A quoted selection appears, each sentence bearing a number.)

____ 1. Which one of the following best states what sentence number one is saying?

a. People are funny.
b. Eliminate the middle man.
c. Two are better than one.

74. Draw a circle around *the word* that best describes the statement.

1. A lion's roar is so frightful that it fills the entire jungle and makes the other animals tremble.

gently   loudly   softly   pleasingly

75. What conditions contributed to the early death of Sally in the story?

1. The lack of - - - - - - - - .   4. Too much - - - - - - - - -- - .
2. The decline - - - - - - - - - - - . 5. Not enough - - - - - - -- - .
3. The large - - - - - - - -- -- - .   6. Her - - - - - - - -- - - .
Circle the correct letter:
a. 1, 2, 3   d. 2, 3, 4
b. 1, 2, 4   e. 1, 4, 5
c. 2, 3, 5   f. all of the above

76. (Quotation precedes.)
In the first two lines, Shakespeare says that:

a. All - - - - . - . --- --- - - .   d. Some men . - - - . - - - - . .
b. Every . . - - - -- - . . .   e. Only a few - - . - . - - - .
c. Man - - - -- -- - . - - - - .

77. (Quotation procedes.)
    The metaphor "she is the bird in the gilded cage" indicates that Words-
    fellow felt that the heroine was: (Circle the correct letter.)

    a. ....   c. ... .
    b. .. ..   d. ... ...

78. (Quotation precedes.)
    1. What is the purpose of the last sentence (lines 6–12)? (Circle the cor-
       rect letter.) The sentence:

    a. restates - .. .. ..   c. gives --- ... .
    b. presents -- - - -   d. introduces -- -- .

79. Each of the numbered passages is particularly important for one of the
    following qualities. Place the letter for the quality at the left of the num-
    ber of the passage.

    a. ... ...   c. ... .
    b. ... .   d. ....

80. Circle the number of the best sentence in each group. All but one sen-
    tence in a group contain errors in grammar or usage, parallel structures,
    word placement, expression, and so on.

    (About four numbered sentences follow to make up a group.)

81. Read the first poem. Then answer questions 1 through 5 by underlining
    the right answer and also by writing the number in the space at the left.

    (Quotation here.)

    _____ 1. The poem is
            a. a sonnet   b. a ballad   c. an ode   d. an elegy.
    _____ 2. Etc.

82. In the following exercise, for each problem you are given a complete
    (correct) sentence which is followed by a partial revision. You are to
    complete the revision mentally. Then darken the one lettered space on
    your answer sheet to designate the correct statement about the revised
    sentence.

    Original sentence: W.. ... ...
    Revised sentence: T. . ... , or .... .

    1. In the revised sentence, the word following *or* should be:
       a. you   b. and   c. either   d. let   e. must

83. The following sentence has a problem: "The . ..."

    1. The sentence would be acceptable if the writer inserted the addi-
       tional word: (Circle the letter.)

       a. of   b. in   c. when   d. for   e. that

84. The stages in the development of the Jones family in ____(Title)____ are, in order: (Circle the best number.)

    1. --- ---- ---, --- -- - -, --- -- --, - ---, and --- .
    2. ----- ----- ----- -, ------, ---------, and ------ -- .
    3. ------ ---, -------, ------, and ---- -- - --- .
    4. ---- ------, ----, --------, and -------- ------ .

85. Classify the following adjectives mentally and decide which of the statements best describes their purpose: (Circle the letter.)

    dazzling murkey blinding etc.

    a. characteristics of light   c. describes movement
    b. signifies color   d. tells the effect of light

Sequencing

86. Darken the space on your answer sheet that tells the earliest work of art.

    a. ---- --- ---   c. ---- --- ----
    b. --- . -----   d. ---- --- -- -

87. Arrange the words in each group below so that the most general comes first and the most specific comes last.

    Bessie Guernsey animal cow dairy cow

88. Arrange the following words in two columns so that for each general term in the left column you will have a specific (picture type) word in the right column.

    food garment pizza disease mumps
    water hat furniture river table

General	Descriptive

89. The sentences in each of the following groups are in scrambled order. Decide what should be the best order. Then answer the questions. Consider "0" to mean that nothing follows.

    (Sample paragraph is printed here with each sentence labeled a, b, c, and d.)

    Circle the answers.

    1. Which sentence did you place first?   a b c d 0
    2. Which sentence did you place after (a)?   a b c d 0
    3. Which sentence did you place after (b)?   a b c d 0
    etc.

90. Suppose that each of the following numbered items is the topic of a paragraph you are to write. After each topic several details are listed. On your answer sheet list the detail letters in what you think would be the most effective order.

1. Why my lawn-cutting job was the last.

    a. (a detail)   d. (a detail)
    b. (a detail)   e. (a detail)
    c. (a detail)

Short Answer

91. Complete each item correctly by placing the proper term to the left of the question number.

    _____ 1. A story which a person writes about his or her own life.
    _____ 2. Where a story takes place.

92. After each number on your paper, write the subject of each sentence below:

1. The dog race was fixed.
2. To see the show was our first choice.

93. Construct sentences from each pattern below:

    a. N LV N   c. N LV Aj
    b. N V N   d. D Aj N V Prep Aj N

94. Combine the following two sentences into one:

1. Tom and Fred's school clothes were soaking wet.
2. They walked home in the rain.

Transform the new sentence four different ways so that it expresses:

1. a causal relationship   3. an expected result
2. a temporal relationship   4. a circumstantial relation

95. Opposite each quotation write the title of the work in which it appears:

    _____ 1. (quotation)
    _____ 2. (quotation)
    etc.

96. Under each poet's name list three themes the poet deals with in his poetry.

    a. Tennyson   b. Longfellow
    1. _____   1. _____
    2. _____   2. _____
    3. _____   3. _____

97. On your answer paper write the *figure of speech* found in each of the following sentences:

1. ....
2. ....
3. ....

True or False

98. Certain conclusions in the following statements may or may not be true. If you think that the statement is true, circle the letter T. If you think it is false, circle the F. Then circle one or more of the five reasons (a, b, c, d, e) which support the judgment you made. Sometimes there is only one correct reason.

    T F 1. (statement)

        a. (reason) d. (reason)
        b. (reason) e. (reason)
        c. (reason

99. Read the following paragraph and the conclusions (questions 1 through 5) below. Decide whether the conclusion is correct or incorrect. Then on your answer sheet, opposite the number, make a heavy mark under the letter T if the conclusion is true and under the letter F if it is false.

    (Paragraph quoted.)

    1. This selection was written by Johanna Smith.
    2. The setting of the story is New York City.

100. Janice is a sophomore in high school. She had just completed her first day at school. What are her thoughts? If she were to write her impressions, she would stick to the topic and use the most appropriate words. If you think the numbered statement should be included on her paper, mark an "X" before the number. If not, mark "0."

    _____ 1. (statement)
    _____ 2. (statement)

101. Examine the picture (cartoon, drawing, diagram, etc.) carefully. Then read the statements about it. If the statement is true, circle the word *true* on your answer sheet; if false, circle *false*.

    1. (Statement)
    2. (Statement)
    3. (Statement)

20 Application

ATTITUDES

987   *"Join 'Em"*

Many extracurricular offerings such as clubs need to be changed periodically according to students' changing interests. Allow club sign-ups annually and offer only those clubs for which there is strong interest. Much "recruiting" can be done by teachers. English teachers, for instance, could find out how many students would be interested in poetry, drama, and writing. If there is sufficient interest in all three, several English and speech teachers could volunteer to be sponsors. Extracurricular clubs are among the best socializing offerings in the school.

988   *"Pat on the Back"*

Platitude or not, praise is still the most effective way to involve students. Any student's work contains something that merits praise. If not, then the assignment or task was not designed flexibly enough so that everyone could succeed in some dimension of it.

989   *"Replacing the Old Text"*

Bring out students' creativity by allowing them, as a class or in groups, to write and illustrate an English textbook. This activity, besides encouraging good grammar and knowledge of various literary forms and techniques, helps create an atmosphere of cooperation. Class members learn from each other and achieve that pride of accomplishment too often absent in the typical classroom.

BOOK REPORTS

990   *"Three-Day Borathon"*

Are oral book reports or individual research reports really of that much value to students who have to listen to them for two or three consecutive days? If the purpose is to share information as well as provide speaking experiences, then one might answer Yes. But often these reports are done with such little imagination that listening becomes so boring that there is no sharing. This book contains many ideas for varying book reports (see the Index). Reporting can be done in so many ways that the teacher need not be locked into any single approach.

BULLETIN BOARDS

991 *"Cut Ups"*

Create more interest in bulletin boards by installing them as class projects. Divide the class into three or four groups, assigning a topic or letting them choose their own. Provide most of the materials (stapler, tacks, and tape, for example) and let them move ahead on their own. Everyone gets a job according to talent. Each group's chairperson must write a report explaining various aspects of his or her group's display and read it aloud for discussion.

DEMONSTRATIONS

992 *"Our Own Thing"*

At the end of a semester, hold a student say-and-do day. Class members show they have learned subject matter by working alone or in groups to present readings, original poetry, parodies, essays, short stories, skits, or the like. The purpose, of course, is to see whether the instruction has been assimilated by the students and whether they are able to apply the knowledge constructively.

DISPLAYS

993 *"Fair Idea"*

If science students can have science fairs and art students art fairs, why not a language arts fair? All English teachers and their students can contribute something from simple haiku poetry booklets to feature-length, student-made films. Prizes are always good for added incentive. The fair can involve a single school or an entire city. This idea can be expanded to an all-school Creative Arts Festival to include all subject fields, interests, crafts, and hobbies.

994   *"Marble Statues"*

Try not to assign home projects that require undue amounts of artistic talent or financial backing. What is desired is not a display of parental artistry or oversized piggy banks but rather a simple, honest demonstration of thought and understanding. Grades should be distributed on the latter, never the former. One way to insure this is to specify the medium and materials, making sure they are inexpensive and readily available to all.

GAMES

995   *"All Lit Up"*

Often this book mentions the use of teams, particularly in games, some of which are takeoffs on popular television quiz shows. These game shows often use elaborate systems of bells or buzzers and flashing lights. Why not have something similar in the classroom? Turn over such a project to the less academic but manually skilled students. The first project could be a light signal system to show which person and which team has the answer. Two lighting panels with nothing more expensive than Christmas tree bulbs can be provided along with push buttons for each participant. They might even try some elaborate way to allow one team who answers first to cut out the push buttons for the other team. This construction project will give much prestige to those who need it most.

INSTRUCTIONS

996   *"Cryptographic Assignment"*

The next time you give an assignment, convert parts of it into some kind of code. Challenge the class to discover the assignment by breaking the code. Although some would just as soon not succeed, all students will appreciate the challenge and the different way of introducing an assignment. One easy approach is to use a code in which each letter is two letters left of the desired letter, for example, "ambc" spells "code."

LETTERS

997   *"Club Amici"*

For
my pen pal.

Form a club Amici. Members choose a foreign correspondent their own age. When specific countries have been selected, distribute names and addresses. Such lists are available from several organizations:

International Letter Exchange
Boy Scouts of America
P.O. Box 61030
Dallas/Fort Worth Airport, TX 75261
(for registered Boy Scouts)

Post Box Secretary
Girl Scouts of the USA
830 Third Avenue
New York, NY 10022
(for registered Girl Scouts)

League of Friendship, Inc.
P.O. Box 509
Mount Vernon, OH 43050
(ages 12–25)

Student Letter Exchange
RR Number 4
Waseca, MN 56093
(ages 10–19)

Letters Abroad
209 East 56th Street
New York, NY 10022
(16 and over)

World Pen Pals
1690 Como Avenue
St. Paul, MN 55108
(ages 12–20)

Pen Pals
International Friendship League, Inc.
22 Batterymarch
Boston, MA 02109
(for ages 7–65)

Students write letters to their pen pals as often as they wish. A bulletin board and large table can be set aside for displaying letters, pictures, and interesting objects from gift exchanges. Club meetings are held frequently so members can report on their correspondence and learn some first-hand history and geography while employing their English skills.

998   *"To the Letter"*

Students do not write enough letters to friends and relatives. They always say that they have "nothing to write about." Prepare a poster for your room. Head it "Have You Written Some-body a Letter Recently?" Under the heading list "some things to write about."

1. Current likes, dislikes, hobbies, or ambitions.
2. Facts about your family: trips, illnesses, new car or other acquisitions, some neat happening.
3. Your thoughts, hopes, and dreams.
4. Descriptions of your house: new furniture, your room, re-decorations, yard, gardens.
5. Descriptions of your school, town, favorite TV show, or a movie—even your latest and best friend.
6. Notes about parties, trips, good times, and even bad times.
7. Your opinions about current events—local, state, or national.
8. Reactions to candidates running for office, new or resigning teachers.
9. Recollections of good time previously had with the person to whom you are writing.
10. Telling about improvements in the town, your school, parks, construction areas, new business.
11. Write about favorite or nonfavorite music groups.
12. Keep cheerful; don't fill a letter with "gripe."
13. Above all, have a "letter box" in which you keep notes on scraps of paper reminding you what to write the next time.

MAGAZINES

999   *"Topical Topics"*

The English classroom needs to provide many speaking oppor-tunities. Magazine articles, because of their availability, are a good source of topics for extemporaneous speeches. Students can enjoy relative freedom of choice in locating an interesting article, reading it, making notes, and then discussing the article before the class. Unlike topics such as "a day in the country" or "my most embarrassing moment," magazine articles provide the student with significant material, chosen because of its interest to each individual, and it leads natur-ally into many opportunities to communicate.

NEWSPAPERS

1,000   *"In the Know"*

This competitive game focuses on current events and moti-vates students to read a daily newspaper regularly. Divide the class into two teams for the purpose of writing questions. Limit questions to top world news events. Groups quiz each other. Give one point for each correct answer. A simple reward like free hours in the library might be given to the winning group.

TIP 1,001

1,001 *"The Beginning, Not the End"*

There is no magic in the number 1,000. It just seemed to be a goal to shoot for and a point at which to halt this collection. Halting was a problem. The writer, completing the final draft, was constantly confronted with new ideas not included here. The temptation to include them was great but the task impossible. Since each reader will uncover new ideas that should be here, good ideas should not be allowed to slip away into oblivion. See the Appendix for suggestions to place ideas on cards similar to the ones used to compile this book.

Appendix

Using Ideas to Frame Cognitive Objectives

Another way to use this book effectively is to employ specific nonbehaviorally stated activities as aids in writing performance objectives. Good daily lesson planning starts with some specific objectives founded upon one or more broad but significant goals.

In the description that follows, the author has chosen to use the term *learning objective* rather than the more broadly used psychological terms that emphasize behavior or performance. To many English teachers "performance objective" is even offensive, and "behavioral objective" reduces their enthusiasm completely for writing any objectives.

The learning objective is used to describe a learning task in terms that make its accomplishment observable if not measurable by quantity or quality. A simple test for a meaningful objective is to see if it answers four questions: Who? What? How? and How well? A well-worded objective tells or implies WHO it is for, WHAT the learner is expected to do, HOW the task is to be accomplished (the tools and activity), and HOW WELL the learner must perform to achieve the objective.

Certainly not all learning objectives can contain each of these criteria, but the more information an objective contains the more specific and measurable it will be. Since all learning objectives should be directed to the learner, it is not necessary to mention this fact in each objective. Thus, wordings like "the student will" are superfluous.

Obviously the ideas in this book are really activities used to carry out learning objectives and are, of course, not phrased as learning objectives. But with a little effort, each idea could be reduced to its essentials and become an objective. Then by changing content—specific titles, for example—the objective could apply to whatever a class is covering at the time.

Study this example from the Narration section of Chapter 2.

88–I   *(Experiment/Cartoons) "Balloon Talk"*

After a study of comics and how they are simple narratives, cut out entire sets of comic strips from Sunday papers. Remove the dialogues from the balloons. Each student receives a strip and supplies dialogue appropriate to the characters and to the situations so that the story can be told succinctly. Print dialogue directly on the strip or on separate paper containing numbers corresponding to numbered balloons. As a continuation of this idea, students could devise their own cartoon characters for a strip, drawing one frame each day. Each new frame is related to the previous day's frame. The final frame at the end of the week concludes the short narrative. Even if drawings are just stick figures, students will receive practice developing simple plots through dialogue, action, and setting, along with good punctuation practices.

To locate needed information for objectives, we know that WHO is the class (more specifically, individuals in the class); WHAT is to experiment with dialogue; HOW is met by supplying new dialogue for that removed from comic strips (the vehicle is the cartoons); HOW WELL is not indicated in the idea but might be added to reflect the teacher's expectations. The resulting objective might look like this:

To experiment with dialogue by writing new and appropriate speeches for those removed from published comic strips (until the dialogue is punctuated correctly and until the story can be accurately and interestingly followed by a reader—the HOW WELL.)

Some may prefer this stimulus-response wording:

Given a published comic strip with balloon speeches removed, learners will experiment with appropriate and imaginative dialogue by supplying their own which is punctuated with 100 percent accuracy and written succinctly and cleverly so a reader can follow a complete story.

With a little help from the ideas in this collection, teachers should be able to produce useful learning objectives. A list of verbs to help phrase statements of specific learning expectations can be found in this Appendix. Also with such help, teachers should be able to produce better, more pertinent learning objectives than subscribing to banks of objectives "cranked out" by others remote from the scene.

When using the Ideabook to formulate objectives, note that the WHO of a learning objective is usually understood if it is written for students; the WHAT is based on the process (or behavior) which appears as the first word in parentheses ahead of an idea; the HOW is the second word (vehicle) in parentheses and is drawn from key words in the activity;

and the HOW WELL is added when known or needed. (See also Mager's *Preparing Instructional Objectives.*[1])

THE COGNITIVE AND AFFECTIVE DOMAINS

Now education has at least four kinds of objectives upon which to build learning experiences: cognitive, affective, psychomotor, and perceptual. Up to now, in the writer's opinion, none of these domains has been effectively translated into practical classroom operations to strongly affect the majority of America's classroom teachers. In focusing on just one domain—the cognitive—and acknowledging the importance of another— the affective—goals on which to base the former, perhaps this book will move English education just a little closer to the sensible utilization of learning objectives.

As educators learned from the second taxonomy produced by Krathwohl, Bloom, and Masia, educational objectives can be classified as either cognitive (dealing mainly with knowledge and recall of information) or affective (stressing "desirable interests, attitudes and character development").[2]

The affective domain, this writer is convinced, really represents the goals on which American education must focus. The cognitive objectives are the measurable steps along the way toward reaching the probably never fully achieved and certainly unmeasurable affective goals. Thus, a daily lesson plan (based on a unit plan founded on affective goals) begins with a statement of affective goals which will be attained, at least in part by achieving the cognitive objectives set forth in the plan.

Keeping in mind that objectives are used for attaining goals, the author has also drawn up affective parallels between his classification system and the affective domain described by Krathwohl et al.[3] The following chart draws this comparison. It will also help generate parallel affective goals for cognitive objectives. The processes listed later in this Appendix help.

No claim is made that each of these classifications is directly parallel. One can readily see, however, that many parallels do exist and that anyone interested in relating cognitive objectives to affective goals could be helped by the chart. The scheme is at least a beginning for those who have had little or no experience in this area. Much educational research must yet be completed to refine methods for writing and using goals and objectives for all teaching but especially for teaching English.

The following serves to illustrate an affective goal which might be found under the classification, Receiving. The goal might read: "Empa-

1. Robert F. Mager, *Preparing Instructional Objectives* (Palo Alto, Calif.: Fearon, 1962).
2. David R. Krathwohl, Benjamin S. Bloom, Bertram B. Masia, *Taxonomy of Educational Objectives, Handbook II: Affective Domain* (New York: McKay, 1965), p. 15.
3. Ibid., pp. 176–185. (Used with special permission to paraphrase for the chart.)

Key Words for
Connecting Affective Goals to Cognitive Objectives

Affective Goals	Ideabook Teaching-Learning Sequences and Processes
Receiving Appreciates Attends Empathizes Listens	*Introduction* Discover (question) Listen Observe Read Research
Responding Complies Enjoys Is interested Participates	*Deliberation* Analyze Consolidate Experiment Interpret Organize
Internalizing Values Accepts Becomes responsible Reasons Shows devotion	. . . (A link between first two . levels and last two) .
Organizing Values Selects Systematizes Synthesizes	*Evaluation* Compare Extrapolate Identify Judge Restructure
Utilizing Values Behaves accordingly Philosophizes beliefs, ideas, attitudes	*Application* Construct Perform Solve Speak Write

thize with the people who lived in the Dust Bowl in the early 1900s to help appreciate the value of conserving natural resources."*

A parallel cognitive objective for Introduction (receiving information) could be "To *read* (the process) the book (the vehicle) John Steinbeck's *The Grapes of Wrath* and be able to tell the main idea orally or in writing and to trace at least one nonliteral symbol which reflects the era." The following hypothetical idea as it might appear in the Literature section (Introduction phase) of the Ideabook could have been the springboard for the affective goal and cognitive objective.

*Note: The affective goal begins with a strong verb. Learning objectives begin with the preposition "to" plus a process-type verb forming an infinitive. The author uses this wording to help distinguish between the two.

000–C,I *(Read/Book) "Ecological Sour Grapes"*

Some reasons for today's ecological concerns are well demonstrated in several famous literary works. A good source is
John Steinbeck's *The Grapes of Wrath.* After some opening
discussion on the matter, students are to keep a notebook list
of nonliteral symbols (repeated images) that reflect the ecological needs of this era in American history. They may then
report—orally or in writing—the fruits of their search.

A SIMPLIFIED BLOCK PLAN

"Weekly plan in the office by 9 a.m. on Monday" is the thought that
often takes the edge off a teacher's weekend until the task is completed.
Yes, many teachers are required to turn in a weekly lesson plan to keep
the administration informed as to what is being covered in the various
classes and to assist in teacher evaluation, as well as to make sure that
a substitute teacher will have a plan to follow should the teacher
become ill.

The best plans, of course, are those that state the objectives to be covered and the procedures to be used to meet the objectives. But in some
cases, block plans* are sufficient. If you can use block plans, the block
format described here will cover most of the essentials: the key words
for at least one learning objective, the procedures used, and the text references. The approach illustrated here is based on the planning suggestions that begin and conclude this book. The specific example reflects a
cognitive objective from *The Grapes of Wrath* idea mentioned earlier.
The following diagram is probably the quickest way to describe this
planning technique.

Expanding the top line (the HOW?) tells a substitute or administrator
that the lesson is in the Introduction Phase (mainly) and is partially for
the entire class and partially for individuals. It also tells that the main
process (activity) will be "scan" and the vehicle (tool) will be the book
(in this case *The Grapes of Wrath*). Combining the top line (the HOW?)
with the content (the WHAT?) in the large box gives an objective something like this "To scan pages 00 to 00 of *The Grapes of Wrath* and list
repeated examples which reflect ecological needs in this era of American
history." Several Process and Vehicle words could generate several
objectives.

Although this planning approach seems almost simplistic, it can be
effective, yet time saving, for the busy English teacher.

---

*Block plans generally consist of a page or two divided into five blocks or sections,
one for each day of the week and with as many blocks as there are periods or subjects
taught in the day. The typical block (area) is shown actual size on the next page.

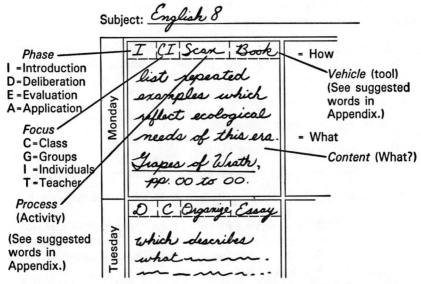

Subject: *English 8*

Phase
I = Introduction
D = Deliberation
E = Evaluation
A = Application

Focus
C = Class
G = Groups
I = Individuals
T = Teacher

Process
(Activity)

(See suggested
words in
Appendix.)

Monday

I CI Scan Book
list repeated
examples which
reflect ecological
needs of this era.
Grapes of Wrath,
pp. 00 to 00.

Tuesday

D C Organize Essay
which describes
what ___ ___.
___ ___ ___...

= How

Vehicle (tool)
(See suggested
words in
Appendix.)

= What

Content (What?)

Note: The more specific word "scan" found under the more general
Process word "read" is used for a narrower day's objective. "Read"
could have been used. See Appendix.

USING THE HANDBOOK FORMAT TO COLLECT AND TO CLASSIFY COLLECTED IDEAS

Reading parts of this book may encourage teachers to do something
about those ellusive ideas that one sees but does not clip or jot down for
future reference.

Most ideas fit into one phase or another of the four-part teaching/
learning sequence which is printed on the following pages. These and the
several other classification features described in this section will make it
easier to file and retrieve those ideas when they are most needed.

This section offers a model card for use in filing and classifying ideas.
Some teachers will want to reproduce specific ideas in this book and
paste them on the cards. Purchasing two books to cut apart will solve
the duplicating problem. Remember, ideas are only worth saving if you
can locate them again, quickly and accurately.

Criteria for the Teaching-Learning Sequence
As Employed in the Ideabook

INTRODUCTION   (1. exposing class to information; 2. initiating, introducing new material, techniques, processes; 3. taking in information to build generalizations)

Discover   (question, inquire)

Listen   (perceive anything oral)

Observe   (perceive anything visual)

Read   (translate literal material for information or pleasure)

Research   (complete an investigation using extraclass resources)

DELIBERATION   (1. deriving meaning from generalizations, reasoning; 2. considering carefully and weighing information recently acquired; 3. placing new knowledge into familiar frameworks; 4. reflecting upon information recently introduced)

Analyze   (distinguish between facts and hypotheses; look for interrelationships, specific arrangements, structures, and techniques)

Consolidate   (select and combine specific information into recognizable formats)

Experiment   (practice using information within its own basic context, usually in-class assignments and exercises)

Interpret   (draw meaning from information received—anything from grasping complete thought of a work to determining purposes, themes, lessons, and so on)

Organize   (classify and order information received)

EVALUATION (1. testing through oral or written methods for significance or usefulness of information; 2. discovering one's own knowledge of material presented; 3. implementing ways to achieve the former two)

Compare (seek similarities and differences among and between situations, ideas, and products usually based on external qualities)

Extrapolate (extend given information beyond the level introduced to determine consequences, effects, implications)

Identify (differentiate among or classify various ideas and structures selecting the meanings—definitions—that belong to each)

Judge (test an idea or product for usability, logic, accuracy, or other internal qualities)

Restructure (sift information, arranging it to fit a function similar to but not exactly like the original context)

APPLICATION (implementing or applying information or knowledge recently learned, preferably in different settings through out-of-class assignments and projects)

Construct (create models, structures, and products that do not generally lend themselves to the processes below)

Perform (present an idea through acting, usually with audible sounds)

Solve (decide a procedure to take; seek a solution)

Speak (present ideas orally)

Write (present ideas on paper)

Model for Collecting and Filing New Ideas

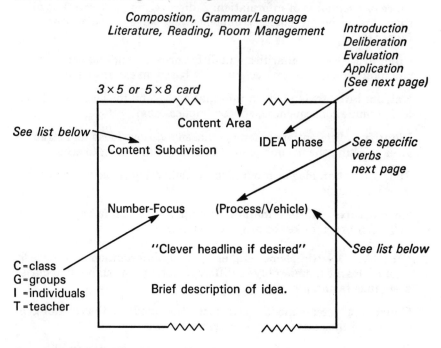

Content Subdivisions

Argumentation ☐ *Description* ☐ *Dialect* ☐ *Drama* ☐ *Exposition* ☐
Film Making ☐ *Humanities* ☐ *Journalism* ☐ *Letter Writing* ☐
Linguistics ☐ *Mechanics* ☐ *Media* ☐ *Narration* ☐ *Nonfiction* ☐
Novels ☐ *Overview* ☐ *Poetry* ☐ *Semantics* ☐ *Short Story* ☐ *Spelling*
Study Skills ☐ *Syntax* ☐ *Usage* ☐ *Vocabulary* ☐ *Words*

Vehicles in the Sequence

Anecdotes ☐ *Artwork* ☐ *Attitudes* ☐ *Audiotapes* ☐ *Authorities* ☐
Biographies ☐ *Books* ☐ *Book Reports* ☐ *Bulletin Boards* ☐ *Cards* ☐
Cartoons ☐ *Chalkboards* ☐ *Charts* ☐ *Circulars* ☐ *Conferences* ☐
Critiques ☐ *Definitions* ☐ *Demonstrations* ☐ *Dictionaries* ☐
Discussions ☐ *Displays* ☐ *Essays* ☐ *Field Trips* ☐ *Filmstrips* ☐
Forms ☐ *Games* ☐ *Handouts* ☐ *Instructions* ☐ *Interviews* ☐
Inventories ☐ *Journals* ☐ *Lectures* ☐ *Letters* ☐ *Libraries* ☐ *Lists* ☐
Magazines ☐ *Mixed Media* ☐ *Models* ☐ *Music* ☐ *Mysteries* ☐ *Myths*
Newspapers ☐ *Notes* ☐ *Oral Readings* ☐ *Papers* ☐ *Paragraphs* ☐
Periodicals ☐ *Pictures* ☐ *Plans* ☐ *Plays* ☐ *Plots* ☐ *Poems* ☐
Problems ☐ *Projectors* ☐ *Puzzles* ☐ *Questionnaires* ☐ *Questions* ☐
Radio ☐ *Recordings* ☐ *Role Playing* ☐ *Senses* ☐ *Selves* ☐ *Sentences*
Short Stories ☐ *Skits* ☐ *Slides* ☐ *Songs* ☐ *Tales* ☐ *Talks* ☐
Television ☐ *Term Papers* ☐ *Tests* ☐ *Topics* ☐ *Transparencies* ☐
Tutors ☐ *Videotapes* ☐

Alternate Process Verbs for Labeling
New Ideas and Writing Objectives

INTRODUCTION PHASE

Discover	*Listen*	*Observe*	*Read*	*Research*
Ask	Apprehend	Examine	Complete	Compile
Contrive	Attend	Follow	Comprehend	Copy
Derive	Catch	Look	Decode	Explore
Determine	Communicate	Notice	Hunt	Inquire
Devise	Hear	Recognize	Interpret	Investigate
Discuss	Heed	Record	Reproduce	Locate
Generalize	Participate	See	Scan	Note
Inquire	Perceive	View	Skim	Study
Question	Understand	Watch	Translate	Survey

DELIBERATION PHASE

Analyze	*Consolidate*	*Experiment*	*Interpret*	*Organize*
Consider	Abbreviate	Convert	Cite	Arrange
Deduce	Assimilate	Manipulate	Define	Classify
Examine	Collect	Practice	Describe	Coordinate
Inspect	Combine	Prove	Explain	Diagram
Probe	Incorporate	Rehearse	Illustrate	Distribute
Scrutinize	Reduce	Speculate	Paraphrase	Group
Search	Simplify	Test	Recite	List
Separate	Summarize	Try	Repeat	Outline
Weigh	Synthesize	Verify	Translate	Sort

EVALUATION PHASE

Compare	*Extrapolate*	*Identify*	*Judge*	*Restructure*
Associate	Amplify	Choose	Appraise	Alter
Contrast	Anticipate	Establish	Criticize	Change
Correlate	Conclude	Find	Decide	Correct
Differentiate	Expand	Fix	Measure	Modify
Distinguish	Estimate	Indicate	Rank	Rearrange
Liken	Finish	Isolate	Rate	Replace
Match	Infer	Label	Select	Restate
Parallel	Predict	Recognize	Try	Revise
Relate	Suggest	Specify	Vote	Substitute

APPLICATION PHASE

Construct	*Perform*	*Solve*	*Speak*	*Write*
Build	Act	Answer	Address	Compose
Create	Demonstrate	Clarify	Converse	Copy
Design	Depict	Decide	Declare	Draft
Develop	Direct	Explain	Discuss	Outline
Devise	Interact	Interpret	Express	Record
Give	Lead	Prove	Persuade	Register
Illustrate	Mimic	Realize	Relate	Relate
Operate	Role Play	Resolve	Respond	Report
Produce	Sing	Unravel	Tell	Transcribe

Glossary

Analyze—the first process under Deliberation in the teaching-learning sequence; distinguishing facts from hypotheses; determining relevance, idea relationships, persuasive techniques, and other aspects. Analysis of literature may be used to recognize form and pattern to derive meaning.

Application—the fourth step in the teaching-learning sequence and fourth letter in the acronym I-D-E-A. This step includes ways a student can put into practice outside of class what he or she has learned in class. Most items in this phase may be regarded as "assignments," but hopefully, assignments will be ways to apply learning to life.

Argumentation—the classic form of rhetoric that comes closest to committing an oral debate to paper; usually included in the quartet of composition studies with narration, description, and exposition.

"C"—not a main classification term, this abbreviation stands for *class* and precedes activities that will involve the entire class.

Compare—the process of seeking similarities and differences among situations, ideas, and products and usually based on observable external qualities. It is a key entry word in the Evaluation phase of the teaching-learning sequence.

Composition—one of the five subject matter divisions used to designate a handbook section. As such, it includes the entire area of written composition from friendly notes to best-selling novels.

Comprehension—as a reading term it typically describes three levels of taking in and processing information: literal, critical, and inferential. As a subject subdivision in this book it denotes being able to read words, understand their meanings, and make generalizations from words as they are combined in sentences.

Consolidate—a process in the Deliberation phase; it is gathering, selecting, and relating specific and useful new information to other previously learned but similar knowledge.

Construct—one of five processes in Application when the learner builds or assembles something having recently learned how. This could be a model of an Indian village, a work of art, a saleable product, or even a magazine.

Deliberation—one of the four steps in the teaching-learning sequence; the second letter in the acronym I-D-E-A. It is the phase when the learner attempts to work with the new information he or she has received in the Introduction phase and to practice with it by placing new generalizations into familiar frameworks, the key to reasoning. It is a time to reflect.

Description—one of the four types of rhetoric typically studied in written composition; a rhetorical principle by which content takes on color, movement, and form.

Dialect—sometimes called "regionalism," this Grammar/Language subdivision refers to the language spoken in particular regions of a country or among particular ethnic groups.

Discover—a process in the Introduction phase by which a learner receives information through a question-answer technique, through methods of inquiry, and even through class discussion.

Drama—used mainly to identify ideas in the Literature section for that genre so important to the study of English. The term may also be found in other sections since drama is not exclusive to literature. For example, drama can be written and be written about, and can stimulate language study to improve reading.

Experiment—this Deliberation process helps identify ideas that allow pupils to practice using new-found learnings in classroom situations such as completing drills and exercises or even playing simulation games.

Extrapolate—originally a mathematician's term which was popularized by Bloom and associates when they prepared their taxonomy of educational objectives—cognitive domain. (See page 296 for citation.) Complicated as it may seem, the term simply refers to an Evaluation process by which the learner tests his or her ability to extend given information and determine or predict implications, consequences, and effects when similar circumstances are applied in another context or situation. Success in this step assures the learner he or she knows the material.

Evaluation—the third step in the teaching-learning sequence; the E in I-D-E-A. It applies to tips that help the learner to know if learning has taken place and helps the teacher discover if material was taught sufficiently. Evaluation also includes material assessment such as whether information is significant, useful, or worth retaining. Sometimes it takes the last step—Application—to prove utility.

Exposition—the area of written composition by which, as its root implies, a writer exposes his or her knowledge about a particular subject, usually how to do or make something, or to tell why the author feels as he or she does about something. Its uniqueness is that it lends itself to organizing supporting details around a topic sentence or developing idea.

Film Making—this skill area has recently been recognized as a valuable subdivision of the English field; a dynamic communication instrument studied as a form of composition and as literature.

"G"—designates activities that lend themselves to *groups* within the classroom setting. The value of grouping for instruction has long been known, but too few teachers take advantage of the many possibilities.

Grammar/Language—one of the content area sections comprising about a fifth of the book and including both traditional and modern approaches. (Because the author supports an integrated study of grammar, many Grammar/Language ideas are scattered throughout the book.)

Humanities—a rapidly growing content area in English; often used to designate many multidisciplinary approaches to the field, sometimes becoming a field by itself with its own discipline. In this book, humanities designates ideas that cross the traditional English boundaries to take in the full range of fine arts. It's a catchword term that threatens to become a catchall.

"I"—this letter symbolizes ideas that are aimed mainly at individuals. Most frequently the ideas concern assignments such as written compositions and term papers for independent study. The term also identifies ideas involving projects designed to meet particular talents and skills.

Identify—a well-known term in the Evaluation phase of instruction, since learners are frequently asked to "identify" something for a test. Sometimes the task is to differentiate among various ideas and structures and to choose one or several that pertain to a particular situation. More typically, learners match meanings and definitions with parallel terms or sources.

Interpret—a process term, indicating activities in the Deliberation teaching-learning sequence. It concerns grasping the complete thought, for example, of a literary work to determine its purpose, theme, moral, or any other nonliteral device.

Introduction—step preceding Deliberation, Evaluation, and Application in the teaching-learning sequence. It names the operation that occurs when learners receive information through one or more senses. It represents a somewhat passive information input-intake operation, but it can become more active through processes of inquiry (questioning) and research.

Journalism—a content subdivision indicating tips that either enhance student knowledge of the field of journalism (includes both newspapers and magazines) or uses the field to help teach English.

Judge—in the Evaluation phase, this process represents what transpires when the learner tests an idea, product, or communication for usability, accuracy, logic, or other internal traits.

Letter Writing—simply the special content subdivision that is often the most practical learning for students working in a composition unit.

Linguistics—content subdivision dealing with the scientific approach to language study; causes English teachers to explain whether they are teaching "the old or the new grammar." The new grammar is scientifically based and entails transforming or generating sentences or treating them from a psychological view. Linguistics is descriptive; "old grammar" is prescriptive.

Listen—needs no definition; included as one of five processes in the Introduction or information-receiving phase of the teaching-learning sequence.

Literature—one of the five subject matter divisions containing ideas for teaching the novel, drama, poetry, and other forms.

Mechanics—Grammar/Language subdivision; includes helps for teaching capitalization and punctuation.

Media—print and nonprint ways for informing the general public. In this book, film, which is generally included in media, is a subdivision by itself.

Narration—one of the content subdivisions primarily, though not exclusively, in the Composition section. It marks those activities concerned with story telling.

Novels—this subdivision entry word in Literature refers to activities devoted to reading and reacting to fiction.

Observe—method by which a learner receives information in the Introduction phase of the teaching-learning process.

Organize—this process under the Deliberation phase denotes what must take place occasionally to facilitate recall, particularly if incoming information is varied and unwieldy.

Overview—one of the twenty-five content area subdivisions; it designates approaches which serve to integrate the several skill areas in the field: composition, grammar/language, literature, and reading.

Perform—one of the five major processes under the Application phase and identifying activities in which the learner participates in some form of role playing such as dramas, skits, simulation games, or in activities that require special skills—reading a poem effectively, singing a song, playing an instrument, and many other skills that be acquired by practice.

Poetry—that content under Literature devoted to producing, reading, and studying various forms of verse.

Process—this is not one of the classifications or descriptors, but since it is used so frequently in the Introduction to the book and in the Glossary, it should be defined briefly. The term refers to the techniques or methods by which people learn and teachers teach; all the twenty ways that permit teaching and learning to transpire through the four generally accepted sequences of Introduction, Deliberation, Evaluation, and Application.

Read—one of the five information-receiving processes listed under the Introduction phase of the teaching-learning process.

Reading—the fourth main section in the book in which are found 250 ideas for teaching reading, most of them emphasizing reading and writing activities for slow learners.

Reading Rate—a subdivision found primarily in the content area of Reading. Ideas are given to increase words per minute and to vary that rate according to reading difficulty.

Research—a process among five in the Introduction section designating one way a learner takes in information. It usually involves out-of-class sources such as libraries and interviews with authorities.

Restructure—in the Evaluation phase of the teaching-learning sequence. This process designates activities that require sifting data and arranging it to fit a function similar to but not exactly like the original source.

Room Management—the last of the five main divisions; contains ideas to help the teacher handle anything from attitudes to tutoring.

Semantics—traditionally, a word referring to a branch of linguistics concerned with word meanings. Its use in this handbook is no exception.

Solve—a process in the Application phase of the teaching-learning sequence typifying the problem-solving and problem-clarifying activities made possible by having learned a body of material or information.

Speak—along with the four other Application processes—construct, perform, solve, and write—the word identifies activities that involve orally sharing knowledge of gathered information.

Spelling—the subject matter subdivisions referring to Grammar/Language ideas to improve this typical but sometimes neglected area of English.

Study Skills—one of the Reading subdivisions designating suggested activities to improve skills in locating, organizing, and recalling information, following directions, selecting and evaluating information. Thus, study skills help sharpen many processes in the first three teaching-learning sequences.

Syntax—this subdivision found mainly in the Grammar/Language section is used in its traditional sense to indicate activities for improving sentence structure, arranging words in normal message-carrying relationships.

"T"—this abbreviation found after many of the idea numbers, indicates tips directed to the *teacher,* mainly for carrying out some aspect of the content area in which they appear. It is not used with ideas for class or groups. The "T" abbreviation also designates tutoring approaches including all types of one-to-one instruction: peer, cross-age, cross-ability.

Usage—a subdivision of the Grammar/Language section; describes ways to use language in speaking or writing.

Vehicle—not a classification or descriptor, this term is the second word in the parentheses that precede each tip. As such, it describes how the process is to be carried out. A suggested list appears in the Appendix. The vehicle word is usually the main tool or teaching aid for facilitating learning.

Vocabulary—subdivision which classifies tips primarily in the Grammar/Language and Reading sections. As usual, the term classifies activities for learning word definitions.

Words—one of the several subdivisions found in the content areas, this one usually in the Grammar/Language and Reading sections. The term signifies an activity dealing with word functions, or, in Reading, word calling. In the Reading area, word identification skills and sight word development are found under "Words."

Write—a process term under Application denoting activities based on written communication as opposed to oral and aural approaches.

READING TERMS

Blend—two or three consonants which when sounded keep their original, separate sounds, e.g., *st* in post, *str* in strong.

Comprehension—the act of reading with understanding; usually includes three levels: translating words and ideas, reacting to ideas, and making inferences (also known as literal, critical, and inferential levels).

Consonant—any letter sounded by momentarily obstructing the movement of air using the tongue, palate, or lips (*b, c, d, t,* etc.).

Context—the parts of a sentence or paragraph that occur just before and after a word and determine its exact meaning; sometimes the entire work or interrelated discourse is needed.

Critical Level—one aspect of comprehension that involves the reader in analyzing the material for author bias, objectivity, accuracy, feasibility, and so on, based on past experience with the same or similar material.

Decoding—translating letter symbols into oral (or thought) language.

Digraph—a combination of two consonants or vowels that give a single unique sound, e.g., *oa* in boat, *ph* in photo.

Diphthong—two vowels which when said together give their separate sounds, often retaining their individual nature, e.g., *oi* in oil, *ou* in out. (Similar to a consonant blend.)

Dolch Service Words—a list of 220 common words that every fourth grader should know by sight (not have to sound out). This list, containing no nouns and developed in the early 1900s by E. W. Dolch, is the widely accepted forerunner of more recent lists such as those offered by Fry, Kucera and Francis, Thorndike and Lorge, and others.

Experiential Level—(See Critical Level.)

Inferential Level—that area of comprehension known as "reading between the lines." It involves extrapolating beyond the given or literal facts.

Literal Level—an area of comprehension that involves translating the words and giving them meaning.

Phonics—the area of reading that focuses on sounds made by individual letters and combinations.

Root—a main word or base to which prefixes, suffixes, and inflections may be added to alter the meaning.

Scanning—searching printed material rapidly to seek out specific information decided upon before the reading.

Skimming—a purposeful, quick reading of a particular piece of material to determine main ideas, subideas, and overall theme.

Speed—also known as rate, is the speed at which a reader can read so many words per minute. Rates vary with the purpose, the difficulty of the material, and the reader's knowledge of the material.

Structure—the analytical aspects of a word in its smallest parts (stems, roots, affixes).

Study Skills—a natural or acquired ability to obtain some information about a subject; usually locating, recalling, selecting, and organizing such information for a specific purpose.

Syllabication—separating words into units of pronunciation following certain accepted patterns and rules, i.e., each syllable contains a vowel sound; blends, digraphs, and diphthongs are not separated; words are always divided between twin consonants and between other consonants unless the first vowel has a long sound (se-cret).

Syntax—words arranged by grammatical pattern, usually in sentence formats.

Tachistoscope—any device used to flash one or several words at variable exposure times, usually speeded up gradually.

Vowel—a letter voiced with the mouth open and unobstructed, such as the letter *a*.

Word Recognition—also known as word attack and word identification; relating symbol to sound by using such aids as context, word structure, phonics, or the dictionary.

Resource Bibliography

Except for a few "classics" in the field, the author has included only sources from 1970 and on. This listing, therefore, is just a fraction of what could or should have been included. But it is a beginning since many of the publications have their own bibliographies. Annotations are used when the title may not give sufficient clues about content. To save additional space, the abbreviation NCTE is used to cite the many publications of the National Council of Teachers of English. For more information about NCTE publications, contact Paul O'Dea at NCTE Headquarters, 1111 Kenyon Road, Urbana, Illinois 61801.

COMPOSITION

All About Letters. United States Postal Service in Cooperation with NCTE, 1979. For students in grades 6 through 12, this sixty-four page booklet provides an excellent "how to" guide on letter writing. It also lists sources available to students for ordering many free and inexpensive items.

Bergman, Floyd L. *Manuscript Diagnosis: The Text-Ray.* Ann Arbor, Mich.: Campus Publishers, 1974. Describes a unique composition evaluation procedure. Relates grammar and composition functionally.

———. *The Write It and Edit Kit.* Ft. Lauderdale: House of Printing, 1980. This twenty-four page booklet, which fits handily into a notebook, is a practical guide for students or adults. The approach, a companion piece and update of *Manuscript Diagnosis* (above), helps writers analyze their own style and edit for clarity. (Copies available only from the author at 2162 NE 59th Court, Ft. Lauderdale, FL 33308.)

Britton, James; Burgess, Tony; Martin, Nancy; McLeod, Alec, and Rosen, Harold. *The Development of Writing Abilities*. London: Macmillan Education, 1975. Offers insights into the nature of the writing process and analyzes typical student writing.

Brown, Harry M. *How to Write: A Practical Rhetoric*. New York: Holt, Rinehart and Winston, 1978. Designed to help students develop skills in expository writing, the book is a good review for teachers of composition. It contains numerous examples.

Carlson, Ruth Kearney. *Sparkling Words*. 2nd ed. (Paladin House, Publishers) NCTE, 1979. Contains 315 ideas to help young authors write creatively.

Christensen, Francis, et al. "The Sentence and the Paragraph." *(College English and College Composition and Communication.)* NCTE, 1966. Articles on rhetoric of English prose including the generative paragraph and the tagmemic approach to paragraph analysis.

Cooper, Charles R., and Odell, Lee, eds. *Research on Composing: Points of Departure*. NCTE, 1978. Researchers and teachers of writing discuss widely individual teaching practices, needed research, and the psychological and physiological composing processes.

Corbett, Edward P. J., ed. *Composition and Its Teaching*. (Ohio Council of English Language Arts), NCTE, 1979.

Cramer, Ronald. *Children's Writing and Language Growth*. Columbus, OH: Charles E. Merrill Publishing Company, 1978. A good source of ideas for those teachers who wish to upgrade their own attitudes about and approaches for teaching writing.

Cunningham, Donald H., and Estrin, Herman A., eds. *The Teaching of Technical Writing*. NCTE, 1975. Presents descriptions of technical writing courses in action. Discusses evaluation and many other aspects of the technical/scientific writing fields.

Day, Robert, and Weaver, Gail Cohen, eds. *Creative Writing in the Classroom*. NCTE, 1978. This is an annotated bibliography of selected references (K–12) from 200 journal articles and books published from 1950 to 1976.

Gerbrandt, Gary L. *An Idea Book for Acting Out and Writing Language K–8*. NCTE, 1974. Practical, proven ideas for individualizing the language arts. Also helpful ideas for teaching writing through completing unfinished sentences, writing fables and stories, and unscrambling sentences.

Glorfeld, Louis E.; Lauerman, David A.; and Stageberg, Norman C. *A Concise Guide for Writers*. 3rd ed. New York: Holt, Rinehart & Winston, 1977.

Holbrook, David. *Children's Writing*. Cambridge, England: Cambridge University Press, 1967.

Hook, J. N. *Guide to Good Writing: Grammar, Style, Usage*. New York: Ronald Press Co., 1962.

Ideaform Theme Paper. NCTE. Packaged (thirty sheets) paper with an evaluation checklist on back to save teacher time. Free sample on request.

Irmscher, William F. *Teaching Expository Writing.* New York: Holt, Rinehart and Winston, 1979. A thorough description of expository writing,
the book is an excellent resource for anyone who is teaching the art
from process to practice.
Katz, Marjorie P., and Arbeiter, Jean S. *Pegs to Hang Ideas On: A Book of
Quotations.* New York: M. Evand and Company, 1973. Distributed by
J. B. Lippincott Co. A collection of quotations from contemporary
newspapers and magazines. Categories relate to personal
development, environment, and major social and political issues.
Koch, Carl, and Brazil, James M. *Strategies for Teaching the Composition
Process.* NCTE, 1978. A book of useful ideas and exercises for
teachers of writing at many grade levels. It also discusses
constructive evaluation.
Kunz, Linda Ann, and Viscount, Robert R. *Write Me a Ream: A Course in
Controlled Composition for Job Training and Adult Education.* New
York: Teachers College Press, 1973.
Lundsteen, Sara W., ed. *Help for the Teacher of Written Composition (K–9):
New Directions in Research.* NCTE, 1976. All the research and
related ideas that you will be able to use in offering perspectives on
written composition.
Macrorie, Ken. *Telling Writing.* New York: Hayden Book Company, 1970.
Useful for the teacher or as a class text through its down-to-earth
discussion about composition.
_____ . *Writing to Be Read.* New York: Hayden Book Company, 1968.
Maxwell, Rhoda, and Judy, Stephen, eds. *Composing: The 1979 Yearbook of
the Michigan Council of Teachers of English.* NCTE, 1979. These
eleven essays explore new areas of theory and practice in
composition.
Mitchell, Richard. *Less Than Words Can Say.* Boston: Little-Brown and
Company, 1979. In his latest condemnation of composition literacy,
the "underground grammarian" presents some provocative thoughts
and suggestions for the harried teacher of composition.
Murray, Donald M. *A Writer Teaches Writing: A Practical Method of
Teaching High School Composition.* Boston: Houghton Mifflin
Company, 1968.
National Writers Club, 1365 Logan St., Denver, CO 80203. Free information
on writing careers.
O'Hare, Frank, *Sentence Combining: Improving Student Writing without
Formal Grammar Instruction.* NCTE, 1973.
Perrin, Porter G. *The Writer's Guide and Index to English.* 6th ed. Revised
by Karl W. Dykema and Wilma R. Ebbitt. Glenview, IL: Scott,
Foresman and Company, 1978.
Simons, George F. *Keeping Your Personal Journal.* New York: Paulist
Press, 1978. Here is a book with many practical ideas for starting and
keeping journals.
Smith, Eugene. *Teacher Preparation in Composition.* NCTE, 1969.
Stanford, Gene, chair, and the Committee on Classroom Practices. *Class-
room Practices 1979–1980: How to Handle the Paper Load.* NCTE,
1979. The twenty-seven authors in this collection describe effective
and less time-consuming methods for teaching composition.

Stanford, Gene, and Smith, Marie. *A Guidebook for Teaching Composition.* Boston: Allyn and Bacon, Inc., 1975. A helpful guide for the composition teacher, this soft-cover book offers ninety-nine reproducible activities as well as work-saving suggestions and ideas for teaching effective writing.

———. *A Guidebook for Teaching Creative Writing.* Boston: Allyn and Bacon, Inc., 1978. This soft-cover book contains many reproducible activities, specific ideas for assignments, and individual and group projects to help teachers of creative writing.

Strunk, William Jr., and White, E. B. *The Elements of Style.* 3rd ed. New York: Macmillan Publishing Co., Inc. 1979. A classic in the field for its succinct usefulness, this tiny book provides rules of usage and suggestions for a style that is brief, clear, and sensible.

Tate, Gary, and Corbett, Edward P. J., eds. *Teaching High School Composition.* New York: Oxford University Press, 1970. A substantially documented collection of articles on composition. An extensive bibliography is included, as well as a suggested minimal reference library.

Wheeler, Thomas C. *The Great American Writing Block: Causes and Cures of the New Illiteracy.* New York: The Viking Press, 1979. The author discusses the effects of television, standardized testing, and other factors that have led to the decline of composition skills. To this are added solutions based on actual experiences.

The Whole Word Catalog. Staff of Teachers and Writers Collaborative. NCTE, 1972. A collection of open classroom assignments to stimulate student writing for both elementary and secondary.

Wilson, Grace E., ed. *Composition Situations.* NCTE, 1966. A collection of topics in forty-five categories under general sections: personal experiences, language study, mass media, and literature study.

GRAMMAR/LANGUAGE

Aarons, Alfred C., et al. "Linguistic-Cultural Differences and American Education." *(Florida FL Reporter.)* NCTE, 1969. Anthology of forty-three articles on problems of cultural pluralism.

Allen, Harold B., ed. *Readings in Applied English Linguistics.* 2nd ed. New York: Appleton Century Crofts, 1967.

Allen, Virginia F., and Forman, Sidney. *English as a Second Language: A Comprehensive Bibliography.* New York: Arno, 1978. Catalog of 1,000 items: books, pamphlets, periodicals, films, filmstrips, records, tapes, charts, maps, games, and models. Categories are Linguistics, Language Culture, Language Learning, Texts, and References.

Berbrich, John D. *101 Ways to Learn Vocabulary.* New York: Amsco School Publications, 1971.

Berger, Allen, and Smith, Blanche Hope, eds. *Classroom Practices in Teaching English, 1972–1973: Language Activities.* NCTE, 1972. Contains over fifty ideas and activities on language development at all educational levels.

Bergman, Floyd L., and Bergman, Virginia B. *A Guidebook for Teaching Grammar.* Boston: Allyn and Bacon, Inc. (Proposed publication date 1982.) This guide is just what grammar teachers have needed for a long time: hundreds of practical and student-motivating activities and exercises to help students understand the grammar that is basic to written composition. As in other books in this series, many exercises are on reproducible pages.

Daiker, Donald A.; Kerek, Andrew; and Morenberg, Max. *The Writer's Options: College Sentence Combining.* New York: Harper and Row, Publishers, Inc., 1979. For the advanced student of the sentence combining approach, this book gives a systematic, disciplined look at the combining process and provides many related exercises.

Davis, A. L. *Culture, Class, and Language Variety.* NCTE, 1972. Ten articles to help teachers work more effectively with language problems of children who speak nonstandard dialects.

Francis, W. Nelson. *The English Language: An Introduction.* New York: W. W. Norton & Co., 1965.

Hayakawa, S. I. *Language in Thought and Action.* 3rd ed. New York: Harcourt, Brace and World, 1972.

Herndon, Jeanne H. *A Survey of Modern Grammars.* New York: Holt, Rinehart & Winston, 1976. Written for in-service and pre-service elementary and secondary teachers of language arts or English.

Labov, William. *The Study of Nonstandard English.* NCTE, 1970. Suggests ways to develop insights on nonstandard English, thus making it an integral part of sociolinguistic structure.

Lefevre, Carl A. *Linguistics, English, and the Language Arts.* New York: Teachers College Press, 1973. An introduction to linguistics, it explains traditional, structural, transformational, and generative grammar and suggests what each contributes to language.

Linguistics and the Classroom Teacher. 1970 edition. Association for Supervision and Curriculum Development. Room 428, 1202 16th St., N.W., Washington, D.C. Introduction to linguistics and its use in developing communication skills.

Loban, Walter. *Language Development: Kindergarten through Grade Twelve.* NCTE, 1976. An essential addition to any language teacher's library; gives many insights into growth in language skills.

Malmstrom, Jean. *Language in Society.* 2nd ed. New York: Hayden Book Company, 1973.

McDavid, Raven I., et al. *Americans Speaking.* NCTE, 1967. Transcriptions of free discourse and readings by speakers in six dialect areas. Available with record and/or pamphlet.

O'Hare, Frank. *Sentence Combining: Improving Student Writing Without Formal Grammar Instruction.* NCTE, 1973. For those who have their doubts as to the value of traditional grammar to improve written composition, this book reports research on a sentence combining system that worked successfully to improve student writing.

Pollock, Thomas C. "Misspelling in Grades 9–12," *English Record* 22 (Fall 1971); 46–53. Analysis of 388 of 50,000 misspelled words submitted by 1,706 teachers.

Pooley, Robert C. *The Teaching of English Usage.* 2nd ed. NCTE, 1974. A rationale for teaching informal standard English with specific suggestions for teaching usage.

Postman, Neil, and Weingartner, Charles. *Linguistics.* New York: Dell, 1966. This book gives detailed suggestions on what works in teaching linguistics; discusses transfer of learnings into actual practice.

Sapir, Edward. *Culture, Language and Personality.* Berkeley: University of California Press, 1961.

Selected List of Materials for Teachers of English to Speakers of Other Languages. Center for Applied Linguistics, 1611 N. Kent Rd., Arlington, VA 22209.

Shipley, Joseph T. *Word Play.* New York: Hawthorn Books, 1972. A valuable resource for the teacher who wants to use word games to develop student interest and competency in language learning.

Smith, E. Brooks; Goodman, Kenneth S.; and Meredith, Robert. *Language and Thinking in the Elementary School.* New York: Holt, Rinehart & Winston, 1976.

Strong, William. *Sentence Combining: A Composing Book.* New York: Random House, Inc., 1973. Frequently used as a classroom text, this book also serves to inform teachers about sentence combining; also provides a good source of sentence combining exercises.

Wardhaugh, Ronald. *Introduction to Linguistics.* New York: McGraw-Hill, 1972.

Weaver, Constance. *Grammar for Teachers: Perspectives and Definitions.* NCTE, 1979. Lays a strong foundation in grammar for improving listening, speaking, reading, and writing.

LITERATURE

American Library Association. *A Basic Book Collection for High Schools* and *A Basic Book Collection for Junior High Schools.* Revised regularly.

Barnfield, Gabriel. *Creative Drama in Schools.* London: Macmillan Company, 1970.

Booklist. American Library Association, 50 E. Huron St., Chicago, IL 60611. A semimonthly with about 150 book reviews each issue.

Book Review Digest. H. W. Wilson Co., 950 University Ave., Bronx, NY 10452. A monthly and an annual accumulation of book reviews which had appeared when a book was first published.

Brooks, Cleanth, and Warren, Robert Penn. *Understanding Poetry.* 3rd ed. New York: Holt, Rinehart & Winston, 1960.

Burton, Dwight L. *Literature Study in the High Schools.* 3rd ed. New York: Holt, Rinehart & Winston, 1970. Discussion on constructive criticism of literature in the secondary classroom. Suggestions for setting up sample bibliographies.

Carlsen, G. Robert. *Books and the Teenage Reader.* New York: Bantam Books, 1979. An introduction to the reading interests of young adults.

Chicorel, Marietta, ed. *Index to Poetry in Collections: Poetry in Print.* Chicorel Library Publishing Corporation, 275 Central Park West, New York, NY 10024. Over 250,000 entries locating poetry by titles, first lines, authors, editors, translators, and collection titles.

Children's Book Council, Inc., 175 Fifth Avenue, New York, NY 10010. Sponsors of National Children's Book Week, the organization will provide materials to stimulate reading. Free information on request in self-addressed, stamped envelope.

Ciardi, John, and Williams, Miller. *How Does a Poem Mean?* 2nd ed. Boston: Houghton Mifflin Company, 1975.

The Combined Paperback Exhibit. Combined Paperback Exhibit, Inc., Scarborough Park, Albany Post Road, Briarcliff Manor, NY 10510. A free catalog—elementary through senior high—of school exhibit information.

Donelson, Kenneth, ed. "Adolescent Literature, Adolescent Reading in the English Class." *(Arizona English Bulletin).* Urbana, IL: National Council of Teachers of English, 1972. Brief articles about contemporary books young people enjoy, all based on interest surveys.

Donelson, Kenneth, ed., and NCTE Committee on the Senior High Booklist. *Books for You: A Booklist for Senior High Students.* NCTE, 1976. An annotated listing of 2,500 titles that students can use to locate appealing, recent books.

Donelson, Kenneth L., and Nilsen, Alleen Pace. *Literature for Today's Young Adults.* Glenview, IL: Scott, Foresman and Company, 1980. A well-rounded theory-to-practice book which will be a continual source of needed information for the teacher of literature or even for those who select and approve literature: parents and librarians alike.

Dreyer, Sharon S. *Bookfinder: A Guide to Children's Literature About the Needs and Problems of Youth Aged 2–15.* Circle Pines, MN: American Guidance Service, 1977. A book to which all teachers should have access, it lists among other problems literature of self-identity, isolation, and the struggle to conform.

Dunning, A. Stephen. *Teaching Literature to Adolescents: Poetry.* Glenview, IL: Scott, Foresman and Company, 1966.

————. *Teaching Literature to Adolescents: Short Stories.* Glenview, IL: Scott, Foresman and Company, 1968.

Gallo, Donald, ed. *Poetry: Reading, Writing, and Analyzing It.* NCTE, 1979. The twenty-eight contributors to this collection offer creative ideas for reading and studying poetry.

Hiatt, Doris, and Klein, Celeste. *Kliatt Paperback Book Guide.* 6 Crocker Circle, West Newton, Mass. 02165. A looseleaf quarterly service that reviews books for young adults.

Hodgson, John, and Richards, Ernest. *Improvisation: Discovery and Creativity in Drama.* London: Methuen, 1977.

Howes, Alan B. *Teaching Literature to Adolescents: Plays.* Glenview, IL: Scott, Foresman and Company, 1968.

Improvisation Handbook. Glenview, IL: Scott, Foresman and Company, 1974. A collection of games and exercises to acquaint students with improvisation techniques. Also contains scenes for practice.

Kujoth, Jean Spealman. *Reading Interests of Children and Young Adults.* Methuen, NJ: Scarecrow Press, 1970.

The New York Times Book Review. The New York Times Co., Times Square, NY 10036. A weekly general book review service of *The New York Times* Sunday edition. About twenty or thirty titles in each issue.

Paperbound Books in Print and *Books in Print.* R. R. Bowker Co., 1180 Avenue of the Americas, New York, NY 10036. All the information needed for ordering books. Perhaps too expensive for teachers, but every library should have these.

Pownall, David. *Articles on Twentieth Century Literature: An Annotated Bibliography 1954–1970.* Kraus Thomson Organization Limited. Millwood, NY 10546. An eight-volume reference work providing access to more than 22,000 journal articles about contemporary literature throughout the world.

Purves, Alan C., ed. *How Porcupines Make Love.* New York: John Wiley & Sons, Inc., 1972. Describes various fresh approaches to teaching literature.

Reid, Virginia M., ed. *Reading Ladders for Human Relations.* (American Council on Education.) NCTE, 1972. Annotated bibliography of more than 1,300 books arranged by maturity level. Focuses on expanding sensitivity toward people.

Rivlin, Asher E., et al. *Poetry Unfolding.* Madison, WI: VEC, Inc., 1979. This book offers a new audiovisual approach to learning poetry. It utilizes transparencies and student worksheets aimed at creative poetry.

Rodrigues, Raymond, and Badaczewski, Dennis. *A Guidebook for Teaching Literature.* Boston: Allyn and Bacon, Inc., 1978. A practical resource for the English teacher, this soft-cover book contains reproducible worksheets, along with games and group and class activities using many, varied approaches for involving students with literature.

School Library Journal. R. R. Bowker Co., 1180 Avenue of the Americas, New York, NY 10036. A monthly with book reviews including sections for junior high and young adults.

Schwartz, Shiela. *Teaching Adolescent Literature: A Humanistic Approach.* Rochelle Park, NJ: Hayden Book Company, Inc., 1979. This book stresses literature that appeals to the personal concerns of young people; describes successful adolescent literature of the past two decades and how to use it in class.

Simmons, Gloria M., and Hutchinson, Helene D. *Black Culture: Reading and Writing Black.* New York: Holt, Rinehart & Winston, 1972.

Stensland, Anna Lee. *Literature by and about the American Indian,* NCTE, 1979. Descriptions of the latest books on the American Indian, biographies of Indian writers, teaching materials, and suggestions for classroom collections.

Turner, Darwin T., and Stanford, Barbara Dodds. *Theory and Practice in the Teaching of Literature by Afro-Americans.* NCTE, 1971.

Walker, Jerry L., ed., and NCTE Committee on the Junior High Booklist. *Your Reading: A Booklist for Junior High Students.* NCTE, 1975. Students can use these 1,600 titles and annotations to locate engaging books which are grouped into forty or more distinct headings.

Warshaw, Thayer. *Handbook for Teaching the Bible in Literature Classes.* Nashville: Abingden, 1978. This book, aimed at literature teachers, provides suggestions to help students discover that the Bible is a source of great literary heritage. The book offers many projects and activities to enhance this approach.

Way, Brian. *Development Through Drama.* New York: Humanities Press, 1967.

MEDIA

Achenbaum, Alvin, et al. "Doublespeak: What is Deceptive Advertising?" NCTE, 1973. (Cassette tape, 87 min.) Focuses on current controversies over advertising aimed at children. Includes audience questions.

Anderson, Chuck. *The Electric Journalist: An Introduction to Video.* New York: Praeger Publications, 1973. How to videotape and edit, also production ideas and their influence on American life (cable TV and public access).

Andersen, Yvonne. *Make Your Own Animated Movies.* Boston: Little, Brown and Company, 1970. Easy-to-understand and step-by-step information for young filmmakers.

"The Arts—How to Become Involved." YWCA National Board. New York, NY 10022. (Color prints.) Shows how to stimulate student involvement through films, music, the dance, fine arts, graphic arts, multimedia events, and so on. (8½" × 11" color prints with supplementary text.)

Audio-Visual Marketplace.: A Multi-Media Guide. R. R. Bowker Co., 1180 Avenue of the Americas, New York, NY 10036. Extensive media bibliography.

Ayer Directory: Newspapers, Magazines, and Trade Publications. Ayer Press, West Washington Square, Philadelphia, PA 19106. Names and addresses in this annual publication which every library should have.

Berger, Arthur Asa. *Pop Culture.* Dayton, OH: Pflaum/Standard, 1973. A book with a variety of subjects to discuss American culture and how our environment tends to shape the unaware.

Betancourt, Jeanne. *Women in Focus.* Dayton, OH: Pflaum/Standard, 38 West Fifth St. 45402. Catalog with reviews of over seventy nonsexist and feminist films for libraries, high schools, universities, and community groups.

Boutwell, William D., ed. *Using Mass Media in the Schools.* New York: Appleton-Century-Crofts, 1962.

COSMEP (Committee of Small Magazine Editors and Publishers). P.O. Box 703, San Francisco, CA 94101. Provides information on the nation's leading "little magazines."

The Creative Person—Richard Williams. National Education Television, 10 Columbus Circle, New York, NY 10019. (Film.) A close look at film animation. 16 mm, b&w, 30 min.

Current Media. Curriculum Innovations, Inc. 501 Lake Forest Avenue, Highwood, IL 60040. A continuing guide to journalism and the language arts for students in grades 7–12.

Edmonds, Robert. *Script-Writing for the Audio-Visual Media.* New York: Teachers College Press, Columbia University, 1978. Experienced in the field, the author covers scriptwriting for all media as well as a discussion of variations among the media.

A Film about Filmmaking. International Film Bureau, 332 S. Michigan Ave., Chicago, IL 60604, 1972. (Film.) A group of college students produce a film from planning to editing. 16 mm, color, 18 min.

Film Quarterly. University of California Press, 2223 Fulton St., Berkeley, CA 94720.

Films in Review. National Board of Review of Motion Pictures, Inc., 210 E. 68th St., New York, NY 10021.

For the Love of the Moon. Pyramid Films, Box 1048, Santa Monica, CA 90406. (Color film, 27 min.) An unusual presentation in which characters are hands with faces drawn on them. A study in illusion for high school students in any setting.

Foster, Harold M. *The New Literacy: The Language of Film and Television.* NCTE, 1979. This book offers practical tips on teaching visual literacy and integrating it into the curriculum. It includes teaching units that could be used for a high school film course.

Four Ways to Drama. University of California Media Center, Berkeley, CA 94720. (Film.) A short dramatic incident is presented four ways: radio, television, stage, and screen. 16mm, b&w, 33 min.

Free-Loan Training Films, A Guide to. Serina Press, 70 Kennedy Street, Alexandria, VA 22305. 16 mm.

Galvin, Kathleen, and Book, Cassandra. *Person-to-Person: An Introduction to Speech Communication.* Skokie, IL: National Textbook Company. Describes communication to improve human relationships. Uses syndicated comic strips, photographs, and posters.

Garrison, Cecil. *1001 Media Ideas for Teachers.* Berkeley, CA: McCutchan Publishing Corp., 1977.

Giblin, Thomas R. *Popular Media and the Teaching of English.* Pacific Palisades, CA: Goodyear Publishing Co., Inc., 1972. A collection of ideas dealing with the *why* and the *how* of popular media study in the secondary English classroom.

Guides to New Educational Media: Films, Filmstrips, Phono Records, Radio, Slides, and Television. American Library Association, 50 E. Huron Street, Chicago, IL 60611.

Heintz, Ann. *Exploring Television.* Chicago: Loyola Press, 1971. Introductory explanation on television for classroom use.

————. *Mass Media.* Chicago: Loyola Press, 1975. Many activities, games, and discussion topics for the classroom.

Hornick, Joanne. *Creative Bulletin Boards for Junior High English.* New York: Citation Press, 1968.

Houk, Annelle, and Bogart, Carlotta. *Media Literacy.* Dayton, OH: Pflaum/Standard, 1974.

The Humanities and the Curriculum. Association for Supervision and Curriculum Development, Room 428, 1201 16th St., N.W., Washington, D.C., 1970.

Jackdaws: Collections of Historical Documents. New York: Grossman Publishers. Packets to enrich the study of history, biography, and classical literary characters.

Katz, John, ed. *Perspectives on the Study of Film.* Boston: Little, Brown & Co., 1971.

K-Eight (Instructional Management and Leadership). North American Publishing Company, 134 N. 13th St., Philadelphia, PA 19107. Ideas for educational innovation.

Littell, Joseph Fletcher. *Coping With Television.* Evanston, IL: McDougal, Littell & Company, 1973. A complete look at television—its workings, content, and influence.

Manchel, Frank. *Yesterday's Clowns: The Rise of Film Comedy.* New York: Franklin Watts, 1973. A visit with some of the screen's greatest comedians; over fifty black and white photographs with bibliography.

McLuhan, H. Marshall. *Understanding Media: The Extensions of Man.* New York: New American Library, 1973.

Mitchell, Wanda. *Televising Your Message.* Skokie, IL: National Textbook Company, 1976. A practical, multi-purpose and very complete discussion of television from many points of view.

Montage. Regional Valley High School, Demarest, NJ 07627. This publication features articles on film education in high school, model programs, and reports on film-making.

The Movies. Indiana University Audio-visual Center. Bloomington, IN 47405 (Film.) The motion pictures examined sociologically. 16 mm, b&w, 29 min.

Potter, Robert R. *English Everywhere: Meaning, Media and You.* New York: The Globe Book Company, Inc., 1971. Covers subjects of interest to students: advertising, movies, television, the newspaper, language of humor and politics.

Schrank, Jeffrey. *The Guide to Short Films.* Rochelle Park, NJ: Hayden Book Company, Inc. An up-to-date comprehensive guide to more than 250 short films for film study.

The Seed Catalog. Boston: Beacon Press, 1974. Multi-media ideas for every classroom.

Schwarz, Ira P., and Karel, Leon C. *Teaching the Related Arts.* Kirksville, MO: Simpson Publishing Co., 1973. Approaches to interrelating the arts: music, painting, sculpture, architecture, crafts, literature, film, and dance.

Smallman, Kirk. *Creative Film-Making.* New York: The Macmillan Company, 1969. A beginner's book on film making, especially Super 8.

Sohn, David. *Film: The Creative Eye.* Dayton, OH: Pflaum/Standard. Features the aesthetic wonders of film.

Teachers Guides to Television. 145 East 69th St., New York, NY 10021. Guides to current TV programs. Write for subscription rates.

3M Loan-a-Library. Minnesota Mining and Manufacturing Co. One-week free loan of printed originals for making overhead transparencies. Contact local 3M dealer.

Time English Program. Chicago: Time, Inc. Requires at least five student subscriptions for weekly issues (9–12 grade).

U.S. Government Films for Public Educational Use. Superintendent of Documents, Government Films for Public Educational Use. Superintendent of Documents, Government Printing Office, Washington, DC 20402.

Valdes, Joan, and Crow, Jeanne. *The Media Works.* Dayton, OH: George Pflaum, 1975.

Videoplayer. Videoplayer Publishing Co., Inc., 13273 Ventura Blvd., Studio City, CA 91604. A news magazine for the international videotape player industry.

Young Filmmakers Foundation. *Young Animators and Their Discoveries.* New York: Praeger Publishers, Inc., 1973. Young filmmakers, age 14 and up, describe their animation experiments. General introduction to animated film production.

READING

Advanced Reading Skill Builder. Pleasantville, NY: Education Division, Reader's Digest Services, Inc. Booklets for students in grades 7, 8, and 9. Cassettes available. Write for information.

Bamman, H. A., and Dawson, Mildred. *Fundamentals of Basic Reading Instruction.* 2nd ed. New York: David McKay Co., 1963.

Burmeister, Lou. *Reading Strategies for Secondary School Teachers,* Reading, MA: Addison-Wesley Publishing Company, 1978.

Carlsen, Robert G. *Books and the Teenage Reader.* New York: Bantam Books, Inc., 1980. Revised and updated edition of a classic reference, the book features a descriptive guide to more than 1,200 books that teens want to read.

Cullinan, Bernice, ed. *Black Dialects and Reading.* NCTE, 1974. Information and practical suggestions regarding black dialect, oral language, and reading.

Cumulative Reading Record. Folder 9½ × 11¾ to record reading and reactions. Special insert available. Free sample on request.

Directory of Learning Resources for Reading. Gales Ferry, CT: Education Systems Inc. A general guide to conferences, meetings, reading journals, training centers, federal agencies, national organizations, statistical data, and publishers of instructional materials.

Donelson, Kenneth, chair., and the Committee on the Right to Read. *The Students' Right to Read.* NCTE, 1972. Updating of information on censorship. Lists sources of assistance.

Fader, Daniel. *The New Hooked on Books.* New York: Berkeley Publishing Corporation, 1976. This is a sequel to Fader's *Hooked on Books* which described results of a study using motivational reading techniques for delinquent students. The new book and its predecessor reveal the many implications to more normal environments.

Fallon, Berlie J., and Filgo, Dorothy, eds. *Forty States Innovate to Improve Reading Programs*. Belmont, CA: Fearon-Pitnam Publishing, Inc., 1973. Describes seventy-five exemplary reading programs, elementary through high school.

Gephart, William J. *The Convergence Technique and Reading*. Bloomington, IN: Phi Delta Kappa, 1969. Interim report on the planning of a reading research program.

Goldman, Frederick, and Burnett, Linda R. *Need Johnny Read?* Dayton, OH: Pflaum/Standard. Discusses the educational power of television and films and their use in schools.

Goltry, M. *Forms in Your Future*. New York: Globe Books Company. Presents twenty-four lessons built around various application blanks and forms which most students will eventually need to use in thier lives. Tear-out, duplicated forms.

Goodman, Kenneth A., ed. *Miscue Analysis*. NCTE, 1973. Applications of miscue analysis in a full range of classroom situations such as teacher training, remedial reading, college programs, and in-service workshops.

Goodman, Kenneth S., and Niles, Olive S. *Reading: Process and Program*. NCTE, 1970. Discusses multiple behaviors in reading along with promising trends, teacher training, preparing reading materials.

Herber, Harold L. *Teaching Reading in the Content Areas*. 2nd ed. Englewood Cliffs, NJ: Prentice-Hall, Inc., 1978. A thorough reading resource book for the teacher who has the desire to teach reading through the subject matter fields.

International Reading Association, Order Dept., 6 Tyre Ave., Newark, DE 19711. Write for publication list.

Karlin, Robert. *Teaching Reading in the High School*. 3rd. ed. Indianapolis: Bobbs-Merrill Co., 1977.

Laubach, Frank C.; Kirk, Elizabeth; and Laubach, Robert S. *Everyday Reading and Writing*. Syracuse: New Readers Press, 1970. Interestingly presented skills workbook which stresses newspapers, instructions, recipes, maps, and business forms, among others.

Maberly, Norman. *Mastering Speed Reading*. Bergenfield, NJ: The New American Library, 1973. Useful for 8th grade and up. Includes charts, diagrams, and tests.

Massey, William J., and Moore, Virginia D. *Helping High School Students to Read Better*. New York: Holt, Rinehart, & Winston, 1965.

Right to Read Office, U.S. Office of Education, 400 Maryland Ave., S.W., Washington, D.C. 20202. For inquiries about reading programs and research.

Ruddell, Robert B., ed. *Accountability and Reading Instruction: Critical Issues*. NCTE, 1973. Contributors discuss behavioral objectives, tests, performance contracting as they relate to reading instruction.

Russell, David H., and Karp, Eta E. *Reading Aids through the Grades*. New York: Teachers College Press, 1975.

Spache, Evelyn B. *Reading Activities for Child Involvement*. Boston: Allyn and Bacon, 1976. Offers activities for any reading program in elementary or middle school.

Spache, George. *The Teaching of Reading.* Bloomington, IN: Phi Delta Kappa, 1972. Summarizes and analyzes the best known information on reading readiness, methods, and ways to reach the disadvantaged.
———— . *Diagnosing and Correcting Reading Disabilities.* Boston: Allyn and Bacon, Inc., 1976.

Staiger, Ralph C., ed. *The Teaching of Reading.* Lexington: Ginn and Company, 1973. This is a sourcebook of key articles from world leaders in the field and was produced as a special project by the International Reading Association on behalf of Unesco.

Strang, Ruth; McCullough, Constance M.; and Traxler, Arthur E. *Improvement of Reading,* 4th ed. New York: McGraw-Hill Book Company, 1967.

Thomas, Ellen Lamar, and Robinson, H. Alan. *Improving Reading in Every Class.* 2nd ed. Boston: Allyn and Bacon, 1977. Describes practical procedures for teaching reading in all high school subject areas. Reference to a variety of related publications.

Verner, Zenobia. *Newsbook of Reading Comprehension Activities.* Houston: Clayton Publishing Company, 1978. Students read newspapers and then engage in self-directed activities from the book.

Wardhaugh, Ronald. *Reading: A Linguistic Perspective.* New York: Harcourt Brace Jovanovich, 1969.

White, Marian E., ed. *High Interest-Easy Reading for Junior and Senior High School Students,* 3rd. ed. NCTE, 1979.

Yellow Pages at every telephone. Bell Telephone Companies. More than phone numbers, these pages are really a course in Western civilization, its mores and ideals. Useful for improving reading skills (as in scanning) and providing topics to discuss.

Your Reading: A Booklist for Junior High Students. NCTE, 1975. This book lists annotated current titles that readers should enjoy. It is periodically updated, so ask for the latest edition.

REFERENCE SHELF
Curriculum and Instruction

Association for Supervision and Curriculum Development. *Individualizing Instruction.* 1701 K Street. N.W., Washington, D.C., 1970.

Bloom, Benjamin. *Individual Differences in School Achievement: A Vanishing Point?* Bloomington, IN: Phi Delta Kappa, 1971. Award winning, lectures which focus on mastery learning proposed as a basis for reorganizing learning.
———— , ed. *Taxonomy of Educational Objectives: The Classification of Educational Goals. Handbook I: Cognitive Domain.* New York: David McKay Company, Inc., 1977.

Burton, Dwight L., et al. *Teaching English Today.* Boston: Houghton Mifflin, 1975.

College Entrance Examination Board. *12,000 Students and Their English Teachers.* NCTE, 1968. Model teaching plans for units in language literature, and composition, grades 9–12.

Curriculum Materials of (current year). Association for Supervision and Curriculum Development, 1701 K Street N.W., Washington, D.C.

20006. Catalogs the current Curriculum Materials Exhibit at ASCD annual conference, K-12 curriculum guides, and other instructional aids developed by school systems.

Dale, Edgar. *Building a Learning Environment.* Bloomington, IN: Phi Delta Kappa, 1972. Clearly discusses the philosophical and the practical needed to create effective learning-teaching situations.

Dixon, John. *Growth Through English.* 3rd ed. NCTE, 1975.

Farrell, Edmund J. *Deciding the Future: A Forecast of Responsibilities of Secondary Teachers of English, 1970–2000 A.D.* NCTE, 1971. Summarizes responses from eighty experts writing on the future of English teaching.

Fisk, Loretta Z., and Lindgren, Henry C. *A Survival Guide for Teachers.* New York: John Wiley & Sons, 1973. Brisk, anecdotal, practical, no-nonsense book that's entertaining, instructive, and will help support you in your first few teaching years "on the other side of the desk."

Gardner, John. *Excellence: Can We Be Equal and Excellent Too?* New York: Harper & Row, 1961.

Hahn, Robert O. *Creative Teachers: Who Wants Them?* New York: John Wiley & Sons, 1973. Determines the climate needed in the public secondary school to keep teachers creative.

Hook, J. N. *The Teaching of High School English.* 4th ed. New York: The Ronald Press, 1972.

Houston, Robert W., and Howsam, Robert B., eds. *Competency-Based Teacher Education.* Chicago: Science Research Associates, 1972. Articles covering five areas: objectives, curriculum design, evaluation, certification, and consortia.

Judy, Stephen. *Explorations in the Teaching of Secondary English.* New York: Dodd, Mead and Company, 1974. One of the more recent English methods books that draws heavily upon the creative mode of students and their teachers.

Kirrie, Marjorie; Maloney, Henry; Gutschow, Deanna, and Tuttle, Frederick. *English for the Verbally Talented.* NCTE, 1979. A collection of convention speeches promoting quality programs for bright students.

Krathwohl, David R.; Bloom, Benjamin S.; and Masia, Bertram B., eds. *Taxonomy of Educational Objectives: The Classification of Educational Goals. Handbook II: Affective Domain.* New York: David McKay Company, 1964.

Loban, Walter; Ryan, Margaret; and Squire, James. *Teaching Language and Literature.* 2nd ed. New York: Harcourt Brace Jovanovich, 1969.

Mager, Robert F. *Preparing Instructional Objectives.* 2nd ed. Belmont, CA: Fearon Publishers, 1967.

Moffett, James, and Wagner, Betty Jane. *Student-Centered Language Arts and Reading: Grades K–13,* 2nd ed. Boston: Houghton Mifflin Co., 1976.

Muller, Herbert J. *The Uses of English.* (Report of the Anglo-American Dartmouth Seminar.) New York: Holt, Rinehart & Winston, 1968.

Neff, Charles and Nancy. *Aids to Curriculum Planning: English Language Arts K–12.* NCTE, 1973.

O'Donnell, Bernard, ed. *Aids to Curriculum Planning: English Language Arts K–12*. NCTE; ERIC/RCS, 1973. Aids to committees developing curriculum guides: philosophy, objectives, evaluation, language, composition, media, reading, and literature.

Parker, J. Cecil, and Rubin, Louis J. *Process as Content: Curriculum Design and the Application of Knowledge*. Chicago: Rand McNally & Company, 1966.

Rice, Frank. *English and Its Teaching*. Professional Educators Publications. Lincoln, NEB: Cliff Notes, 1972. One of the first in a series of professional books, summaries to English teaching in its present state. Describes new developments and teaching methods.

Shuman, R. Baird, ed. *Creative Approaches to the Teaching of English: Secondary*. Itasca, IL: F. E. Peacock Publishers, 1974.

Squire, James R., ed. *The Teaching of English*. Chicago: University of Chicago Press, 1977. Written by the Yearbook Committee of the National Society for the Study of Education, this book is the first one devoted exclusively to the study of English. It is an indispensable aid for the active teacher and administrator.

Stanford, Barbara Dodds, and Amin, Krima. *Black Literature for High School Students*. NCTE, 1978. A guide for introducing black literature into the curriculum: issues, problems, and goals plus a survey of black American literature from colonial times to the present.

Stanford, Gene, chair, and the NCTE Committee on Classroom Practices. *Classroom Practices in Teaching English, 1978–79: Activating the Passive Student*. NCTE, 1978. Twenty-seven articles focus on methods for teaching reading, composing, poetry, and doing research with special emphasis on the "tuned-out" student.

Taba, Hilda. *Curriculum Development: Theory and Practice*. New York: Harcourt Brace & World, 1962.

Winkeljohann, Rosemary Sr. *Recommended English Language Arts Curriculum Guides, K-12*. NCTE, 1979. Educators will find this valuable when writing or revising their own guides.

Evaluation

Berger, Allen, and Smith, Blanche Hope, eds. *Classroom Practices in Teaching English, 1972–73: Measure for Measure*. NCTE, 1972. Focuses on measurement, testing, evaluation, and grading.

Burns, Paul C. *Diagnostic Teaching of the Language Arts*. Itasca, IL: F. E. Peacock Publishers, Inc., 1974. A practical guide to diagnosis: where to begin when individualizing English language arts.

Buros, Oscar Krisen, ed. *English Tests and Reviews*. Edison, NJ: The Gryphon Press, 1975. A comprehensive index for all English tests with references and reviews. An important source for a school needing to improve its testing program.

Carruthers, Robert B. *Building Better English Tests*. NCTE, 1963

Cooper, Charles R., and Odell, Lee. *Evaluating Writing: Describing, Measuring, Judging*. NCTE, 1977. This book will help any English teacher who has felt the pressure of reading and evaluating student writing.

Elbow, Peter. *Writing Without Teachers*. Oxford, England: Oxford University Press, 1973. This book presents useful strategies on teaching students how to critique their own writing and that of their classmates. It also offers suggestions to improve writing fluency.

ETS Publications. Educational Testing Service, Princeton, NJ 08540. Free catalog including free or inexpensive items.

Ideas

Brand, Stuart, ed. *The Last Whole Earth Catalog*. Menlo Park, CA: Portola Institute, Inc., 1971. Distributed by Random House. An unorthodox catalog of just about anything to stimulate thought, discussion, and even writing.

Citation Press, 50 West 44th St., New York, NY 10036. Write for free catalog describing such aids as *Films Deliver, Teaching Creatively with Film. 100 Novel Ways with Book Reports, Learning Discussion Skills through Games, Creative Bulletin Boards for Junior High English*.

Clapp, Ouida, chair. *Classroom Practices in Teaching English 1977–78: Teaching the Basics—Really!* NCTE, 1977. The chair and the NCTE Committee on Classroom Practices has prepared a comprehensive source of suggestions for teaching every area of English.

Classroom Interaction Newsletter. Research for Better Schools, 1700 Market Street, Philadelphia, PA 19103.

Daniels, Steven. *How 2 Gerbils, 20 Goldfish, 200 Games, 2,000 Books and I Taught Them How to Read*. Philadelphia: The Westminster Press, 1971.

Davis, Kenneth, and Hollowell, John. *Inventing and Playing Games in the English Classroom*, NCTE, 1977. A handbook for teachers who are looking for and designing simulation games to teach English. Includes complete descriptions of several games and lists sources of commercially prepared games.

Haskins, Mary Glen. *Half-Hour Notice, Fifty Mini-Lessons for High School Substitutes*. Citation Press, 50 West 44th St., New York, NY 10036. Fifty self-contained assignments with follow-up activities and suggested readings.

Hillcocks, George. *Alternatives in English: A Critical Appraisal of Elective Programs*. ERIC/RCS, 1972. Appraises data from one hundred schools in thirty-seven states.

Judy, Stephen N. *Explorations in the Teaching of Secondary English: A Source Book for Experimental Teaching*. New York: Dodd, Mead & Co., 1974. Covers composition, dramatics, language arts, literature, media, oral English, semantics, and curriculum planning.

Judy, Stephen, and Judy, Susan. *The English Teacher's Handbook*. Cambridge, MA: Winthrop Publishers, Inc., 1979. This handbook can serve as both a methods book and idea book. Teachers are stimulated to use their own ideas by the many suggestions.

Michel, Lois A. *Another Way Out*. New York: Holt, Rinehart & Winston, 1974. A multiform, multilevel, multiethnic anthology to develop communication skills in essays, editorials, fables, letters, reviews, puzzles, short stories, and speeches.

Miller, Lynne, and Batten, Carol. *Short Span Activities: Ideas for Utilizing Spare Minutes in the Classroom.* New York: Citation Press, 1973. More than eighty games and activities for different subject areas and grade levels. Language arts activities include usage, spelling, memory, creative writing, and pantomime.

Orbit. Ontario Institute for Studies in Education, Publication Sales, 252 Bloor Street West, Toronto, M5S/V6 Ontario, Canada. Innovative programs described along with practical suggestions for elementary and secondary classroom teachers.

Poteet, G. Howard. *Tom Swift and His Electric English Teacher.* Dayton, OH: Pflaum/Standard, 1974. A fun-and-games teacher resource book.

Reeves, Ruth, ed. *Ideas for Teaching English: Successful Practices in the Junior High School.* NCTE. A looseleaf binder containing more than 400 detachable pages detailing about 100 proven practices for composition, dictionary and language study, literature, listening, mass media, speech, spelling, and reading.

Schrank, Jeffrey. *Teaching Human Beings: 101 Subversive Activities for the Classroom.* Boston: Beacon Press, 1972.

Wurman, Richard Saul, ed. *Yellow Pages of Learning Resources.* Boston: The MIT Press, 1972.

Zavatsky, Bill, and Padgett, Ron. *The Whole Word Catalogue 2.* New York: McGraw-Hill Paperbacks, 1977. Contains many ideas for creative approaches to teaching various aspects of English: includes activities for writing poetry and drama.

Learning Theory

Bruner, Jerome. *Toward a Theory of Instruction.* 2nd ed. New York: W. W. Norton, 1968.

Cry Help! NBC Educational Enterprises, 30 Rockefeller Plaza, New York, NY 10020. (Color film; 34, 30, 19 minutes.) A three-part color film which discusses mental disturbance among adolescents. Includes essays, poems, art work. For secondary school English and humanities classes.

Dobson, James. *Dare to Discipline.* Wheaton, IL: Tyndale House, 1970. A book of practical suggestions on how to understand why students do what they do.

Erikson, Erik. *Identity: Youth and Crisis.* New York: W. W. Norton, 1968.

Gagné, Robert M. *The Conditions of Learning,* 3rd ed. New York: Holt, Rinehart & Winston, 1977.

————. *Expectations for School Learning.* Bloomington, IN: Phi Delta Kappa, 1973. Award lecture dealing with questions and answers regarding educational goals.

Ghiselin, Brewster, ed. *The Creative Process.* New York: Mentor Books, 1955.

Gowen, John C., et al., eds. *Creativity: Its Educational Implications.* New York: John Wiley & Sons, 1967.

Johnson, Eric W. *How to Live Through Junior High School.* New York: Lippincott, 1975. This book, based on actual teaching experiences in the junior high school, can even be helpful to parents.

Kagan, Jerome, ed. *Creativity and Learning.* Boston: Beacon Press, 1967.

Langer, Susanne. *Mind: An Essay on Human Feeling.* Baltimore, MD: Johns Hopkins Press, 1973.

Life Skills in School and Society. Association for Supervision and Curriculum Development, Room 428, 1201 16th St. N.W., Washington, D.C. 1970 edition. Views the cognitive and affective capabilities needed for truly functional education.

Long, Nicholas J.; Morse, William C.; and Newman, Ruth G. *Conflict in the Classroom: The Education of Children With Problems.* 3rd ed. Belmont, CA: Wadsworth Publishing Co., 1976.

Schwebel, Milton, and Ralph, Jane, eds. *Piaget in the Classroom.* New York: Basic Books, 1973.

Simon, Sidney B., and Clark, Jay. *Beginning Values Clarification: A Guide for the Use of Values Clarification in the Classroom.* LaMesa, CA: Pennant Press, 1975.

Simon, Signey B., Howe, Leland W.; and Kirschenbaum, Howard. *Values Clarification: A Handbook of Practical Strategies for Teachers and Students.* New York: Hart, 1972. This is a useful guide for activities that give students the opportunity and the right to their own ideas.

Stanford, Gene. *Developing Effective Classroom Groups.* New York: Hart, 1977. An extensive analytical book that explores the reasons why some groups fail and others succeed. Contains suggestions for evaluating one's own methods of discussion.

Thelen, Herbert. *Dynamics of Groups at Work.* Chicago: University of Chicago Press, 1967.

Lists

Consumer Information Catalog: A Catalog of Selected Federal Publications of Consumer Interest. Consumer Information Center, Pueblo, CO 81009. This is a free catalog of over 200 items, half of which are free on request. Provides addresses to which students can write, obtaining practical writing practice.

Educators Grade Guide to Free Teaching Aids; Educators Guide to Free Filmstrips; Educators Guide to Free Tapes, Scripts, and Transcriptions; Educators Index of Free Materials. Educators Progress Service, 214 Center Street, Randolph, WI 53956. These are four separate booklets.

ERIC/RCS, 1111 Kenyon Road, Urbana, IL 61801. Write for ordering information and index to obtain current research developments in the field. Index also in Resources in Education, available three times annually from NCTE (same address).

Free and Inexpensive Learning Materials. Office of Educational Services— F & I, George Peabody College for Teachers, Nashville, TN 37203. Lists inexpensive and free materials for classroom use and provides good sources of addresses for letter writing assignments.

Interpreting Language Arts Research for the Teacher. Association for Supervision and Curriculum Development, Room 428, 1201 16th St. N.W., Washington, D.C. Comprehensive list of practical classroom aids; over 1,100 reference sources.

National Council of Teachers of English. *NCTE Guide to Teaching Materials for English, Grades 7–12.* 1111 Kenyon Road, Urbana, IL 61801. Detailed, objective descriptions of commercially available instructional materials for students of English and language arts: anthologies, textbooks, workbooks, and other print-based materials. Ask for current edition as well as past.

————— . *Professional Publications for the Teacher of English and Language Arts.* (current year). Free catalog. Lists publications from the Council, its affiliates, and other sources. Includes maps, filmstrips, and recordings.

National Education Association Catalog of Publications. National Education Association, 1201 16 Street N.W., Washington, D.C. 20036. Although this is a general list, many items are useful for the English classroom.

Saalheimer, Harriet. *Free for the Asking: A Super Treasury of Valuable Things You Can Get Free or for Next to Nothing.* New York: Parker Publishing Company, Inc. A periodically updated source of hundreds of items students can use and could write for to gain practice.

Salisbury, Gordon. *Catalog of Free Teaching Materials.* Riverside, CA: Ribidoux Printing Co., 1973.

Standard Periodical Directory. 6th ed. Oxbridge Communications, Inc., 183 Madison Avenue, New York, NY 10016. A comprehensive listing of periodicals, their publishers, addresses, editors, and phone numbers. Some annotations are included. Lists are by subject fields. The education section is extensive.

Weber, J. Sherwood, ed. *Good Reading.* 21st ed. New York: R. R. Bowker Company, A guide to more than 2,500 books with annotations, evaluations, and full bibliographic data on each book.

Weisinger, Mort. *1001 Valuable Things You Can Get Free.* New York: Bantam Books, 1979. A giveaway list of products, kits, maps, plans, films, Bible selections, manuals, and services. These are offered by American industries, profit and nonprofit organizations, and by local and national governments.

Periodicals

College English. NCTE, 1111 Kenyon Road, Urbana, IL 61801. Official monthly journal (September through May) especially for teachers in higher education.

College Composition and Communication. NCTE. Quarterly publication of the NCTE Conference on College Composition and Communication (CCCC). Includes articles for composition and communication teachers in two- and four-year colleges.

Communication Education. Speech Communication Association, 5205 Leesburg Pike, Falls Church, VA 22041. Official journal of interest to speech and English teachers.

Curriculum Review. Published five times a year by Curriculum Advisory Services, 500 S. Clinton, Chicago, IL 60607. This publication evaluates in depth texts, kits, and supplements for the K–12 curriculum.

Elementary English. NCTE. Official monthly journal (September through May).

English Education. NCTE. Published four times annually: October, December, February, and May. Official journal of the Conference on English Education (CEE), mainly for those in teacher education programs.

English High Lights. Glenview, IL: Scott, Foresman & Co. Free service bulletin of classroom happenings, teaching ideas, plus a page for the bulletin board.

English Journal. NCTE. Official monthly journal; nine issues annually (September through May).

English Teaching Techniques, Journal of. University of Michigan, Flint. 1321 E. Court Street, Flint, MI 48503.

ERIC Clearninghouse on Reading and Communication Skills. ERIC/RCS, 1111 Kenyon Road, Urbana, IL 61801. Vast collection of unpublished research and abstracts. Send for information on ordering.

Exercise Exchange. Charles Duke, ed. Department of English, Murray State University, Murray, KY 42071. A journal for English teachers junior high through college, this publication seeks manuscripts on any practical classroom English teaching applications.

Film—English/Humanities Association, Journal. 265 Ernst Bessey Hall, Michigan State University, East Lansing, MI 48823.

Idea Factor, The. This periodical is published four times a year by the JH/MS Assembly of the National Council of Teachers of English. Currently available through Becky Johnson, No. 50B, Braeburn Drive, Richmond, VA 23233. This material is written by language arts and English teachers who teach early adolescents.

Learning: The Magazine for Creative Teaching. Subscription Department, P. O. Box 2580, Boulder, CO 80322.

Linguistic Reporter, The. Center for Applied Linguistics Publications, 1611 N. Kent Street, Arlington, VA 22209. An international source of language-related issues: language teaching and learning, sociolinguistics, bilingual-bicultural education, psycholinguistics, language planning, and English as a second language.

Media and Methods. Philadelphia: North American Publishing Co., 401 North Broad Street, Philadelphia, PA 19108. A magazine (nine issues) devoted to general discussions and ads covering broad segments of the electronic and graphic media. Frequently contains tips for teaching language arts.

Media Mix. Claretian Publications, 221 W. Madison St., Chicago, IL 60606. A newsletter published eight times a year. Reviews and articles on films, filmstrips, TV programs, records, cassette tapes, books, teacher aids. Provides consumer reports and sources of "freebies."

Mersand, Joseph, Dept. of Teacher Preparation, York College of CUNY, 150-14 Jamaica Avenue, NYC 11432. Free reprints by enclosing postage and self-addressed clasp envelope. Write for list and specifications.

National Education Association, 1201 16th St. N.W., Washington, D.C. 20036. Send for English publications list.

National Park Service, Office of the Director, U.S. Department of the

Interior, Washington, D.C. 20240. Write for information on environ-
mental education programs.

Phi Delta Kappa Fastbacks, Phi Delta Kappa, Inc., Bloomington, IN 47401.
Selections from the fifty available titles. Write for catalog.

Public Doublespeak Newsletter, The. NCTE, 1111 Kenyon Road, Urbana,
IL 61801. Published quarterly, this newsletter contains activities of
the NCTE Public Doublespeak Committee as well as information on
available materials and suggestions for teaching about doublespeak:
the dishonest and sometimes inhumane uses of language.

Publications of Interest to Teachers of English. Modern Language Association of America, Materials Center, 62 Fifth Ave., New York, NY
10011. (Free.)

Reading, Journal of. International Reading Association, 800 Barksdale
Road, Newark, DE 19711.

Research in the Teaching of English. NCTE. Issued threee times annually.

School Bulletin. National Geographic Society, 17th and M Streets, N.W.,
Washington, D.C. 20036. Thirty issues. Write for publications list.

Speech Journal. Southern Connecticut State College, Department of
Speech, New Haven, CT 06515.

Standard Periodical Directory (see Lists page 330)

The Teacher Paper. 2221 N.W. 23rd, Portland, OR 97212. A quarterly
journal written by teachers for teachers.

This Magazine Is about Schools, 3 Church St., Suite 401, Toronto M5E/M2/
Ontario, Canada. A straightforward alternative education magazine.
Contains many useful ideas and discussions to make schools
relevant.

Today's Education (NEA Journal). National Education Association, 1201
16th Street N.W., Washington, D.C. 20036. This is the official
publication of the NEA. It contains articles for improving instruction
and keeping teachers informed on educational developments.

The Writer. The Writer, Inc., 8 Arlington St., Boston, MA 02116. Student
subscription rate available.

Indexes

BIOGRAPHICAL INDEX

Specific activity numbers are in **boldface** type; page numbers are in Roman type. Capital C designates composition activities; G/L designates grammar and language; L designates literature; R designates reading; and RM designates room management.

333

TITLE INDEX

TOPIC INDEX